D0821686

PICTORIAL AND DECORATIVE TITLE PAGES FROM MUSIC SOURCES

PICTORIAL AND DECORATIVE TITLE PAGES FROM MUSIC SOURCES

201 EXAMPLES FROM 1500 TO 1800

Selected, Introduced and Annotated

BY

GOTTFRIED S. FRAENKEL

Dover Publications, Inc., New York

Published in Canada by General Publishing Company, Ltd., 30 Lesmill Road, Don Mills, Toronto, Ontario.
Published in the United Kingdom by Constable and Company, Ltd., 10 Orange Street, London WC 2.

Pictorial and Decorative Title Pages from Music Sources (formerly *Decorative Music Title Pages*) is a new work, first published by Dover Publications, Inc., in 1968.

DOVER *Pictorial Archive* SERIES

International Standard Book Number: 0-486-21915-1
Library of Congress Catalog Card Number: 67-27232

Manufactured in the United States of America
Dover Publications, Inc.
180 Varick Street
New York, N. Y. 10014

Foreword

Habent sua fata libelli • *Each book has its history.*

All books are, or ought to be, the outcome of some personal experience of the author. This one stems from a life-long interest in the early original prints of music, editions issued in past centuries, at the time of the composer, by the composer himself or in his behalf. Everybody who has handled such old editions is familiar with the charm and beauty of many of the title pages. Reproductions of such pages can be seen in many books on music, but apart from earlier and mostly incomplete treatments of the subject, little known and long out of print, no comprehensive treatise on decorative title pages of music exists today.

From the first concept of a book in the mind of a prospective author to the finished product there is a long series of hurdles, none more formidable than that of catching the ear, fancy and purse of a publisher. It gives me special pleasure to express my appreciation to the President of Dover Publications, Inc., Mr. Hayward Cirker, for giving this rather unusual project his wholehearted support.

A book is necessarily written and published with a public in view. Who are these prospective buyers and readers, and we hope ultimate appreciators, of this particular work? We have in mind four groups:

1. The student of the history of music, for whom it is a collection of previously unavailable source material.

2. The lover of music, whose enjoyment and understanding are enhanced by relating the music to the contemporary currents in the figurative arts.

3. The student of the history of the graphic arts, for whom this collection provides a record of stylistic and technical trends and developments over a span of 300 years in a field which has probably escaped his attention for the lack of conveniently available material.

4. Finally, the expert and connoisseur in the art of printing and book production, for whom this book presents a unique display of lettering and layout of pages, and a combination of textual and decorative elements in a dazzling variety of techniques and styles.

The presentation of the illustrations in this book differs from several similar ventures in that the material, with very few exceptions, was photographed directly from the originals, for the most part in the great libraries of the world. For helpful cooperation in this special thanks are due to Mr. A. Hyatt King of the British Museum, London; Drs. A. Halm and K. Dorfmüller of the Bayerische Staatsbibliothek, Munich; Prof. Napoleone Fanti of the Civico Museo Bibliografico Musicale, Bologna; and to the staff of these libraries and of the University Library, Uppsala; the Library of Congress, Washington; the New York Public Library; the Bibliothèque Nationale, Paris; and the Österreichische Nationalbibliothek, Vienna.

The source of each reproduction is stated in the accompanying caption, and a listing by collections will be found on page 223.

Urbana, Illinois G. S. F.
June, 1967

Contents

List of Plates

ENGLISH PUBLISHERS, ELIZABETHAN AND JACOBEAN PERIODS

ITALIAN PUBLISHERS, FIRST HALF OF SEVENTEENTH CENTURY

GERMANY AND OTHER LANDS, FIRST HALF OF SEVENTEENTH CENTURY

149 Johann Mattheson. *Pieces de Clavecin*. I. D. Fletcher, London, 1714.
150 Domenico Scarlatti. *Essercizi per gravicembalo*. London, 1738.
151 George Frideric Handel. *Suites de Pieces Pour le Clavecin*. Printed by Wright & Co., London, *c*. 1784.
152 George Frideric Handel. *Julius Caesar*. John Cluer, London, 1724.
153 George Frideric Handel. *Alexander*. John Cluer, London, 1726.
154 George Frideric Handel. *Rinaldo*. John Walsh, London, 1711.
155 George Frideric Handel. *Parthenope*. John Walsh & Joseph Hare, London, 1730.
156 George Bickham, Jr. *The Musical Entertainer. Vol. I.* George Bickham, London, 1737.
157 George Bickham, Jr. *The Musical Entertainer*. George Bickham, London, 1738.

ALL COUNTRIES, LATER EIGHTEENTH CENTURY

158 Antoine Mahaut. *Maendelyks musikaels Tydverdryf*. A. Olofsen, Amsterdam, 1751/2.
159 Jean-Jacques Rousseau. *Les consolations des miseres de ma vie*. De Roullède de la Chevardière, Paris, 1781.
160 Andrea Basili. *Musica universale*. Venice, 1776.
161 Ferdinando Giuseppe Bertoni. *Orfeo*. Innocente Alessandri & Pietro Scattaglia, Venice, 1776.
162 Vincenzo Manfredini. *Sonate da Clavecimbalo*. Imperial Academy of Sciences, St. Petersburg, 1765.
163 Thomas Carter. *The Rival Candidates*. Robert Bremner, London, 1775.
164 E. T. P. A. *Talestri, Regina delle Amazzoni*. Bernhard Christoph Breitkopf & Son, Leipzig, 1765.
165 Wenzel Pichl. *Trois concerts*. Johann Julius Hummel, Berlin, 1775.
166 *Lieder der Deutschen*. George Ludewig Winter, Berlin, 1767.
167 Johann Adam Hiller. *Cantaten und Arien verschiedener Dichter*. Schwickert, Leipzig, 1781.
168 Karl Friedrich Abel. *Six Sonates pour le Clavecin, ou Piano-Forte, avec accompagnement d'un Violon*. Published by the composer, London, 1777.
169 Karl Friedrich Abel. *Six Quartetto*. Printed by Robert Bremner, London, 1760's.
170 Johann Christian Bach. *Six sonates pour le clavecin ou le piano forte*. London, *c*. 1770.
171 Johann Christian Bach. *Six Sonatas for the Harpsichord or Piano Forte; with an Accompagnament for a Violin*. Welcker, London, 1775 (?).
172 Luigi Boccherini. *Six Trios*. Johann Julius Hummel, Amsterdam, *c*. 1785.

HAYDN

173 Joseph Haydn. *Six Quatuor*. Johann Julius Hummel, Amsterdam, 1769.
174 Joseph Haydn. *Sei quartetti concertante*. Huberty, Paris, 1773.
175 Joseph Haydn. *Six Quatuor*. Robert Bremner, London, after 1765.
176 Joseph Haydn. *Three Quartettos*. William Forster, London, after 1785.

177 Joseph Haydn. *Three Quartetts.* Longman, Clementi & Co., London, 1799.
178 Joseph Haydn. *Trios simphonies.* Christoph Torricella, Vienna, 1784.
179 Joseph Haydn. *Sei Sonate.* Artaria, Vienna, 1780.
180 Joseph Haydn. *Trio.* Artaria, Vienna, 1798.
181 Joseph Haydn. *Die Jahreszeiten. Partitur.* Breitkopf & Härtel, Leipzig, 1802.
182 Joseph Haydn. *The Seasons. Klavierauszug.* Breitkopf & Härtel, Leipzig, 1801.
183 Joseph Haydn. *The Seasons. Klavierauszug.* Breitkopf & Härtel, Leipzig, 1801.
184 Joseph Haydn. *Oeuvres Complettes. Cahier I.* Breitkopf & Härtel, Leipzig, 1800.
185 Joseph Haydn. (*Oeuvres Complettes. Cahier 9.*) *Gesaenge.* Breitkopf & Härtel, Leipzig, after 1803.

MOZART

186 Wolfgang Amadeus Mozart. *Sei Quartetti.* Artaria, Vienna, 1785.
187 Wolfgang Amadeus Mozart. *Six Sonates Pour le Clavecin, ou Pianoforte avec l'accompagnoment d'un Violon.* Artaria, Vienna, 1781.
188 Wolfgang Amadeus Mozart. *Grand concert pour le clavecin ou forte-piano.* Artaria, Vienna, 1785.
189 Wolfgang Amadeus Mozart. *Fantaisie et Sonate Pour le Forte-Piano.* Artaria, Vienna, 1785.
190 Wolfgang Amadeus Mozart. *Trio.* Artaria, Vienna, 1790.
191 Wolfgang Amadeus Mozart. *Die Entführung aus dem Serrail.* Bernhard Schott, Mainz, 1785 (?).
192 Wolfgang Amadeus Mozart. *Die Zauberflöte.* Nicolaus Simrock, Bonn, 1793.
193 Wolfgang Amadeus Mozart. *Grand Concerto pour le Piano-Forte.* Johann Anton André, Offenbach, 1802.
194 Wolfgang Amadeus Mozart. *Così fan tutte* (piano score). Maurice Schlesinger, Paris, 1822.
195 Wolfgang Amadeus Mozart. *Musikalischer Spass.* Johann Anton André Offenbach, 1802.
196 Wolfgang Amadeus Mozart. *Oeuvres Complettes.* Breitkopf & Härtel, Leipzig, 1806.

ALL COUNTRIES, ABOUT 1800

197 Ludwig van Beethoven. *Trois Trios.* Artaria, Vienna, 1795.
198 Nicolas-Marie Dalayrac. *Le Poëte et le Musicien ou Je Cherche un Sujet.* Duhan, Paris, 1811 (?).
199 Johann Friedrich Reichardt. *Schillers Lyrische Gedichte.* Breitkopf & Härtel, Leipzig, 1810.
200 Johann Sebastian Bach. *Clavier Sonaten Mit obligater Violine.* Hans Georg Nägeli, Zurich, 1804.
201 Johann Sebastian Bach. *Clavier Sonaten Mit obligater Violine.* Hans Georg Nägeli, Zurich, 1804.

PICTORIAL AND DECORATIVE TITLE PAGES FROM MUSIC SOURCES

Introduction

I Scope and arrangement of the present collection

Modern editions of great musical works of the past often bear little resemblance to the original publications. Constant editing and reediting have sometimes reduced the music itself to a travesty of the composer's intentions; but what concerns us here is the appearance of the books: more specifically, their title pages. In addition to the invaluable bibliographical information they afford, many early music titles, with their artistic and historical values, give us a glimpse into the spirit of their period. While this is true of books in all fields, the music title page, because of the delightful subject matter—often because of its sheer size—seems to have presented designers, printers and publishers with a special challenge to fill the spaces with decorations. Imaginative use was made of the visual elements of music—instruments, performers and performances—producing title pages of great beauty.

All too few modern music reprints include reproductions of the original title pages and, as we shall see, anthologies of such reproductions are all but nonexistent. The present volume is unique in offering over 200 of the most striking and most interesting music titles produced between 1500 and 1800.

Sources of the Plates

The collection of suitable material for this book was greatly facilitated by the existence of two previous illustrated accounts of the art and development of the music title. The first such work (1904) was *Les titres illustrés*, by a great expert in the arts of the book, John Grand-Carteret (see Bibliography, p. 17). Considering the pioneering nature of his undertaking, his book was an outstanding achievement. The illustrations, however, were not always well selected, their reproduction was poor, and the larger and more valuable part of the volume dealt with light music of the nineteenth century, a period outside the scope of this book.

In 1921 the German bibliophile Walter von zur Westen brought out a sumptuous folio entitled *Musiktitel aus vier Jahrhunderten* as a festschrift for the seventy-fifth anniversary of the noted printing firm of C. G. Röder in Leipzig. It contains 96 superbly reproduced illustrations, many full-page, the last third covering nineteenth-century music. These two very rare collections, both with a continuous text, have been the only books so far dealing specifically with music titles, and they were invaluable guideposts for the selection of material in the present volume. But they were not the only sources of information and suggestions.

The most extensive single repertory today of illustrated music titles (although these are reproduced at very great reductions) is the German encyclopedia *Die Musik in Geschichte und Gegenwart* (see Bibliography). Twelve volumes have been published so far (spring, 1967), up through the article "Symphonische Dichtung." The *MGG*, as this vast work is familiarly called, is also the most reliable comprehensive source of musical biographies and bibliographies now available, and where applicable, I have here followed the *MGG* entries for preferred forms of composers' names, dates of composers' lives, dates of editions and similar information.

Other suggestions for title illustrations came from Georg Kinsky's *A History of Music in Pictures* and the Italian *Enciclopedia della Musica* (see Bibliography), as well as from catalogues of libraries, booksellers and auctions, and individual biographies of composers too numerous to mention.

With a list of possible choices compiled from these publications, augmented by suggestions gathered from the literature, the next step was to locate good copies of the originals. This undertaking was made difficult by the absence of printed catalogues of many of the important music collections. The few that exist, such as those of the British Museum, the Paris Bibliothèque Nationale (very incomplete) and the music libraries in Bologna and other Italian cities, give no information on the character or state of the title pages. The same applies to the catalogue of the New York Public Library, which only appeared after the collection of material for this book was completed. The great collections at Munich, Vienna and Washington do not even possess printed catalogues. The best general source for the locations of originals is still Robert Eitner's *Quellen-Lexikon* (see Bibliography). Eitner's work, however, is not only restricted to Europe and entirely lacking in descriptions of titles, but also very incomplete, long outdated and unreliable because of the wholesale destruction and dislocation of material during the Second World War.

Even final location of a work is not necessarily the end of the search, because title pages have the unfortunate habit of getting lost, especially if they are attractive, or of being damaged or soiled. They may have been made from cracked plates, or something may have been written or pasted over them, or else they may have been taken from an edition other than the one anticipated. These considerations made it necessary to check most of the material at the source. Even after diligent searching on the spot and following up every possible suggestion, I am only too conscious of my failure to attain anything approaching completeness in the collection. It is utterly impossible for anyone not on the staff of a library to look through shelf after shelf in search of material, so there is no way of judging how much was missed. Nevertheless, many of the illustrations in this book are reproduced for the first time.

It should be pointed out here that even when the criterion of artistic merit is not applied, the ornamental title page is not as typical as the perusal of this book may suggest. In fact, the large majority of music titles, like those of most books, simply contain lettering, set in type or engraved, without any decorative elements.

Criteria for Selection

In the selection of the material I used in general the following criteria: (1) limitation to the period between 1500 and 1800; (2) limitation to actual music prints rather than works about music; (3) emphasis on title pages proper, as distinct from frontispieces and other pages; and (4) decorative qualities that go beyond mere type or calligraphy. There were various reasons for these restrictions, and for the handful of exceptions I permitted myself in each category.

1. The starting date for this selection was set by history, since the publishing of music in mensural notation, it is now generally agreed, started with a print by the Venetian Petrucci in the year 1501 (Plate 1). The decision to end the book at approximately 1800 was somewhat arbitrary, but had its reasons. For one thing, it would have been impossible to do justice to the subject had it been followed up to the present time. For another, the year 1800 has often been used in music bibliography as a dividing line between "old" and "recent" music. It represents the natural end of one epoch and the beginning of another, not only in compositional style, but also in publishing, since it was then that cheap methods of mass production became prevalent, with a concomitant lowering of taste. Not that the nineteenth century did not produce title pages of decorative interest; but these are found predominantly in sheet music of songs and dances, few publishers of serious music devoting attention to decoration. The Grand-Carteret and von zur Westen books mentioned above give many graceful examples of nineteenth-century sheet music.

The eight titles included here that date from after 1800 are all by eighteenth-century composers and all of special interest. The latest item (Plate 194), dating from 1822, is also the only lithographic page I have included, but I felt that the Mozart section would be enriched by this delightful and justly famous *Così* title.

2. It was not always possible to draw a sharp line between actual printed music and theoretical works, since early books often contain both types of material and the character of the title pages is frequently similar in the two kinds of publications. Three notable titles of theoretical works are illustrated in the second, historical, part of this Introduction (Figures 2, 3 and 4); others are shown in Plates 9, 10, 11, 39, 63, 76, 81, 146 and 160.

3. Frontispieces have been excluded because they are not title pages, but independent works of art with stylistic values of their own. In the one case where I have shown a frontispiece, the actual title appears on the same plate (108). Plates 2, 3 and 157 represent a special exception, since they are picture pages that fall within a book, but the unique interest of the books they come from seemed to justify their inclusion.

4. As for the exclusion of titles of merely typographical or calligraphical merit, here again I have not been entirely consistent, because often the script or type arrangement can itself be considered as the artistic expression of the period, and may be typical of a particular publisher. Examples of such inclusions are the titles of Bach's *Clavier Übung* (Plate 142) and Handel's *Partenope* (Plate 155, typical of many Walsh editions). Moreover, a sharp distinction between script and other decoration is impossible because the script is often an integral part of the pictorial design, and the calligrapher is credited on the title along with the designer (see, for example, Plates 121 and 129).

Order of Presentation

The natural sequence to be followed in any anthology encompassing a long period of time is the historical one. The period covered in the present volume comprises some 300 years, from 1501 to the beginning of the nineteenth century. A strictly chronological order would have been an easy solution of the delicate task of presentation, but would have been lacking in logic, because styles do not change in strictly chronological order, especially when very different national cultures are involved. It seemed preferable to group the material by cultural periods. The breakdown is approximately as follows (see the List of Plates for further details):

PLATES	
1–17:	All countries, first half of sixteenth century
18–29:	Italian publishers, second half of sixteenth century
30–37:	French publishers, second half of sixteenth century
38–42:	Antwerp, second half of sixteenth century
43–53:	German publishers, second half of sixteenth century
54–67:	English publishers, Elizabethan and Jacobean periods
68–85:	Italian publishers, first half of seventeenth century
86–101:	Germany, Austria, Netherlands, Denmark, first half of seventeenth century
102–105:	English publishers, later seventeenth century
106–109:	Corelli
110–133:	French publishers, seventeenth and most of eighteenth centuries
134–145:	Germany and Switzerland, later seventeenth and first half of eighteenth centuries
146–157:	English publishers, first half of eighteenth century
158–172:	All countries, later eighteenth century
173–185:	Haydn
186–196:	Mozart
197–201:	All countries, about 1800

Even within each of these categories, strict chronological order is not always observed. Works issued by one publisher, or works written by one composer, are generally grouped together. One of my chief concerns was for the pictorial values of the page layouts in this volume—an interesting sequence of illustrations, harmonious facing pages, and the like. Three great composers whose publications were truly international—Corelli, Haydn and Mozart—have groupings of their own.

The captions all begin in a standard way, with the composer's name, the name of the work illustrated (original spelling), the name of the publisher (or printer, or both), the place of publication and the year of publication—to the extent that these items are known. Next I identify the owner of the particular copy that has been reproduced in this edition. The remaining part supplies a minimum background on the composer's life (except for extremely well-known figures), the work in question and its printing history, the publisher, the designer and engraver of the title page, the iconography of the title and so on, as applicable.

II *Music printing and the history of the title page*

Printing Techniques, 1470–1800

It is necessary to deal briefly with the technique of music printing, since it bears on the development of the title page. In the earliest stages of book printing, musical passages were inserted into the text by hand. By 1473 the printing of neumatic music (choral notation) had begun. It now appears that movable type was used even before wood and metal blocks. In 1501 the Venetian printer-publisher Petrucci (Figure 1) produced the earliest known book in modern mensural notation, a collection of songs (Plate 1), still printing staff lines and notes in separate operations. It was Gardane (Plate 12) who introduced to Italy the method developed in France (by Pierre Hautin about 1525?) of printing notes and staff simultaneously.

Decorative title pages in this early period were produced by woodcut, a technique which had reached a high state of perfection early in the sixteenth century. Lettering was either part of the block or set in type. For about a hundred years this was practically the exclusive means of title decoration. Its only serious rival was the ornament called the *fleuron*, or printer's flowers. Invented in France in the mid-sixteenth century, the *fleuron* was an arrangement of cast metal pieces of different shapes in patterns of endless variety which could form ornamental borders framing the type-set text of the title. This rapidly became a favorite method of decorating music titles, first in Brabant, where it was much used by the music

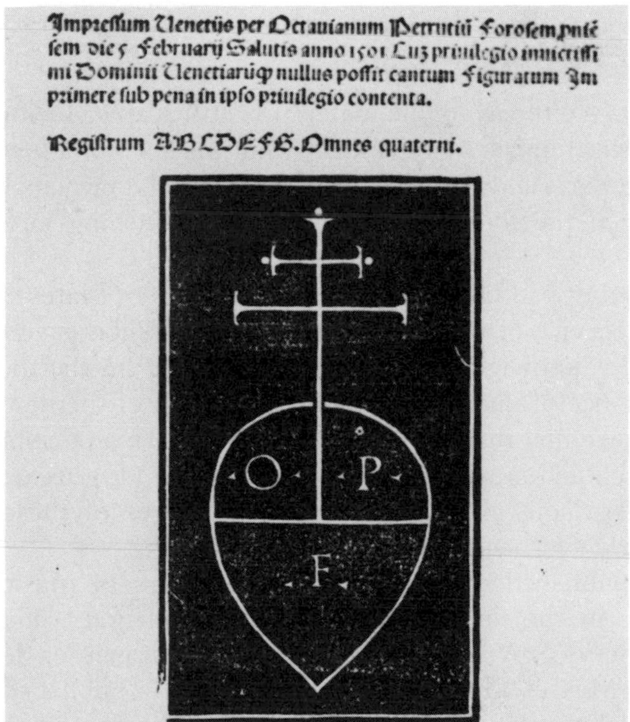

Impressum Venetiis per Octauianum Petrutiũ Forosempronié
sem die 5 Februarij Salutis anno 1501 Cũ priuilegio inuictissi
mi Dominii Venetiarũ q nullus possit cantum Figuratum Im
primere sub pena in ipso priuilegio contenta.

Registrum ABCDEFG. Omnes quaterni.

Fig. 1
The only colophon design used by the Venetian printer Petrucci. The initials stand for Octavianus Petrutius Forosemproniensis (= of Fossombrone). (Civico Museo Bibliografico Musicale, Bologna.)

house of Phalèse in Louvain and Antwerp (Plate 42), and toward the end of the century in England, where it became the predominant style for madrigal titles (Plates 58 and 59).

The technique of engraving, applied for the first time to music by the Roman printer Verovio (Plates 28 and 29) in 1586, was a major advance; for example, this allowed polyphonic voices for a single instrument to be printed simultaneously. The art of engraving had then been known for over a hundred years, experiencing its first great flowering in Italy and Germany early in the sixteenth century. It seems inconceivable today that a technique so eminently suited to music reproduction, so much simpler and more adaptable than typesetting, was not used sooner by music printers. Once introduced, it became the leading technique during the course of the seventeenth century. Naturally, engraving also quickly replaced the woodcut in decorative title pages. In fact, even before engraving had become the general method of printing music, some books had engraved titles and type-set music. In the present selection many of the titles dating from 1600 to 1650, and practically all the titles from then on, are engraved.

During the 1750's, J. G. I. Breitkopf (see Plate 164) developed a method of one-step typesetting of chords and polyphonic strands on a single staff which he hoped would restore the prestige of type-set music, but the esthetic effect was inferior to that of engraved music, and his method, though of great importance as a technical achievement, has found use mainly for brief musical examples within texts.

In 1799 Senefelder patented his new lithographic technique. Lithography became so convenient and inexpensive a method for printing music (and titles) that it gradually replaced engraving. With certain technical modifications, it is the method commonly used today. But this is already beyond the historical limits of the present book.

Brief Survey of the Present Collection

In the earliest period, up to about 1540, the available material is still scarce. From Venice the new art of printing mensural music by type had within the span of a few years spread to Rome and Milan, to Paris and Augsburg. Venice, then the principal center of printing in Italy, remained the foremost Italian music publishing city for over 150 years.

In Germany the new music printing had begun in Augsburg by 1507 (Plates 2 and 3), and rapidly spread, in the service of the Reformation, to Wittenberg and nearby Leipzig. Luther, himself a knowledgeable and enthusiastic musician, immediately recognized the importance of music for the popularization of the new faith (see caption to Plate 7). Thus we find that some of the earliest German prints in this selection are by Luther himself and musicians of his circle: Rhaw (Figure 2; Plate 7), Walter (Plate 6) and Agricola (Figure 3). The title pages of these works are splendid examples of early German Renaissance woodcut art.

The great majority of music published during the first 150 years of music printing was vocal—secular music in the form of chansons and madrigals, and sacred music for use in the church service. As early as 1516, the Roman printer de Antiquis issued a gigantic folio of Masses (Plate 4), the first of many published during the century, with huge text lettering and note heads, and often decorated

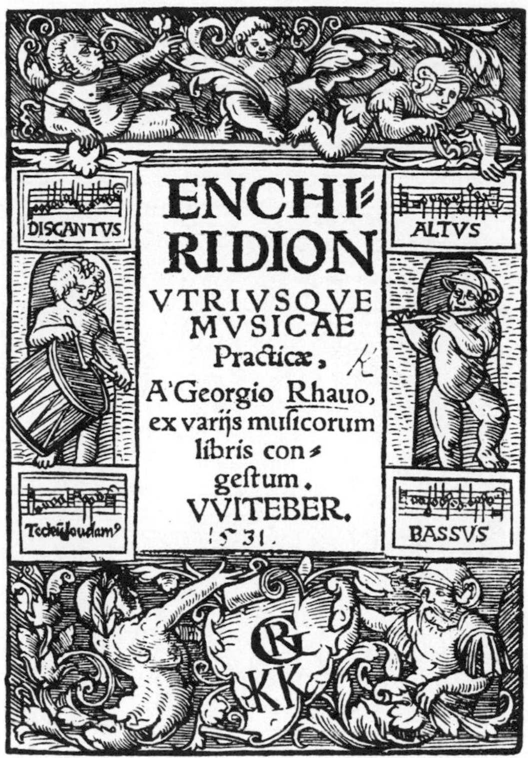

DISCANTVS

ALTVS

ENCHI-
RIDION
VTRIVSQVE
MVSICAE
Practicæ,
A'Georgio Rhauo,
ex variis musicorum
libris con-
gestum.
VVITEBER.
1531.

BASSVS

Fig. 2

GEORG RHAW (compiler)
Enchiridion Utriusque Musicae Practicae.
Rhaw, Wittenberg, 1531.
British Museum, London.

This handbook was first published by J. Rhau-Grunenberg, Wittenberg, in 1517. This 1531 title page seems to be that of the fifth edition (out of at least thirteen). For more information on Rhaw, see Plate 7.

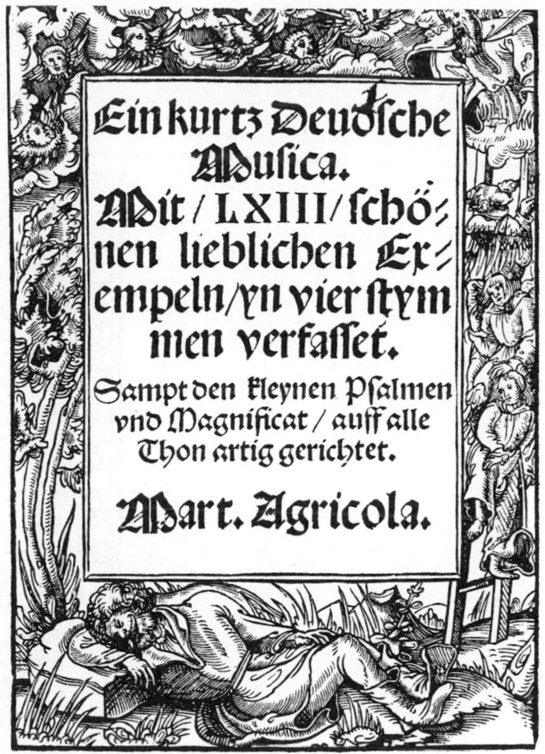

Ein kurtz Deudsche
Musica.
Mit / LXIII / schö-
nen lieblichen Ex-
empeln/yn vier stym-
men verfasset.
Sampt den kleynen Psalmen
vnd Magnificat / auff alle
Thon artig gerichtet.
Mart. Agricola.

Fig. 3

MARTINUS AGRICOLA (Martin Sore)
Ein kurtz Deudsche Musica. Georg Rhaw, Wittenberg, 1529.
Bayerische Staatsbibliothek, Munich.

Agricola (1486?–1556) was a musician of Luther's circle and an important theorist. This was his first book (first edition 1528), a textbook written—not in Latin, but in a German inspired by Luther's Bible translations—for the Protestant Lateinschule in Magdeburg, where Agricola was Cantor; the musical examples are by the author. The woodcut border has been variously attributed to a "Meister der Jakobsleiter" or the studio of Lucas Cranach at Wittenberg. On the printer Rhaw, see Plate 7.

with illuminated initials; by their sheer size these tomes called for beautifully designed title pages. Such books, placed on a lectern, were large enough to be read by a whole group of singers, as shown in an early treatise by Gaffurius (Figure 4). Other examples of this type in the present collection were issued by Attaingnant (Plate 5), Le Roy and Ballard (Plate 30) and du Chemin (Plate 31) in Paris, the brothers Dorico in Rome (Plates 18 and 19) and the famous printers Plantin in Antwerp (Plate 38) and Berg in Munich (Plate 44).

Following in the line of Petrucci's production, many of the earliest printed music books were collections of chansons. The triumphal spread of the Renaissance madrigal, which had its origin in the first decades of the sixteenth century, could hardly have occurred had there been no music printing. Beginning with one of the earliest madrigal collections (by Verdelot) issued by Gardane (Plate 13), the

Practica musicae vtriusq; cãtus excellẽtis Frã
chini gaffori laudẽsis. Quattuor libris modula
tissima: Sũmaq; diligẽtia nouissime ipressa.

Fig. 4

FRANCHINUS GAFFURIUS (Franchino Gafori)
Practica musicae. Venice, 1512.
Bayerische Staatsbibliothek, Munich.

The first edition of this theoretical work appeared in Milan in 1496, but this ornamental title is new in the 1512 Venice edition. Gaffurius (1451–1522), also an important composer, was in charge of the music at the Milan Duomo from 1484 until his death.

reader will find the titles of numerous issues of madrigals from Italy, France, Germany and England up to the middle of the seventeenth century.

Venice remained the hub of music printing until late in the seventeenth century. Its most prolific publishing firm was that of Gardane (later Italianized to Gardano), whose prodigious output between 1538 and 1611, continued by their successor Magni until 1685, included much of the madrigal production of Italy, France and Germany. The Gardano emblem, a lion and a bear with a rose, can be seen on many of their titles, often filling the whole page (Plate 13). Gardano's most notable competitors in Venice were the Scotto family, active from 1481 to at least 1609, and the Vincenti family, active from 1583 to 1665. Vincenti's emblem, a pine cone, appears on most of his title pages (Plate 24). These firms continued to use woodcut borders and to print by type even after some of their more up-to-date contemporaries, like Verovio (published between 1586 and 1608; see Plates 28, 29 and 73) and Borbone (active from 1615 to 1637; see Plates 78 and 79) at Rome, were making full use of engraving both for title design and music. The Renaissance border remained the principal ornament of music titles in Italy far into the seventeenth century. Several other music publishers were active in Venice in that century: Raverii, for a short but prolific period, 1606–1609; the Magni family, 1611–1685 (Plate 85), successors to Gardano; and Amadino, who published between 1583 and 1621 (Plate 69). Elsewhere in Italy, in Milan (Plate 75), Siena (Plate 76), Florence (Plates 68 and 80), Rome (Plates 74 and 77, for example) and Palermo (Plate 70), music remained a sideline of general book printers.

In France the first music printer of importance, Attaingnant, issued many books of chansons in addition to the monumental folios of church music already mentioned. A royal *privilège* gave the firm of Le Roy and Ballard (Plates 30, 32 and 33), later Ballard (Plate 34), a virtual monopoly of music printing in France for over 200 years starting in the mid-sixteenth century. Under the imprint of Le Roy and Ballard there appeared between 1551 and 1598 no fewer than 319 separate works of music, among them, as mentioned above, many large tomes of church music similar in style to those issued by the rival firm of du Chemin. Many of Le Roy and Ballard's music publications in the 1570's and 1580's featured the woodcut title exemplified here by a work of Lasso (Plate 32). This title, like the two following it, are in the Fontainebleau style, which derived its characteristics from the frescoes at Fontainebleau in which mythological figures are placed in a framework of stucco and painted architectural elements. In their general composition these Le Roy and Ballard titles greatly resemble a book title by Cousin the Younger which appears as Plate 58 in Alexander Nesbitt's *200 Decorative Title-Pages* (see Bibliography). In the seventeenth century the house of Ballard ignored the newer stylistic trends and issued many old-fashioned titles (Plate 35). Outside Paris the only important French center of music printing was Lyons. A Lyons title of 1583 (Plate 37) is also typical of the Fontainebleau style.

Throughout the sixteenth century in Germany numerous decorative music titles were produced in the best tradition of German woodcut art, and by some of the most noted masters of the medium. Southwestern and southern Germany remained the centers of this activity, notably Augsburg (Plates 50 and 51), Strassburg (Plate 49), Frankfurt (Plates 48 and 53), Nuremberg (Plates 46 and 47) and Munich (Plates 43–45). In general, music was not published by specialized music printers, as in Venice and Paris, but by ordinary book-printing firms, large and small. Beautiful music prints were produced by the famous presses of Jobin in Strassburg, Feyerabend in Frankfurt (Plate 48), Berg in Munich and—somewhat outside this area—Plantin in Antwerp (Plate 38).

In this period the only specialized music printer on a large scale outside Venice and Paris was the house of Phalèse (active from *c.* 1545 to *c.* 1650), situated first at Louvain and later at Antwerp. Their titles, however, usually show little decoration, apart from a liberal use of printer's flowers (Plate 42).

In the seventeenth century, music in the German-speaking area continued to be printed in the many cultural centers and residences which then flourished. Our group of fourteen prints dating from 1603 to 1676 were produced in no fewer than eleven cities: Augsburg (Plates 86 and 93), Helmstedt (Plate 88), Nuremberg (Plates 89 and 96), Wolfenbüttel (Plates 90 and 91), Leipzig (Plate 95), Königsberg (Plate 97), Dresden (Plate 98), Berlin (Plate 101), Wittenberg (Plate 94), Zittau (Plate 99) and Innsbruck (Plate 100). To this array of cities we might have added Erfurt, Lüneburg, Hamburg, Cologne, Lübeck, Jena and many others. Slightly outside this area were Utrecht (Plate 87) and Copenhagen (Plate 92). All this production was by local printers who did not specialize in music. The title pages were executed in woodcut or engraving and are good examples of German Baroque book art of the seventeenth century.

Music printing in England started only toward the middle of the sixteenth century, and was at first almost entirely confined to Psalm settings and similar devotional music. It had a short, but great, flowering during the English musical renaissance at the turn of the century, when much of the extensive production of "Elizabethan" madrigals appeared in print. The British publishers were particularly unoriginal in the decoration of their title pages, indiscriminately using designs and blocks from earlier periods, often imported from abroad. For example, the first work issued by the famous composers Tallis and Byrd as publishers (Plate 54) used a slightly altered version of an old Le Roy and Ballard title, while songs by Dowland (Plate 57) were adorned with a Moresque title copied from a French book of 1544, and a 1612 title to music by Corkine (Plate 60) was adapted from a Plantin print of 1566. But the most commonly used ornamental device of early English music, especially in the output of the music publisher East (Este), was printer's flowers (Plates 58 and 59).

The first English musical renaissance gradually came to an end in the first decade of the seventeenth century, and little music was published until the middle of the century. The Commonwealth fostered a more popular type of music: rounds, catches and country dances. The new music house of the Playfords, father and son, catered to the new development, producing this type of music cheaply and in a handy size. They dominated the English music market during the second half of the century. Our three titles by the elder Playford (Plates 102–104) conveniently illustrate the mood and nature of the music they introduce. Later the Playfords became the publishers of Purcell, and so played an important role in the second English musical renaissance.

In Venice, as we have seen, the great music publishing houses had ceased their activities by the middle of the seventeenth century. For the next 150 years Italy exported musicians rather than printed music. The works written by these cosmopolitan composers, like those of the Italian masters who stayed at home, were published in Amsterdam, Paris and London. Few Baroque music titles of distinction came out of Italy in the later seventeenth and early eighteenth centuries. Corelli's works appeared first in Rome (Plates 106–108) and Bologna, but were soon reprinted on a far larger scale in Amsterdam (Plate 109) and London.

In France through the first half of the seventeenth century, music publishing was still entirely dominated by the firm of Ballard, which by its refusal to follow the trends of the times missed the opportunities provided by engraving in the design of decorative title pages. A large proportion of the printed music of the period consisted of lute pieces. The great flowering of the arts during the second half of the century at the court of Louis XIV brought with it the rise of French grand opera and the supremacy of the harpsichord as a solo instrument. Music titles were adorned in the French style of Baroque known as "Louis XIV"; among the designers and engravers were some of the great masters of the graphic arts: Richer, Jollain, Lepautre and the team of Bérain and Scotin. Our selections include titles of works by the great harpsichordists Chambonnières (Plates 112 and 113) and d'Anglebert (Plate 116) and the celebrated court violist Marais (Plates 114 and 115).

The pompous magnificence of French Baroque changed gradually in the early eighteenth century to the graceful and playful Rococo. Though the harpsichord still enjoyed great popularity (Plates 120 and 126), the violin now became the favorite instrument (Plates 121, 125 and 128). Music titles have never been a more fitting expression of the musical and artistic language of their period, and we find among the designers some of the foremost masters of the Rococo: Lancret, Lebas, Lemire and Gravelot.

Compared with the wealth of music titles of artistic distinction in the France of Louis XIV and Louis XV, Germany (like Italy) has little to offer—with such notable exceptions as the magnificent titles from Mainz, 1695 (Plate 135), and Augsburg, 1736(?) (Plate 141). The old traditions of printing and engraving were still very much alive in these cities and in Nuremberg, which had all been among the earliest centers of printing. The works of Bach's contemporaries, as well as the few pieces published by the master in his lifetime (Plates 142 and 143), have title pages of only moderate interest.

Decorative music titles in England during the first half of the eighteenth century were still mostly in typical Baroque style. Several new music houses came into existence, by far the most important being the firm of Walsh, which published almost all that Handel wrote in England, in addition to much contemporary Italian, French and German music. During the first two decades of the century many of Walsh's titles were decorative, if rather stiff. The same blocks were used over and over again for many publications. Walsh's later titles are not ornamental in the strict sense, but are frequently distinguished by a bold lettering in monumental proportions (Plate 155). Also shown are two well-known titles of Handel operas issued by another contemporary publisher, Cluer (Plates 152 and 153).

The Rococo eventually spread from France to the other countries of Europe. Designs of delightful elegance and cosmopolitan style appeared in Germany (Plate 166, for instance), Holland (Plate 158), Italy (for example, Plate 161) and even faraway St. Petersburg (Plate 162). An English print, Bickham's *Musical Entertainer*, represents one of the high points of Rococo book art (Plates 156 and 157); it shows the direct influence of French book illustration, especially in the participation of one of the French masters of the genre, Gravelot, who was living in England at the time.

Rococo book art, however, never took deep root in England. Neoclassical trends began to develop as early as the 1760's, doubtless through the influence of Italian artists who had made England their home. Among them were Cipriani and Bartolozzi, the incomparable designer-engraver team whose enormous graphic output included several music titles (Plates 169 and 170).

In the 1770's the center of music publishing suddenly shifted to the German-speaking countries. Vienna, which had had an ancient tradition of music-making, but little music printing of distinction, now became for a few decades not only the musical capital of the world, but also a most important center of music publishing. Most of the music of Haydn and Mozart which appeared in their lifetime was first brought out by Artaria, a firm of Italian origin (see caption to Plate 179). Their titles utilize a great variety of motifs, but are on the whole in the tradition of neoclassicism; unfortunately none are signed.

Haydn's popularity throughout Europe was immense, numerous editions of his symphonies, piano works and chamber music appearing almost simultaneously in Vienna (Plates 178–180), Paris (Plate 174), Amsterdam (Plate 173) and London (Plates 175–177). Our selection of Haydn titles from these four centers shows the high standard of title designs in that period.

With the flourishing of music in the German lands, the last decades of the eighteenth century saw the foundation of those great German music houses which dominated the scene all through the nineteenth century and up to our own times: Schott in Mainz (from 1770), André in Offenbach (from 1784), Simrock in Bonn (from 1793) and Peters in Leipzig, whose beginnings date back to 1800. The Breitkopf family in Leipzig had started to publish music long before, but became the leading music publishers after Härtel joined the firm in 1795. Among the earliest productions of these publishers were works by Haydn and Mozart, which, in the tradition of the time, had well-designed title pages—a feature these publishers soon discarded. In the years around 1800 Breitkopf & Härtel issued the *"Oeuvres Complettes"* of Haydn (Plates 184 and 185) and Mozart (Plate 196), each volume of which has a title with a specially designed vignette by some well-known contemporary artist. The scores of Haydn's *Seasons* (Plates 181–183) have title pages in the same vein.

Toward the turn of the century the last remnants of Rococo gaiety and neoclassical grace had disappeared, and the pseudo-antique ruled once again, in the noble tones of the French Empire style (Plate 198) and its north German counterpart, the Schinkel style (Plate 199).

As already mentioned, few publishers of serious music in the nineteenth century were concerned with the decoration of their title pages, and there has been no improvement in this situation in more recent years. But it is only just—as well as a true pleasure—to illustrate here (Figure 5) an outstanding example of what can be accomplished in the twentieth century: Picasso's title to Stravinsky's *Ragtime*.

THE MOTIFS OF MUSIC-TITLE ORNAMENT

Obviously, music titles cannot be discussed or appreciated outside the context of general book titles of their time. Such a comparison, however, is difficult to make because of the rarity of comprehensive, well-illustrated and easily available works on book titles. The best bibliographical documentation is available for incunabula of the fifteenth century (too early for the period covered here) and for Renaissance titles of the sixteenth century in Germany (Johnson, 1929) and in England (McKerrow & Ferguson). Engraved English book titles to 1691 have been exhaustively described in Johnson's 1934 catalogue. A study of Baroque titles was made by Philip Hofer. Two comprehensive collections deal with decorative book titles from the beginning of printing. *One Hundred Title Pages*, by Johnson, is well documented for the Renaissance and the eighteenth century, but has very few Baroque titles. The latest and most comprehensive collection of book titles is the Nesbitt book mentioned on page 9. (For all books in this paragraph, see Bibliography.)

Fig. 5

IGOR STRAVINSKY

Ragtime. J. & W. Chester, London, 1919. Collection of G. S. Fraenkel.

Picasso worked with Stravinsky for several years beginning in 1917. This is the title page of the composer's piano arrangement of *Ragtime*; Picasso also illustrated the wrapper.

The characteristic designs of early titles of music books are similar in style and subject matter to those of other books. Indeed, the same designs were often used indiscriminately for publications of widely diverse subjects. The typical book title of the Renaissance was purely decorative without direct relation to the content of the book. Thus we find in early music books the various motifs of contemporary Renaissance book art: scrollwork (Plate 7), arabesque and Moresque patterns (Plate 57). Another early practice, inherited from the Gothic, but of amazing persistence through the centuries, was the use of grotesque motifs, such as fantastic combinations of animal and human figurative elements (for example, Plate 6) or facial contortions (for example, Plate 43). These gave way later, in the Baroque and Rococo periods, to playful groupings of animals, monsters or devils engaged in all sorts of musical activities (for example, Plate 131). Other recurring themes of title decoration were the archway forming a frame to the text of the title (for example, Plate 65) and the putto, displayed in liberal numbers (for example, Plate 110).

At the same time, music titles from the very beginning adopted pictorial designs with specifically musical associations—instruments and instrumental performers. Some titles are valuable source material for the design and development of musical instruments. Perhaps the greatest historical interest is attached to pictures representing the music-making of their period and showing the size, composition and arrangement of bands, orchestras, chamber ensembles and choirs. Of the many examples in this book I might mention in particular here the picture of the Mass at the court of Francis I in 1532 (Plate 5), the choral group in front of a lectern singing from one of the huge folios of the early sixteenth century (Figure 4), Lasso's Munich orchestra of the 1570's (Plate 44), ensembles of viols and recorders in early sixteenth-century Italy (Plates 10 and 11), the English lady at the virginals (Plate 64), the elaborate groupings of instrumentalists and singers in the church music of Praetorius (Plate 89), the gaiety of music-making in the "galant" era (Plate 126), and so on, up to the charming vignette of a piano-violin-cello trio in action in Haydn's time (Plate 180).

The custom of using title designs for many different prints, often over a lengthy period, developed very early. In the sixteenth and seventeenth centuries it was general practice for a printer to make repeated use of a woodcut or engraved border. A design perfectly suited to the work for which it was originally created often lost its meaning on the title of a music work. Some of the best-known music titles have such a history. The title of Morley's *Plaine and Easie Introduction* of 1597, also used in several other music prints of the period, was originally designed for a work on cosmography (Plate 63). The title design of Ward's madrigal collection of 1613 is partly unintelligible because of the deletion of the figure of Queen Elizabeth (Plate 61). The most familiar examples are from England, but this custom was also very common in Italy and Germany. The title design of a 1582 Florentine collection of madrigals was taken over from an earlier print of Lorenzo de' Medici's poetry (Plate 25). The well-known title of Caccini's *Euridice* of 1600 (Plate 68) had been used fifty years earlier by Torrentino of Florence for an edition of Pausanias.

Another, more legitimate, practice was the adoption of a design of general musical content for a whole series of publications; these titles are known nowadays as *passe-partout* titles. Le Roy and Ballard used the same woodcut border for about thirty vocal works in the 1570's and 1580's (Plate 32). The Roman printers Valerio and Luigi Dorico used a border of musical instruments and scenes of music-making for a series of huge tomes of church music (Plates 18 and 19). Walsh in London used a Collins title 22 times between 1695 and 1720 (Plate 148), and the title design to Handel's *Rinaldo* (Plate 154) 17 times between 1711 and 1720. The Empire title of Dalayrac's *Le Poëte et le Musicien* (Plate 198) figured in the scores of many French operas of the early nineteenth century.

Coats-of-arms frequently form the centerpiece of title pages in the sixteenth and seventeenth centuries. In most cases these emblems belong to the noble dedicatee of the work or patron of the composer. Music printed in Rome often carried the arms of the reigning pope (Plate 4), and local hierarchs are represented elsewhere (Plate 41). I have attempted to identify some of these heraldic devices in the captions, but, as is well known, this is often impossible, given the chaotic state of the systematics of heraldry. A title motif similar in character is the printer's sign or publisher's seal, often prominently displayed, as in early Gardane prints (Plate 13).

Finally, another common decorative device on musical title pages is the *fleuron* (printer's flowers), discussed above on page 5.

Artists Represented in the Present Collection

A few words must be said about the designers and engravers who created these title pages. Only about a third of the illustrations in this book are signed. In a few more cases we have stylistic or historical clues to the authorship. In most cases where signatures were present, it was possible to identify the artists readily by referring to the splendid work commonly known as "Thieme-Becker" (see Bibliography). This reference work was adopted as the standard here in citing names and dates of artists.

Unfortunately, almost all the sixteenth-century woodcuts are unsigned, and experts frequently disagree about attributions. An early Strassburg title (Plate 9) has often been attributed to Hans Baldung-Grien, and a contemporary title from Wittenberg (Figure 3) variously to a "Meister von der Jakobsleiter" or the studio of the Cranachs. There is almost general agreement on the attribution of a Luther print (Plate 6) to Cranach or his school on the grounds of location and style. One of the few signed German titles of the high Renaissance is the magnificent Feyerabend title by Jost Amman (Plate 48), who did much work for this publisher, and there is little doubt that Tobias Stimmer designed for Jobin in Strassburg the title shown in Plate 49. The famous Lasso title (Plate 44) used about the same time by Berg in Munich is considered to be the work of Hans Nelt.

No artist identification has been possible for any of the Italian or French titles in this collection dating from the sixteenth and the first half of the seventeenth centuries. With the advent of engraving, signatures become more frequent. Thus we know the authorship of some German and English Baroque titles, among them good examples by the Augsburg engravers Lucas Kilian (Plate 93) and Mathäus Küsel (Plate 100).

This uncertainty about signatures is removed during the great period of French book design and illustration in the ages of Louis XIV and Louis XV, when the major French graphic artists produced outstanding book and music titles. The present selection contains beautiful examples of titles by Richer (Plate 110), Jollain (Plate 112), Trouvain (Plate 114), Lepautre (Plate 117), Bérain (Plate 118), Krafft (Plate 120), Rigaud and Aubert (Plate 121), Guérard (Plate 125), Lancret and Thomassin (Plate 126), Lebas (Plate 127), Lemire (Plate 131) and Gravelot (Plate 133). From eighteenth-century England we present examples of title pages by Collins (Plate 148), Pine (Plate 147), van der Gucht (Plate 149) and the designer-engraver team Cipriani and Bartolozzi (Plates 169 and 170).

In contradistinction to their French contemporaries, most German, Italian and English title artists of the later eighteenth century did not sign their work. This is especially regrettable in the case of the many well-designed titles in Hummel's publications in Amsterdam (Plate 172) and Berlin (Plate 165) and Artaria's in Vienna (Plates 179, 180, 186–190, 197). Notable exceptions are the signed Haydn and Mozart titles dating from the beginning of the nineteenth century issued by Breitkopf & Härtel in Leipzig (Plates 183, 184 and 196).

Urbana, Illinois G. S. FRAENKEL
June, 1967

Bibliography

References for Music Titles

Die Musik in Geschichte und Gegenwart: Allgemeine Enzyklopädie der Musik, ed. by F. Blume, Bärenreiter-Verlag, Kassel and Basel, 1949–1965, 12 vols. so far.

Enciclopedia della Musica, Ricordi, Milan, 1963–1964, 4 vols.

Grand-Carteret, J., *Les titres illustrés et l'image au service de la Musique*, Bocca Frères, Turin, 1904.

Kinsky, G., *A History of Music in Pictures* (Eng. trans.), J. M. Dent and Sons, Ltd., London, 1930.

Larousse de la Musique, Librairie Larousse, Paris, 1957, 2 vols.

Smith, W. C., *A Bibliography of the Musical Works Published by John Walsh During the Years 1695–1720*, The Bibliographical Society, London, 1948.

von zur Westen, W., *Musiktitel aus vier Jahrhunderten*, Festschrift anlässlich des 75jährigen Bestehens der Firma C. G. Röder G.M.B.H., Leipzig, 1921.

References for Music Printing and Music Bibliography

Eitner, R., *Biographisch-Bibliographisches Quellen-Lexikon der Musiker und Musikgelehrten der christlichen Zeitrechnung bis zur Mitte des neunzehnten Jahrhunderts*, 1st ed.: Breitkopf & Härtel, Leipzig, 1900–1904, 10 vols.; 2nd ed.: Akademische Druck- u. Verlagsanstalt, Graz, 1959–1960, 11 vols.

Grove's Dictionary of Music and Musicians, 5th ed., ed. by E. Blom, St. Martin's Press, Inc., New York, 1954, 10 vols.

King, A. Hyatt, *Four Hundred Years of Music Printing*, Trustees of the British Museum, London, 1964.

Marksdale, A. B., *The Printed Note: 500 Years of Music Printing and Engraving*, Toledo Art Museum, Toledo, Ohio, 1957.

References for General Decorative Book Titles

Hofer, P., *Baroque Book Illustration*, Harvard University Press, Cambridge, 1951.

Johnson, A. F., *A Catalogue of Engraved and Etched English Title-Pages Down to the Death of William Faithorne, 1691*, printed for The Bibliographical Society, Oxford University Press, London, 1934 (for 1933).

———, *German Renaissance Title-Borders*, printed for The Bibliographical Society, Oxford University Press, London, 1929.

———, *One Hundred Title-Pages, 1500–1800*, John Lane, London, 1928.

McKerrow, R. B., and Ferguson, F. S., *Title-page Borders Used in England & Scotland, 1485–1640*, printed for The Bibliographical Society, Oxford University Press, London, 1932 (for 1931).

Nesbitt, A., *200 Decorative Title-Pages*, Dover Publications, Inc., New York, 1964.

References for the Graphic Artists

Allgemeines Lexikon der bildenden Künstler von der Antike bis zur Gegenwart ("Thieme-Becker"), ed. by U. Thieme and F. Becker, later by H. Vollmer, Leipzig, 1907–1950, 37 vols., Vols. 1–14 pub. by Wilhelm Engelmann, Vols. 15–37 by E. A. Seemann; plus 6 vols. of additions, ed. by H. Vollmer, pub. by E. A. Seemann, Leipzig, 1953–1962.

Hausenstein, W., *Rokoko: französische und deutsche Illustratoren des 18. Jahrhunderts*, 2nd revised ed., R. Piper & Co., Munich, 1958.

Hind, A. M., *A History of Engraving & Etching from the 15th Century to the Year 1914*, Dover Publications, Inc., New York, 1963.

———, *An Introduction to a History of Woodcut*, Dover Publications, Inc., New York, 1963, 2 vols.

Jessen, P., *Der Ornamentstich*, Verlag für Kunstwissenschaft, Berlin, 1920.

Plates

Harmonice Musices
Odhecaton

Canti.B.numero
Cinquanta

OTTAVIANO PETRUCCI

1 *Harmonice Musices Odhecaton*. Venice, 1501 (*A*) and 1502 (*B. Canti*).
Civico Museo Bibliografico Musicale, Bologna.

In 1498 Petrucci (1466–1539) obtained his license to print music in Venice. This work, which he compiled and printed, is considered to be the first in which movable metal type was used for printing mensural notation. The printing was done in three steps: first the staff lines, then the notes, then the text, initials and folios. These two booklets, *A* and *B*, were the first of a series that included three- and four-part chansons and motets by some of the most important composers of the time. *A* includes works by the Flemish composers Josquin Desprez (*c.* 1440–1521?), Hayne van Ghizeghem (or Gijzegem; fifteenth century), Jacob Obrecht (1450?–1505), Marbrianus de Orto (d. 1529), Johannes Japart and Alexander Agricola (1446–1506). *B* contains music by all the above-named, as well as by Pierre de la Rue (d. 1518).

PETRUS TRITONIUS

2 & 3 *Melopoeae sive Harmoniae tetracenticae super xxii genera carminum.* Erhart Öglin, Augsburg, 1507. Staats- und Stadtbibliothek, Augsburg.

Melopoeae is the first known mensural music book printed in Germany with movable type. The Austrian composer Tritonius (real name Peter Treibenreif or Traybenreiff), in association with

the Viennese humanist Conrad Celtes, produced these simple note-for-note polyphonic settings of Horatian odes that respect the original Latin meters. The title page is strictly typographical; these two plates reproduce leaves inserted into the musical portion of the book. Plate 2 represents Apollo entertaining an assembly of divinities on Mount Parnassus. In Plate 3 Apollo, Jupiter, Mercury, Minerva and Pegasus are surrounded by the Muses.

LIBER QVINDECIM
MISSARVM ELECTA
RVM QVAE PER EXCEL
LENTISSIMOS MVSICOS
COMPOSITAE FVERVNT

ANDREA DE ANTIQUIS [ANTIQUUS, ANTICO]

4 *Liber quindecim Missarum.* Rome, 1516.
British Museum, London.

The printer de Antiquis brought Petrucci's techniques to Rome, receiving the Vatican's permission to print church music in 1516. This folio volume, printed from wood blocks, contains Masses by Josquin Desprez (*c.* 1440–1521?), Anton Brumel (*c.* 1460–1520's), Antoine de Févin (*c.* 1470–1511/2), Pierre de la Rue (d. 1518), Jean Mouton (*c.* 1459–1522), Matthaeus Pipelare and Pietro Roselli (Pierre Rousseau?). The illustration shows de Antiquis presenting his work to Pope Leo X of the Medici family, with the Papal arms and Medici shield below.

Secundus liber tres missas continet.

Prima est Tua est potentia Auth. Mouton fo.xxxix

Secunda est Missa.ix.lc. Claudin fo.lij

Tertia est Surge ⁊ illuiare P.de Mãchicourt fo.lxiij

Cum gratia et priuilegio christianissimi Francorum Regis ad sexenniũ vt patet primo libro.

M.D.xxxij

Registrũ G.H.I.K.L.M.oẽs sunt terni p̃ter M.q̃ est quatern⁹ 19

PIERRE ATTAINGNANT

5 *Secundus liber* of the seven books of Masses *Primus* [*–septimus*] *liber viginti missarum musicalium*. Paris, 1532.
Österreichische Nationalbibliothek, Vienna.

This is the second of the seven volumes of Masses published by Attaingnant (d. 1552) in 1532; it contains works by Jean Mouton (*c.* 1459–1522), Claudin de Sermisy (*c.* 1495–1562) and Pierre de Manchicourt (*c.* 1510–1564). Attaingnant, a printer and music dealer in Paris since at least 1514, most of whose publications are collections of chansons, was the first in his city to print polyphonic music with movable type. In these volumes the notes and segments of staff lines were printed together. The title illustration, by a (German?) artist F. I., depicts a Mass attended by Francis I and other members of the French court.

Deudsche
Messe vnd ord-
nung Gottis
diensts.

Wittemberg.

MARTIN LUTHER

6 *Deudsche Messe.* Michael Lotter, Wittenberg, 1526.
British Museum, London.

An enthusiastic amateur musician, Luther (1483–1546) assigned music an important role in the popularization of the church service, writing his own songs and hymns and prompting others to write more. In this version of the German Mass, on the music of which he collaborated with Conrad Rupff (the Kapellmeister of the Elector of Saxony) and Johann Walter (or Walther; 1496–1570), Luther introduced vernacular elements into the service. The title design, which also appears on tracts by Luther issued by the same publisher, is generally attributed to Lucas Cranach the Elder (1472–1553), who lived in Wittenberg at that time and worked closely with Luther.

GEORG RHAW [RHAU]

7 *Symphoniae iucundae.* Wittenberg, 1538.
Bayerische Staatsbibliothek, Munich.

Rhaw (1488–1548), Cantor of St. Thomas' in Leipzig from 1519 on, published music and other books and pamphlets in the service of the Reformation in Wittenberg from about 1523 until his death; his most important publications contain Protestant music for church and home use. *Symphoniae iucundae* consists of 52 polyphonic vocal pieces, some secular, by such important contemporary composers as Ludwig Senfl (*c.* 1486–1542/3), Henricus Isaac (*c.* 1450–1517), Anton Brumel (*c.* 1460–1520's), Georg Forster (*c.* 1510–1568), Johann Walter (or Walther; 1496–1570), Philippe Verdelot (?–1567?) and Pierre de la Rue (d. 1518). The collection received official sanction from the highest Protestant authorities, Luther himself contributing the famous Latin introduction in praise of music. The titles of the discant and tenor parts are here illustrated.

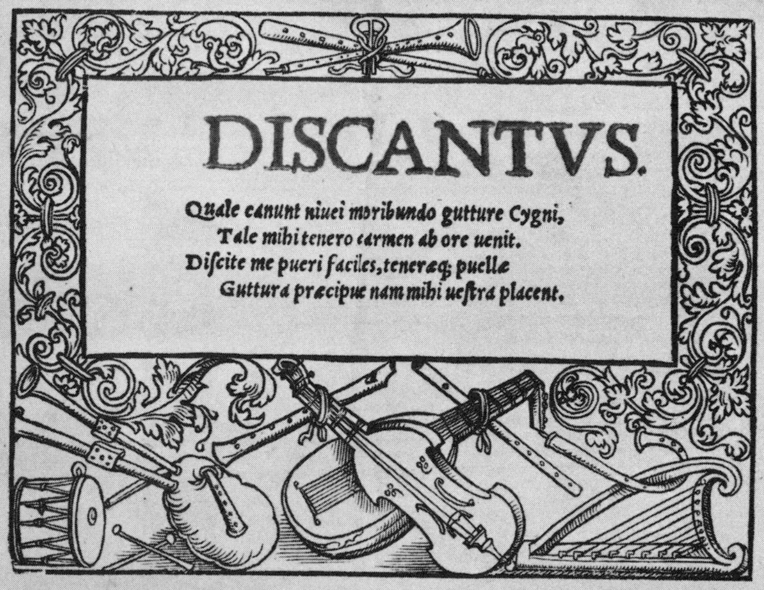

DISCANTVS.

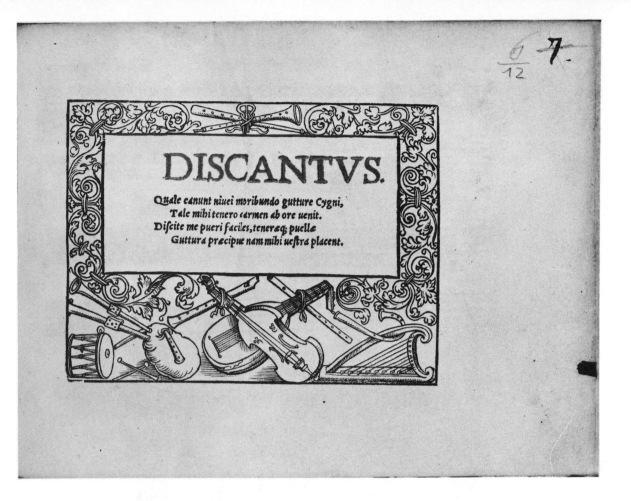

Quale canunt niuei moribundo gutture Cygni,
Tale mihi tenero carmen ab ore uenit.
Discite me pueri faciles, teneræq; puellæ
Guttura præcipue nam mihi uestra placent.

SYMPHONIÆ IV- CVNDAE ATQVE ADEO BREVES

QVATVOR VOCVM, AB OPTIMIS QVIBVSQVE MVSICIS COMPO-
sitæ, ac iuxta ordinem Tonorum dispositæ, quas vulgo mutetas appellare solemus,
Numero quinquaginta duo.

TENOR.

Vox ego sum simplex, tenuiq; canenda labore,
Hinc mea conueniens carmina nomen habent.
Vtq; ego, sic facili resonant modulamine cantus,
Quos breuis hic omni parte libellus habet.
Hi tibi quisquis amas Musarum sacra placebunt,
Seu quia dulce canunt, seu quia sacra canunt.

Cum Præfatione D. Martini Lutheri.

Vitebergæ apud Georgium Rhau.
Anno XXXVIII.

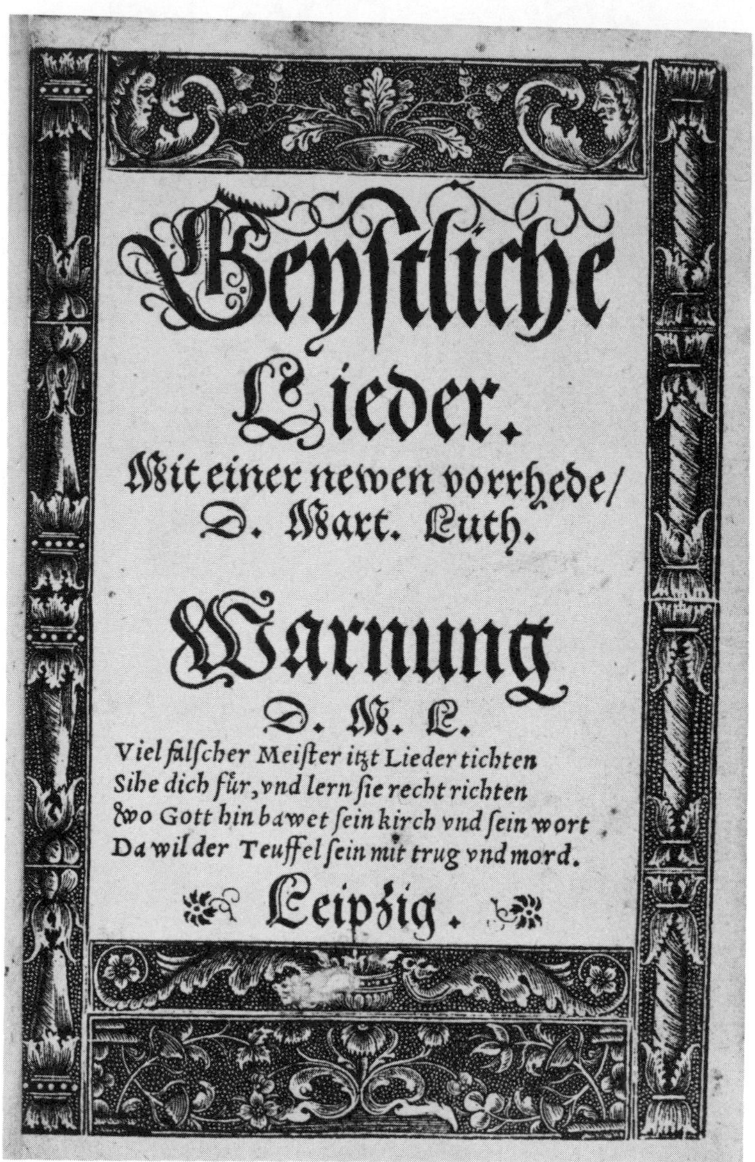

Geyſtliche Lieder.

Mit einer newen vorrhede/ D. Mart. Luth.

Warnung D. M. L.

Viel falſcher Meiſter itzt Lieder tichten
Sihe dich für, vnd lern ſie recht richten
Wo Gott hin bawet ſein kirch vnd ſein wort
Da wil der Teuffel ſein mit trug vnd mord.

Leipzig.

MARTIN LUTHER

8 *Geystliche Lieder*. Valentin Babst, Leipzig, 1545. British Museum, London.

The last of many books of "sacred songs" by Luther and the composers of his circle to appear under Luther's personal supervision, this collection of 101 hymns was printed entirely from wood blocks. Babst printed much Protestant devotional literature.

RERVM

MVSICARVM

OPVSCVLVM RARVM AC IN-
ſigne,totius eius negotii rationem mira in-
duſtria & breuitate complectens, iam
recens publicatum.I O A N.
FROSCHIO,
Autore,

JOHANN FROSCH

9 *Rerum musicarum opusculum.* Peter Schöffer & Mathias Apiarius, Strassburg, 1535.
Reproduced from von zur Westen, *Musiktitel aus vier Jahrhunderten.*

This is a posthumous edition of a theoretical tract, with many musical examples, by the Lutheran theologian Frosch (*c.* 1480–1533), who like Luther himself was a keen musician. The woodcut illustration used to be attributed to Hans Baldung-Grien (*c.* 1480–1545). The shield contains Schöffer's printer's sign.

SYLVESTRO DI GANASSI DAL FONTEGO

10 *Opera Intitulata Fontegara.* Published by the author, Venice, 1535.
Civico Museo Bibliografico Musicale, Bologna.

Ganassi (1492–?) was a virtuoso performer on the recorder and the viola da gamba at the Doge's court and San Marco in Venice. *Fontegara,* his instruction book for recorder playing, contains the earliest detailed sixteenth-century theory of improvisational ornaments.

SYLVESTRO DI GANASSI DAL FONTEGO

11 *Regola Rubertina.* Published by the author, Venice, 1542. Civico Museo Bibliografico Musicale, Bologna.

Like Ganassi's other instruction book (Plate 10), this manual for viol performers (named for an aristocratic pupil, Roberto Strozzi) is addressed to the virtuoso rather than the beginner. The title design is historically important, since it shows the playing position of the various members of the viol family and proves that the entire family was already fully developed by this time. A second part of *Regola Rubertina* appeared in 1543.

TENOR.

PRIMVS LIBER CVM SEX VOCIBVS.

CVM GRATIA ET PRIVILEGIO

MOTTETTI DEL FRVTTO A SEI VOCI

I

ALTVS.

PRIMVS LIBER CVM SEX VOCIBVS.

A. G.

CVM GRATIA

ET PRIVILEGIO.

MOTTETTI DEL FRVTTO A SEI VOCI

N

✤ BASSVS ✤

DI VERDELOT TVTTI LI MADRIGALI DEL PRIMO ET SE-
condo Libro, a Quatro Voci: Nouamente riſtampati, & da molti errori emen-
dati. Con la Gionta de i Madrigali del medeſmo Auttore.

AGGIONTOVI ANCHORA ALTRI MADRIGALI
nouamente Compoſti da Meſſer Adriano, & da altri Eccellentiſsimi Muſici.

M D XXXXI

Excudebat Venetiis, apud Antonium Gardane. Verdelot primi, & ſecundi. BB

ANTONIO GARDANE

12 *Mottetti del Frutto a sei voci.* Venice, 1539.
Bayerische Staatsbibliothek, Munich.

Gardane (d. 1570/1; of French origin) introduced to Italy the technique—already developed in France—of printing notes and staff lines simultaneously. He began to print music in Venice in 1538 and the house he founded (called Gardano from 1555 on) was the most important Italian music publisher until well into the next century. The emblem that appears most often on Gardano title and end pages (see Plate 13) shows a lion and a bear holding a rose. The six-voice *Mottetti del Frutto* contains motets by Nicolas Gombert (*c.* 1500–*c.* 1556) and other masters. The title design of the alto part, in which the Gardano lion and bear are mangling a monkey, is a spiteful allusion to a rival collection, the *Moteti de la Simia*, published earlier the same year at Ferrara by J. de Buglhat, H. de Campis and A. Hucher.

PHILIPPE VERDELOT

13 *Tutti li Madrigali del Primo et Secondo Libro.* Antonio Gardane, Venice, 1541.
Civico Museo Bibliografico Musicale, Bologna.

The Flemish composer Verdelot (?–*c.* 1567), active in Florence and Venice, was one of the first Renaissance madrigalists. This early Gardane print features his house emblem. Also represented by madrigals in this collection is Adriaan Willaert ("Messer Adriano"; 1490–1562), as well as other major Flemish composers active in Italy.

MARCO ANTONIO CAVAZZONI DA BOLOGNA, DETTO D'URBINO

14 *Recerchari, Motetti, Canzoni*. Bernardino Vercellense, Venice, 1523.
British Museum, London.

Cavazzoni (before 1490–after 1559), who was active at Venice, Chioggia, Padua and Rome, is considered the first important composer for the organ in Italy. This collection of organ pieces, probably prepared from metal blocks, is one of the earliest printed books of instrumental music.

CANTVS

MADRIGALI A

QVATRO VOCI DE SIMON

BOYLEAV NOBILE FRANCESE DA LVI NO

uamente composti & coretti

& posti in luce.

A QVATRO VOCI

M. D. XLVI

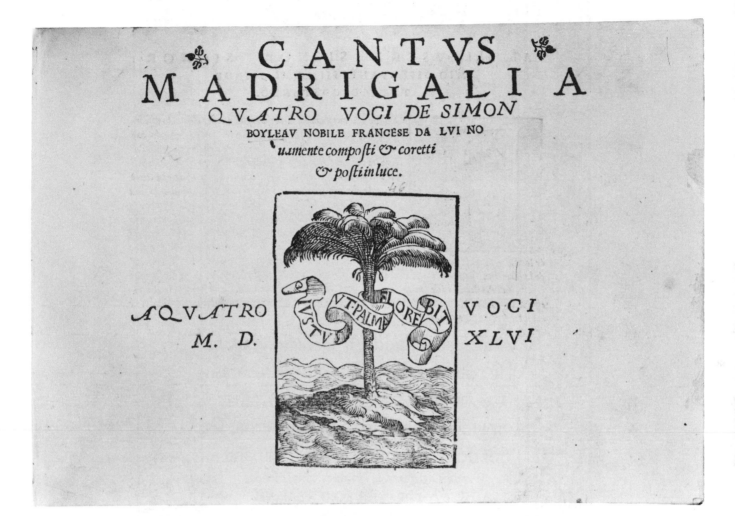

SIMON BOYLEAU

15 *Madrigali a quatro voci.* Francesco & Simone Moscheni (?), Milan, 1546. British Museum, London.

Boyleau was music director at the Milan Duomo from 1551 to 1557 and from 1573 to 1577. The printer's sign is a palm tree with the motto "Iustus ut palma florebit" (The just man shall flourish like the palm tree).

PL VS VL TRA

·BDS·

LIBRO DE MVSICA PARA
Vihuela, intitulado Orphenica lyra. Enl
ql ſe cõtienen muchas y diuerſas obras.
Cõpueſto por Miguel de Fuenllana.
Dirigido al muy alto y muy poderoſo ſe
ñor don Philippe principe de Eſpaña,
Rey de Ynglaterra, de Napoles. &c. nro ſeñor.
CON PRIVILLEGIO REAL.
1554

·BDS·

Taſſado en veynte y ocho reales.

MIGUEL DE FUENLLANA

16 *Orphenica lyra*. Seville, 1554.
Bibliothèque Nationale, Paris.

Fuenllana (born *c.* 1500), blind from birth, court musician to Philip II, was a virtuoso performer on and composer for the vihuela. *Orphenica lyra* contains a theoretical introduction and six books of fantasias and tientos, five for vihuela and one for Spanish guitar. The coat-of-arms on the title page is that of the Spanish royal house; the artist's initials BDS may be seen in two places. The part titles of this book also feature beautiful Renaissance borders.

LIBRO DE MVSICA DE VIHVELA, AGORA NVEVA mente compueſto por Diego Piſador, vezino dela ciudad de Salamanca, dirigido al muy alto y muy poderoſo ſeñor don Philippe principe de Eſpaña nueſtro Señor.

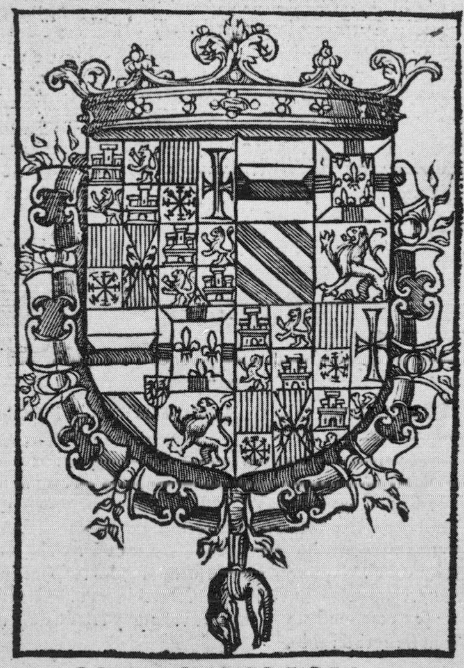

CON PRIVILEGIO.
Eſta taſſado en [illegible] marauedis.
1552

DIEGO PISADOR

17 *Libro de musica de vihuela.* Published by the author, Salamanca, 1552. British Museum, London.

Pisador (*c.* 1509–after 1557) was a vihuela performer at Salamanca. This book contains vihuela tablature settings of vocal music by Josquin Desprez (*c.* 1440–1521?), Jean Mouton (*c.* 1459–1522), Nicolas Gombert (*c.* 1500–*c.* 1556) and Cristóbal de Morales (*c.* 1500–1553).

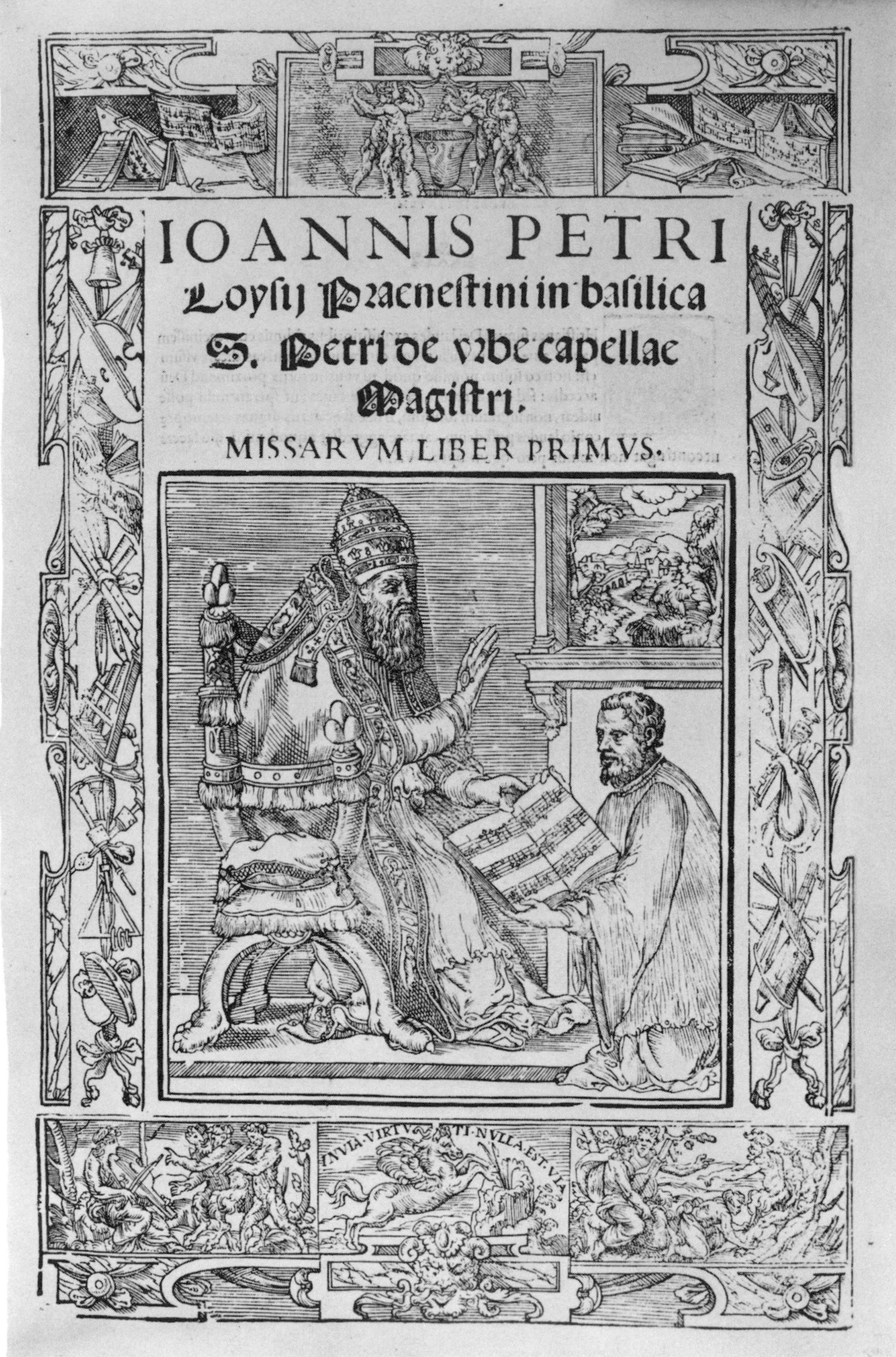

IOANNIS PETRI
Loysij Praenestini in basilica
S. Petri de vrbe capellae
Magistri.
MISSARVM LIBER PRIMVS.

GIOVANNI PIERLUIGI DA PALESTRINA

18 *Missarum liber primus.* Valerio & Luigi Dorico, Rome, 1554.
British Museum, London.

This was the first printed work by the great reformer of Catholic church music Palestrina (*c.* 1525–1594). It was the first in a series of monumental tomes of sacred music with identical borders (see Plate 19) published by the Dorici. The central scene of this title, which represents the composer handing his work to Pope Julius III, is merely a slightly retouched version of a scene that appeared on the title page of a book of Masses by Morales in 1544, so that the accuracy of the portraits is questionable.

Canticum B. Mariae Virginis
a Jo: Animuccia Urbis Basi-
licae S. Petri Magistro
ad omnes modos
Factum.

GIOVANNI ANIMUCCIA

19 *Canticum B. Mariae Virginis*. Valerio & Luigi Dorico, Rome, 1568. British Museum, London.

Animuccia (*c.* 1500–1571), a Roman composer who supplied music for Filippo Neri's Oratorio San Girolamo and who succeeded Palestrina as music director of St. Peter's from 1555 to 1571, wrote church music in the "new" style of Palestrina that emphasized the meaning of the text. The border is the same as in Plate 18.

CONSTANTII PORTAE
ALMAE ECCLESIAE DEIPARAE
VIRGINIS LAVRETANAE
MAGISTRI MVSICES.
MISSARVM LIBER PRIMVS.
Venetijs apud
Angelum Gardanum
M. D. lxxviij.

COSTANZO PORTA

20 *Missarum liber primus.* Angelo Gardano, Venice, 1578. Civico Museo Bibliografico Musicale, Bologna.

Porta (*c.* 1529–1601), a composer of sacred music and madrigals, was music director in churches at Padua, Ravenna and Loretto. The center of this title page shows the shrine of the Virgin that is said to have been lifted up by angels and flown across the seas from Nazareth to Loretto in 1294.

INTAVOLA-
TVRA DE
LIVTO

DI IVLIO CESARE
BARBETTA PADOANO

Doue ſi contiene Padoane Arie Baletti
Paſs' e mezi Saltarelli per Ballar
à la Italiana, & altre coſe
diletteuoli ſecondo
l'uſo di queſti
tempi,

Accommodato per Sonar con Sei
e Sette ordeni de corde.

In Venetia Appreſſo Angelo Gardano
M. D. LXXXV.

GIULIO CESARE BARBETTA

21 *Intavolatura de liuto.* Angelo Gardano, Venice, 1585.
Library of Congress, Washington.

This is a collection of lute compositions in tablature, based on dances of the period, by the Paduan lutenist Barbetta (*c.* 1540–after 1603).

ALTO
DI ANDREA GABRIELI
ORGANISTA DELL'ILLVSTRISS.
Signoria di Venetia in S. Marco.

Il Primo Llibro de Madrigali a Sei voci.
Nuouamente Composti
& dati in Luce.

CON PRIVILEGIO.

VIR TVS

In Venet. Ap. li Figl. d'Ant'Gard. 1574.

I

ANDREA GABRIELI

22 *Il Primo Llibro de Madrigali a Sei voci.* Sons of Antonio Gardano [Angelo Gardano], Venice, 1574. Civico Museo Bibliografico Musicale, Bologna.

Andrea Gabrieli (born between 1510 and 1520, died 1586; uncle of Giovanni Gabrieli), organist at San Marco in Venice from 1564 on, was a popular and prolific composer in all genres of music, best known for his *stile concertato* and the tone color of his polychorality. His madrigals, too, are distinguished by a perfect adaptation of musical ideas to the meaning of the text.

CANTO

IL TRIONFO
DI DORI,

DESCRITTO DA DIVERSI,
Et poſto in Muſica, à Sei Voci,
da altretanti Autori.

In Venetia Appreſſo Angelo Gardano.

M. D. LXXXXII.

ANGELO GARDANO

23 *Il trionfo di Dori.* Venice, 1592.
Library of Congress, Washington.

This is a collection of 29 six-part madrigals by some of the most celebrated composers of the time, among whom were Felice Anerio (1560–1614), Gasparo Costa (active 1581–1590), Giovanni Croce (*c.* 1557–1609; see next plate), Giovanni Gabrieli (*c.* 1555–1612/3), Luca Marenzio (1553/4–1559), Philipp (Filippo) de Monte (1521–1603), Palestrina (see Plate 18), Porta (see Plate 20) and Orazio Vecchi (1550–1605). Angelo Gardano was the publisher and editor. All the texts end: "Viva la bella Dori!" This book was no doubt the direct inspiration for the collection edited by Thomas Morley in 1603 (?) in honor of Queen Elizabeth, *The Triumphes of Oriana*, in which each song ends: "Long live fair Oriana!"

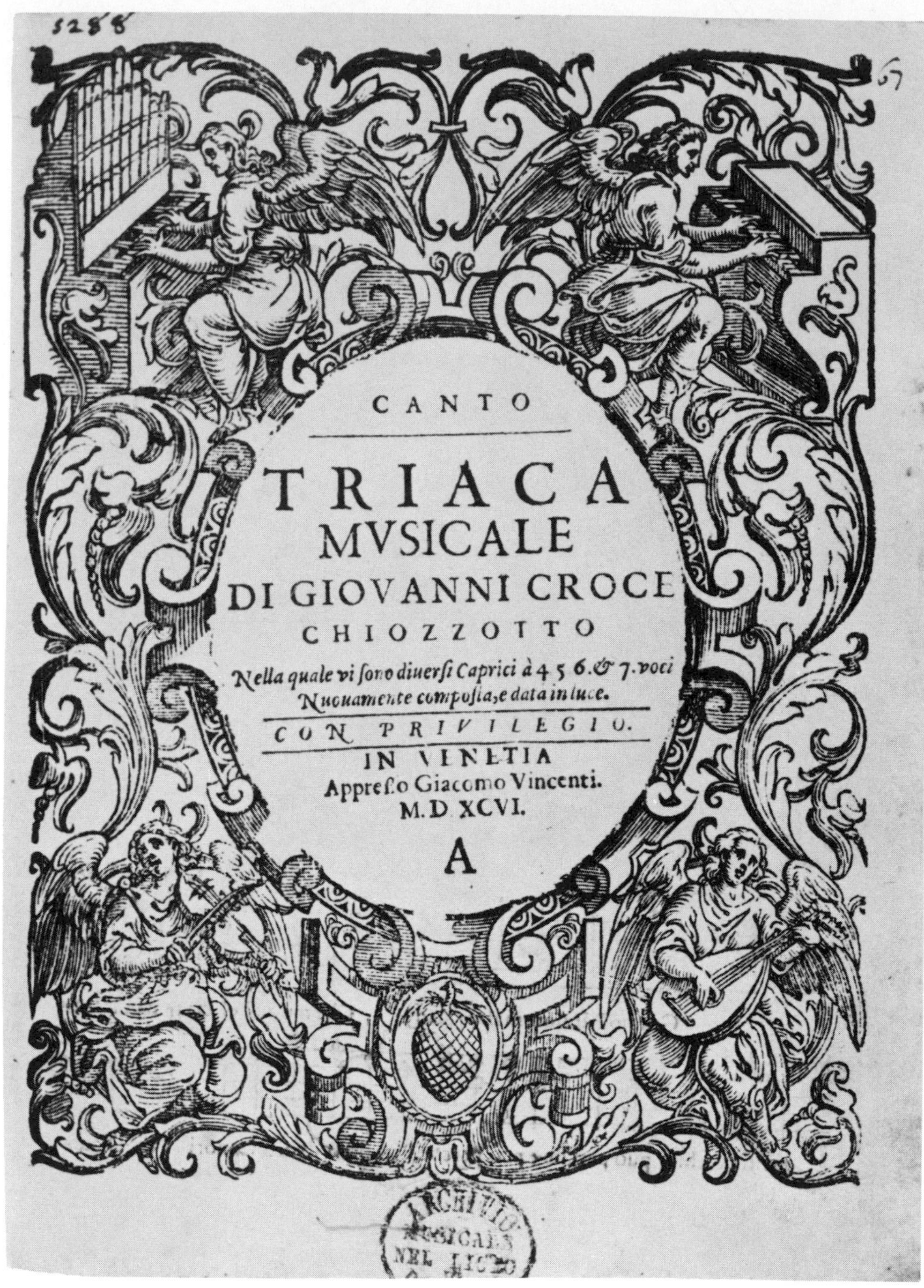

CANTO

TRIACA
MVSICALE
DI GIOVANNI CROCE
CHIOZZOTTO

*Nella quale vi sono diuersi Caprici à 4 5 6. & 7. voci
Nuouamente composta, e data in luce.*

CON PRIVILEGIO.

IN VENETIA
Appresso Giacomo Vincenti.
M.D XCVI.

A

GIOVANNI CROCE

24 *Triaca musicale.* Giacomo Vincenti, Venice, 1596.
Civico Museo Bibliografico Musicale, Bologna.

Croce (*c.* 1557–1609) was music director of San Marco in Venice and an important composer of secular and liturgical music. *Triaca musicale* (first published 1595) is a madrigal-comedy, a form of musical theater that immediately anteceded the opera (see Plates 68 and 69); *triaca* means "cure-all" or "nostrum." For another work by Croce, see Plate 59. Vincenti was one of the most prolific Venetian music printers of his time. His emblem, seen on most of his productions, is a pine cone.

DELLA

SCELTA DI MADRIGALI

de piu eccellenti Autori

DE' NOSTRI TEMPI

A TRE VOCI.

LIBRO PRIMO.

CAN  TO.

IN FIRENZE MDLXXXII.

Appresso Giorgio Marescotti.

25 *Scelta di madrigali*. Giorgio Marescotti, Florence, 1582.
Österreichische Nationalbibliothek, Vienna.

This is the title page to the first book of this collection of madrigals by Alemano Layolle (Aiolli), Vincenzo Ferro (first half of sixteenth century), Andrea Gabrieli (see Plate 22), Ihan (Jehan, Jan) Gero (mid-sixteenth century), Orlando di Lasso (*c.* 1532–1594; see Plates 32, 33 and 44–46), Lerma, Giovanni Nasco (d. 1561), Matteo Rampollini (first half of sixteenth century), Francesco Rosselli (Roussel?) and anonymous composers. The title vignette had already appeared on the title of Marescotti's edition of *Selve d'amore* by Lorenzo de' Medici.

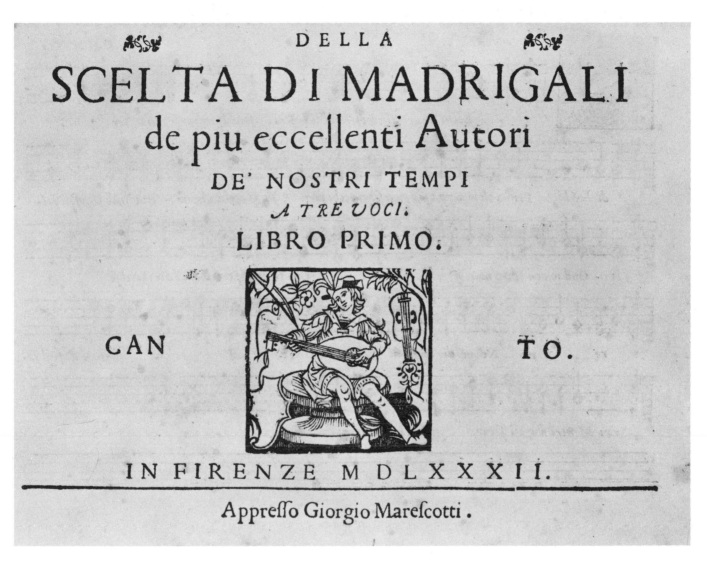

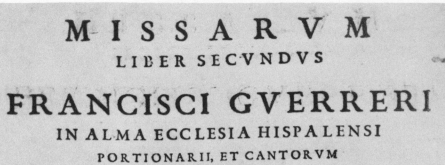

MISSARVM
LIBER SECVNDVS
FRANCISCI GVERRERI
IN ALMA ECCLESIA HISPALENSI
PORTIONARII, ET CANTORVM
PRAEFECTI.

ROMAE.
Ex Typographia Dominici Basæ.
MDLXXXII.
De santtiago delos españoles de Roma

FRANCISCO GUERRERO

26 *Missarum liber secundus*. Domenico Basa, Rome, 1582.
Civico Museo Bibliografico Musicale, Bologna.

A student of Morales, Guerrero (1527/8–1599) was director of the Seville choir school. Most of the music of the Seville composers was printed in Italy at that time.

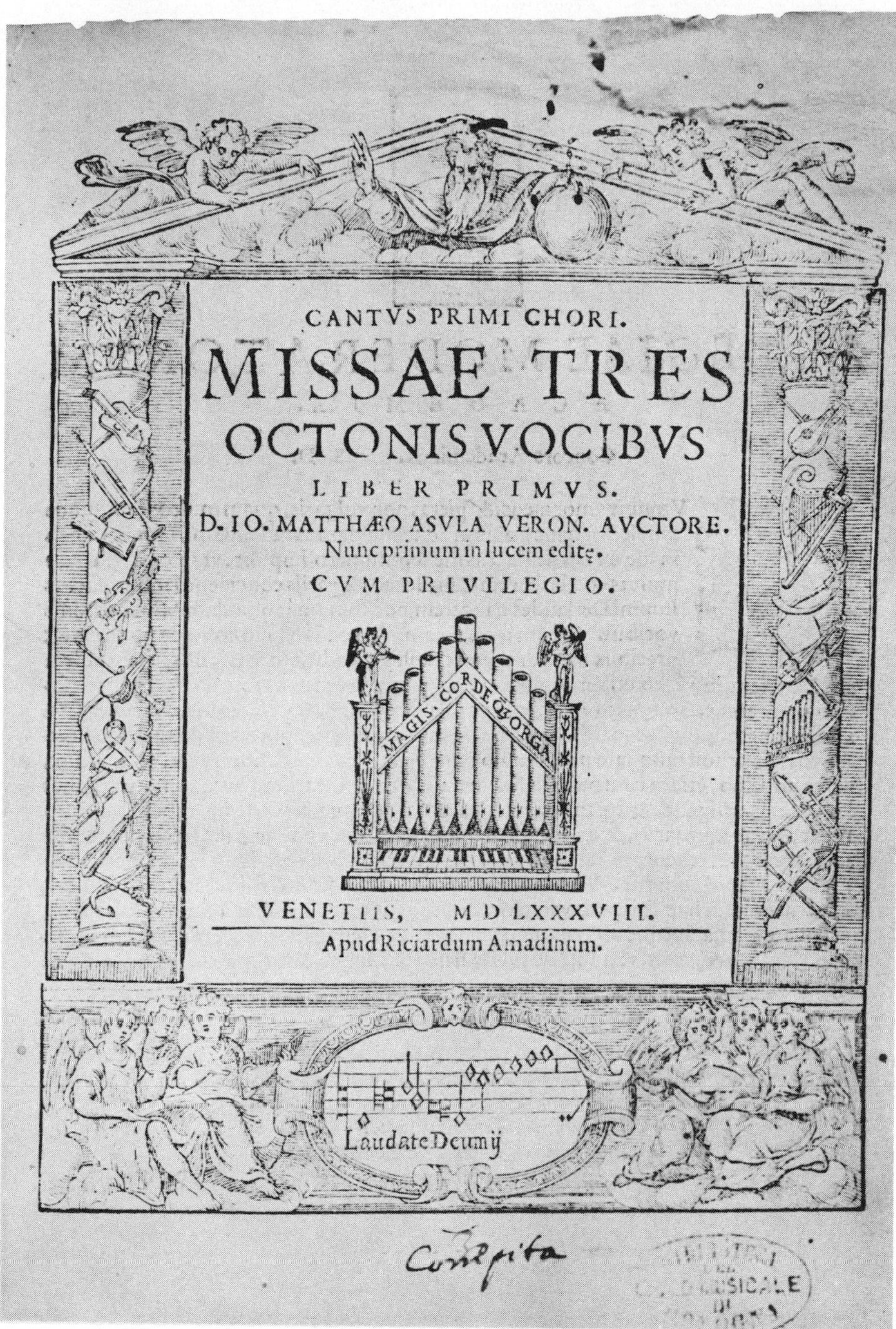
CANTVS PRIMI CHORI.
MISSAE TRES
OCTONIS VOCIBVS
LIBER PRIMVS.
D. IO. MATTHÆO ASVLA VERON. AVCTORE.
Nunc primum in lucem editę.
CVM PRIVILEGIO.
MAGIS. CORDE. Q. ORGA
VENETIIS, MDLXXXVIII.
Apud Riciardum Amadinum.
Laudate Deum ij

GIOVANNI MATTEO ASOLA

27 *Missae tres octonis vocibus*. Ricciardo Amadino, Venice, 1588. Civico Museo Bibliografico Musicale, Bologna.

Asola (*c.* 1524–*c.* 1609) was music director in cathedrals and churches at Treviso, Vicenza, Venice and Verona. He is noted as one of the first composers to write figured basses for the organ accompaniment of sacred music.

GHIRLANDA

DI FIORETTI

MVSICALI

Composta da diuersi Ecc. Musici a 3. voci
Con l'intauolatura del Cimbalo, et
LIVTO

Raccolte et stampate da Simone Verouio

In Roma 1589. Con licentia de Superiori

SIMONE VEROVIO

28 *Ghirlanda di fioretti musicali.* Rome, 1589.
British Museum, London.

Verovio, the editor and publisher of this historic work, was born at s'Hertogenbosch. A composer and music printer at Rome between 1586 and 1595, he is credited with having been the first to use engraved plates, with Martin van Buyten (*fl.* 1588–1613) as his engraver. The *Ghirlanda* is a collection of 25 madrigals by Felice Anerio, Gasparo Costa, Luca Marenzio (for these three, see Plate 23), Palestrina (see Plate 18), Antonio Orlandini, Giovanni Battista Zucchelli and others.

LODI DELLA MVSICA
A.3. Voci.
Composte da diuersi Ecc.ti
Musici con l'intauolat.a
del Cimbalo et liuto
Libro Primo.
Raccolte intagliate et
stampate da Simone
Verouio In
Roma
1595.
Con licentia de Superiori.

SIMONE VEROVIO

29 *Lodi della Musica.* Rome, 1595.
British Museum, London.

This Verovio collection, similar to the foregoing, contains 18 madrigals by Felice Anerio (see Plate 23), Ruggiero Giovannelli (*c.* 1560–1625), the Nanino brothers, Giovanni Maria (*c.* 1545–1607) and Giovanni Bernardino (*c.* 1560–1623), and others.

MISSÆ

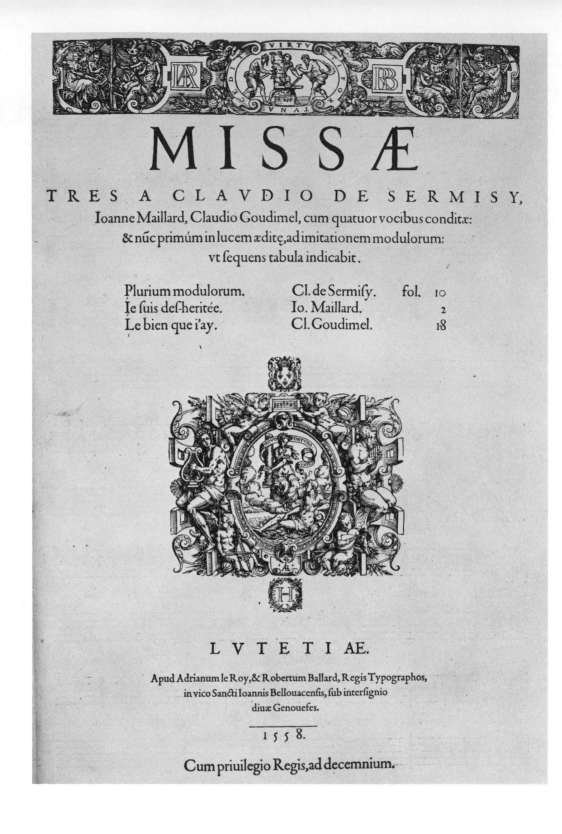

TRES A CLAVDIO DE SERMISY,
Ioanne Maillard, Claudio Goudimel, cum quatuor vocibus conditæ:
& nũc primúm in lucem æditę, ad imitationem modulorum:
vt ſequens tabula indicabit.

Plurium modulorum.	Cl. de Sermiſy.	fol.	10
Ie ſuis deſ-heritée.	Io. Maillard.		2
Le bien que i'ay.	Cl. Goudimel.		18

LVTETIAE.

Apud Adrianum le Roy, & Robertum Ballard, Regis Typographos,
in vico Sanƈti Ioannis Bellouacenſis, ſub interſignio
diuæ Genouefes.

1558.

Cum priuilegio Regis, ad decemnium.

CLAUDIN DE SERMISY (and others)

30 *Missae tres.* Adrian Le Roy & Robert Ballard, Paris, 1558.
Library of Congress, Washington.

Sermisy (1490–1562) was a French composer of sacred music and chansons, a royal musician and a canon of the Sainte-Chapelle. Also represented in this volume are Jean Maillard (*fl.* 1538–1570) and Claude Goudimel (*c.* 1514–1572), who became known for his Protestant Psalm settings written at Metz and elsewhere.

MISSARVM
MVSICALIVM, CERta vocum varietate, ſecundum varios quos referunt modulos & cantiones diſtinctarum,

LIBER SECVNDVS, EX DIVERſis, iiſdemque peritiſsimis auctoribus collectus.

Quorum nomina ſingulis Miſsis adſcripta ſequens tabella indicat.

Miſſa.	Vidi ſpecioſam.	5.	Vocibus diſtincta Auctore.	Val. Sohier.
	Pro Mortuis.	5.		Bonneſond.
	Alma redemptoris.	4.		Cadeac.
	Ie ſuis deſ-heritée.	4.		Guyon.
	Quo abijt dilectus.	4.		Manchicourt.
	De beata Maria.	4.		P. Cler'eau.
	Ie ſuis deſ-heritée.	4.		Gombert.
	Si bona ſuſcepimus.	4.		Do. Finot.
	Ie n'en puis plus.	4.		Daulphin.
	O gente brunette.	4.		De Marle.

PARISIIS,

Ex typographia Nicolai du Chemin, ſub inſigni Gryphonis argentei, via ad D. Ioannem Lateranenſem.

M.D.LXVIII.

Cum priuilegio Regis.

NICOLAS DU CHEMIN

31 *Missarum musicalium . . . liber secundus*. Paris, 1568.
Bibliothèque Nationale, Paris.

Du Chemin (d. 1576), an important Parisian publisher whose first music print dates from 1549, collected and published these Masses by French and Flemish composers. Represented are: Mathieu (or Valentin) Sohier (d. 1560), Simon de Bonefont, Pierre Cadéac (mid-sixteenth century), Jean Guyon (*c.* 1514–after 1574), Pierre de Manchicourt (*c.* 1510–1564), Pierre Cléreau, Nicolas Gombert (*c.* 1500–*c.* 1556), Dominique Phinot (Finot), Pierre Daulphin and Nicolas de Marle.

PRIMVS
LIBER MODVLORVM,
QVINIS VOCIBVS
CONSTANTIVM,
ORLANDO LASSVSIO AVCTORE.

LVTETIÆ PARISIORVM.
Apud Adrianum le Roy, & Robertum Ballard,
Regis Typographos ſub ſigno
montis Parnaſſi.
1571
Cum priuilegio Regis ad decennium.
CONTRATENOR.

ORLANDO DI LASSO

32 *Primus liber modulorum*. Adrian Le Roy & Robert Ballard, Paris, 1571.
Bayerische Staatsbibliothek, Munich.

Orlando di Lasso (Orlandus Lassus; *c*. 1532–1594) was one of the most important and prolific composers of the sixteenth century. His works were published and reprinted in innumerable editions in Germany, France, Italy and the Netherlands. The ornamental border of this title page was used by Le Roy (*c*. 1520–1598) and Ballard (d. 1588) for many publications between 1570 and 1590 (Plate 34 is similar). The author of the decorative design, which is very much in the Fontainebleau style of Jean Cousin the Younger (*c*. 1522–*c*. 1594), is not known. (See Alexander Nesbitt, *200 Decorative Title-Pages*, Plates 52 and 58, for similar French designs of the same period.) More works by Lasso will be found on Plates 33, 44, 45 and 46 of the present volume.

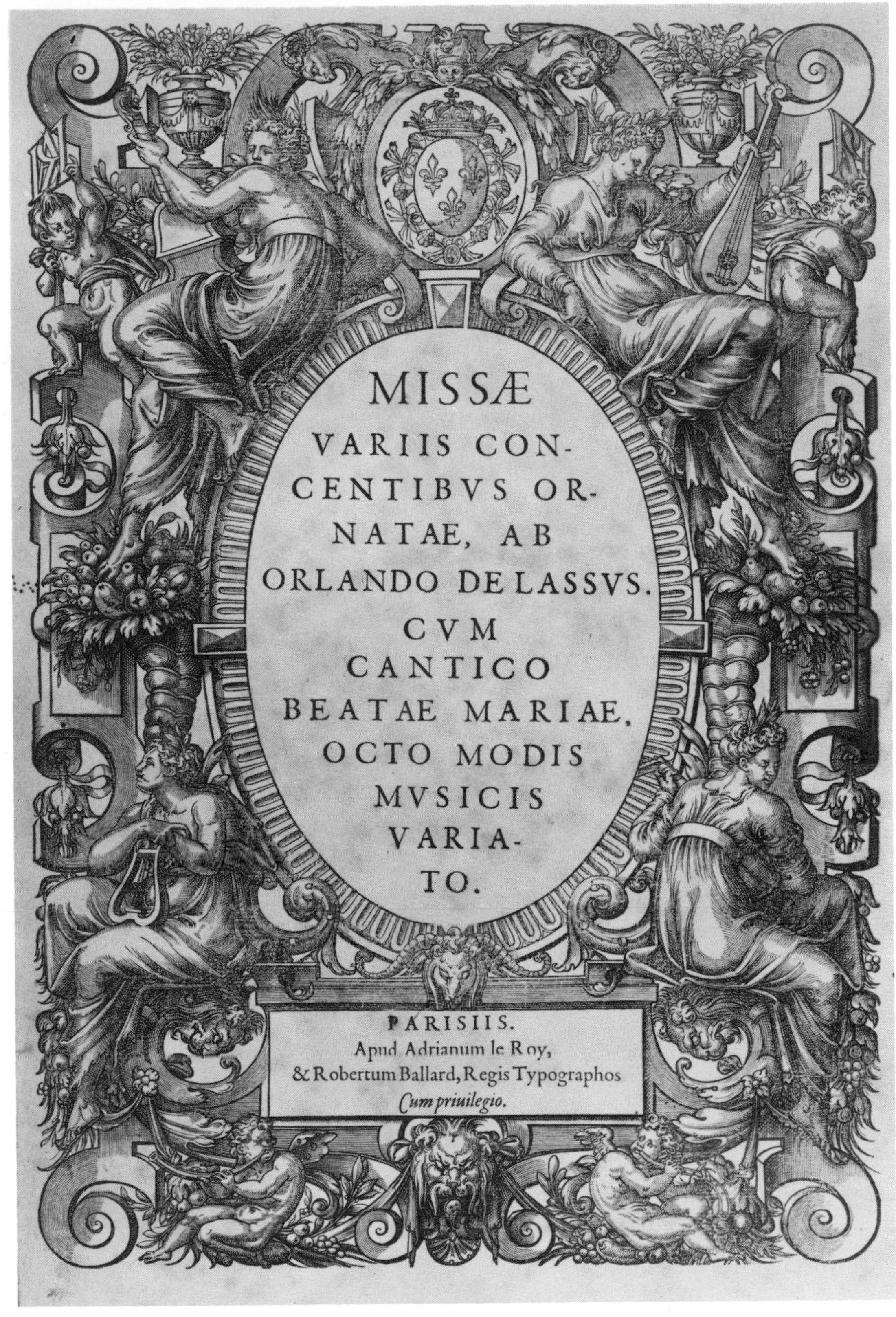
MISSÆ
VARIIS CON-
CENTIBVS OR-
NATAE, AB
ORLANDO DE LASSVS.
CVM
CANTICO
BEATAE MARIAE.
OCTO MODIS
MVSICIS
VARIA-
TO.
PARISIIS.
Apud Adrianum le Roy,
& Robertum Ballard, Regis Typographos
Cum priuilegio.

ORLANDO DI LASSO

33 *Missae variis concentibus ornatae.* Adrian Le Roy & Robert Ballard, Paris, 1577.
Österreichische Nationalbibliothek, Vienna.

Le Roy and Ballard used another title design in the style of the Fontainebleau school for this monumental folio edition of Masses by Lasso.

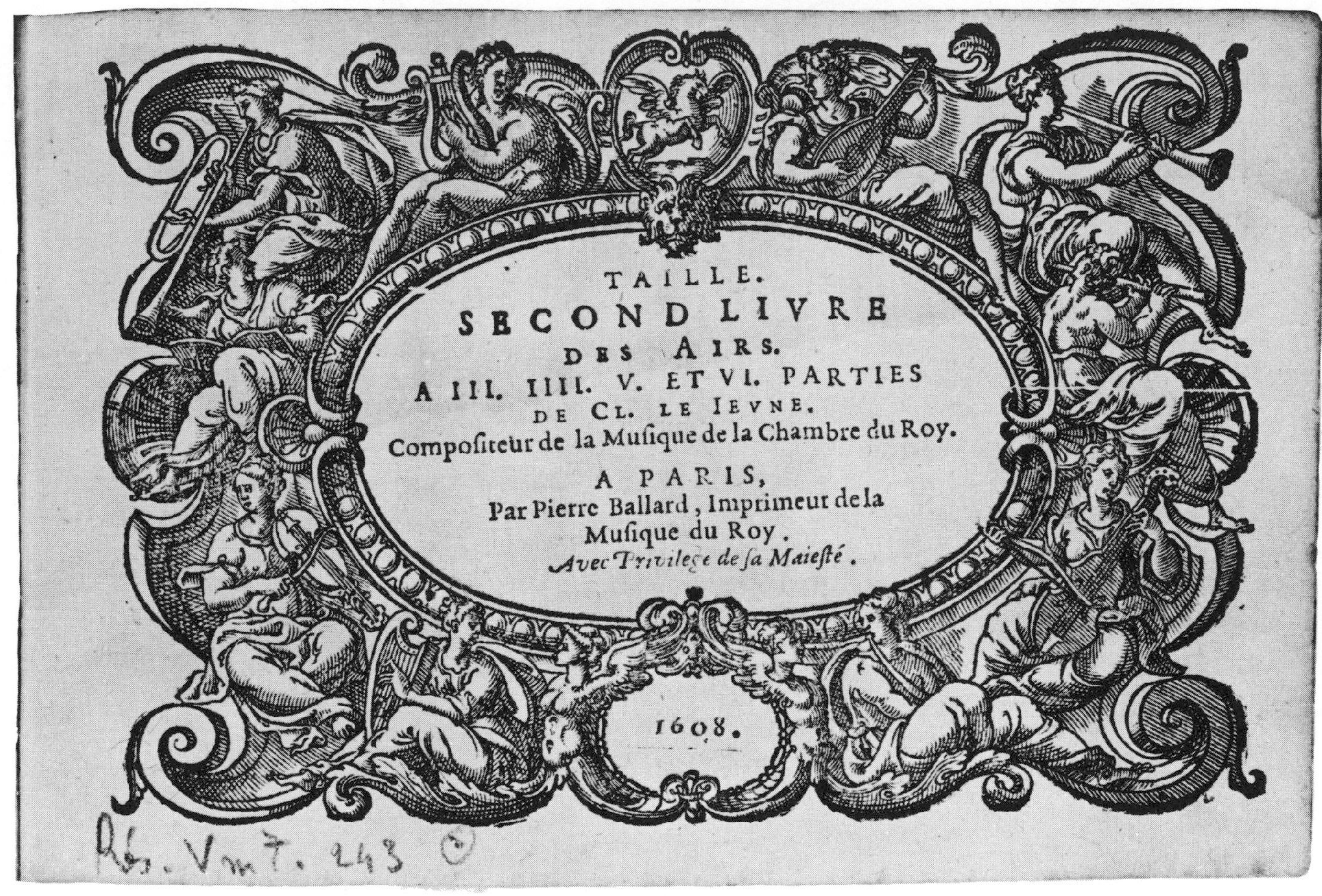

TAILLE.

SECOND LIVRE

DES AIRS.

A III. IIII. V. ET VI. PARTIES

DE CL. LE IEVNE.

Compoſiteur de la Muſique de la Chambre du Roy.

A PARIS,

Par Pierre Ballard, Imprimeur de la

Muſique du Roy.

Avec Privilege de ſa Maieſté.

1608.

CLAUDE LE JEUNE

34 *Second Livre des Airs*. Pierre Ballard, Paris, 1608.
Bibliothèque Nationale, Paris.

Le Jeune (*c.* 1530–1600) was one of the most important French composers of the second half of the sixteenth century, especially noted for his chansons and airs and for his Protestant Psalm settings. This posthumous publication (by a younger Ballard who took over the firm in 1606) uses another passe-partout title similar in style to the two preceding.

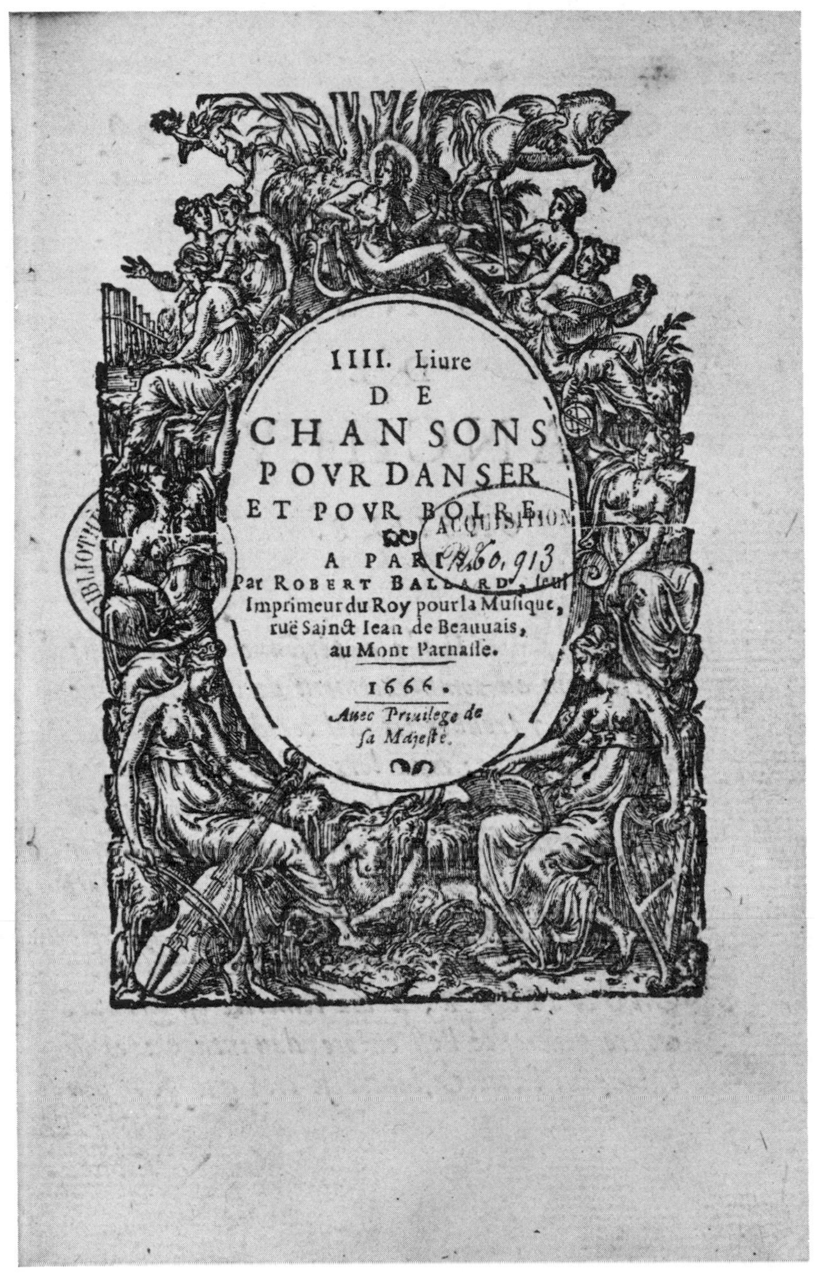

IIII. Liure
DE
CHANSONS
POVR DANSER
ET POVR BOIRE
A PAR
Par ROBERT BALLARD, seul
Imprimeur du Roy pour la Musique,
ruë Sainct Iean de Beauuais,
au Mont Parnasse.
1666.
Auec Priuilege de
sa Majesté.

35 *IIII. Liure de Chansons pour danser et pour boire*. Robert Ballard, Paris, 1666. Bibliothèque Nationale, Paris.

Even late in the seventeenth century the firm of Ballard was still producing music books in the style of a hundred years before. This is a volume (not the first edition) from the series of popular songs "for dancing and drinking" issued by the firm between 1627 and 1692. None of the composers has been identified. This Robert Ballard succeeded his father Pierre (see preceding plate) in 1640.

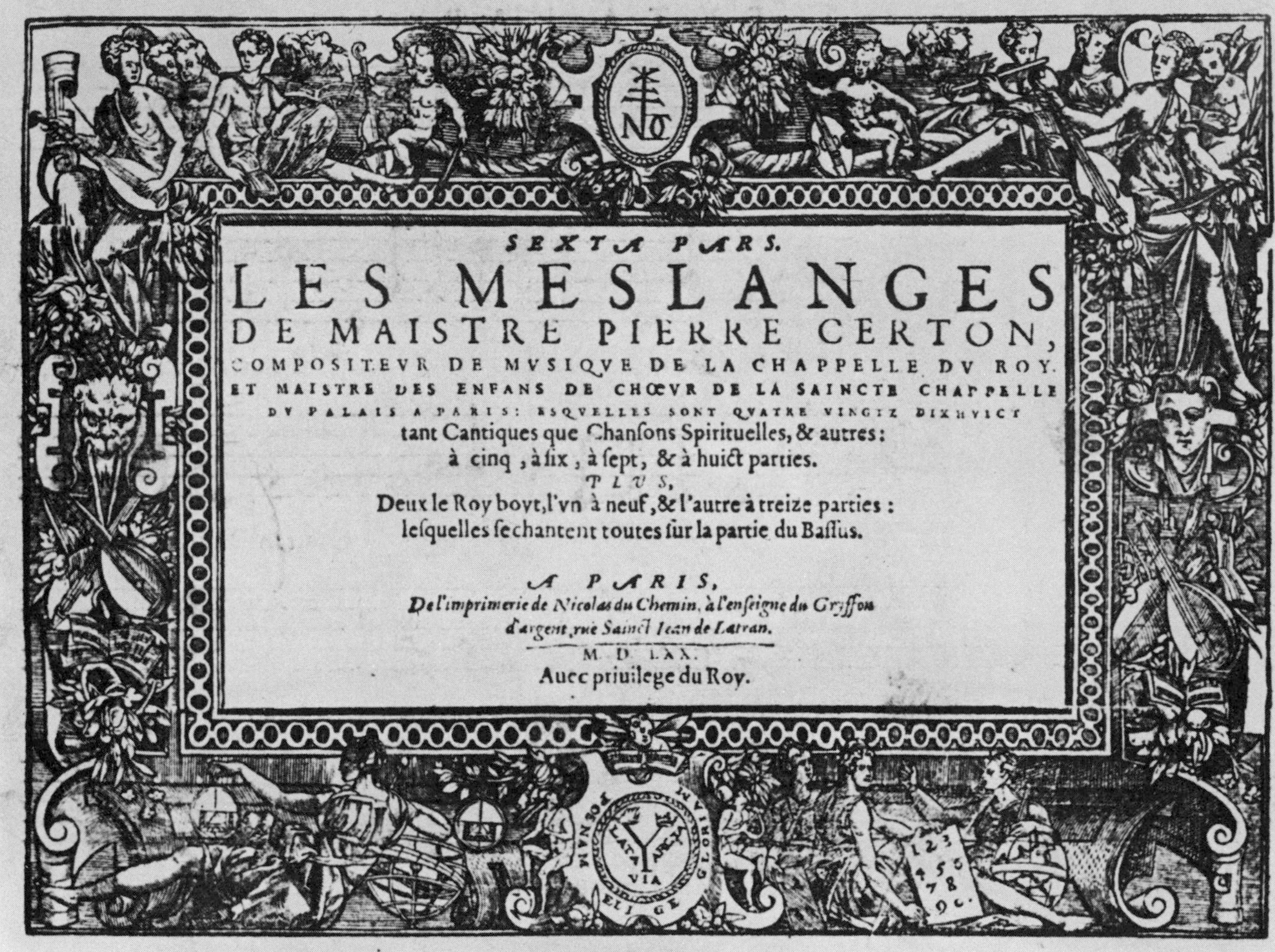

SEXTA PARS.

LES MESLANGES

DE MAISTRE PIERRE CERTON,

COMPOSITEVR DE MVSIQVE DE LA CHAPPELLE DV ROY.

ET MAISTRE DES ENFANS DE CHŒVR DE LA SAINCTE CHAPPELLE

DV PALAIS A PARIS: ESQVELLES SONT QVATRE VINGTZ DIXHVICT

tant Cantiques que Chanſons Spirituelles, & autres:

à cinq, à ſix, à ſept, & à huict parties.

PLVS,

Deux le Roy boyt, l'vn à neuf, & l'autre à treize parties:

leſquelles ſe chantent toutes ſur la partie du Baſſus.

A PARIS,

De l'imprimerie de Nicolas du Chemin, à l'enſeigne du Gryffon

d'argent, rue Sainct Iean de Latran.

M. D. LXX.

Auec priuilege du Roy.

PIERRE CERTON

36 *Les Meslanges*. Nicolas du Chemin, Paris, 1570.
Uppsala University Library.

A prolific composer of Masses, motets and chansons (over 300), Certon (?–1572) was master of the choir school at the Sainte-Chapelle in Paris. This collection of sacred songs is distinguished within the composer's output by the great variety of voice-parts called for (from 5 to 13). On the publisher du Chemin, see Plate 31.

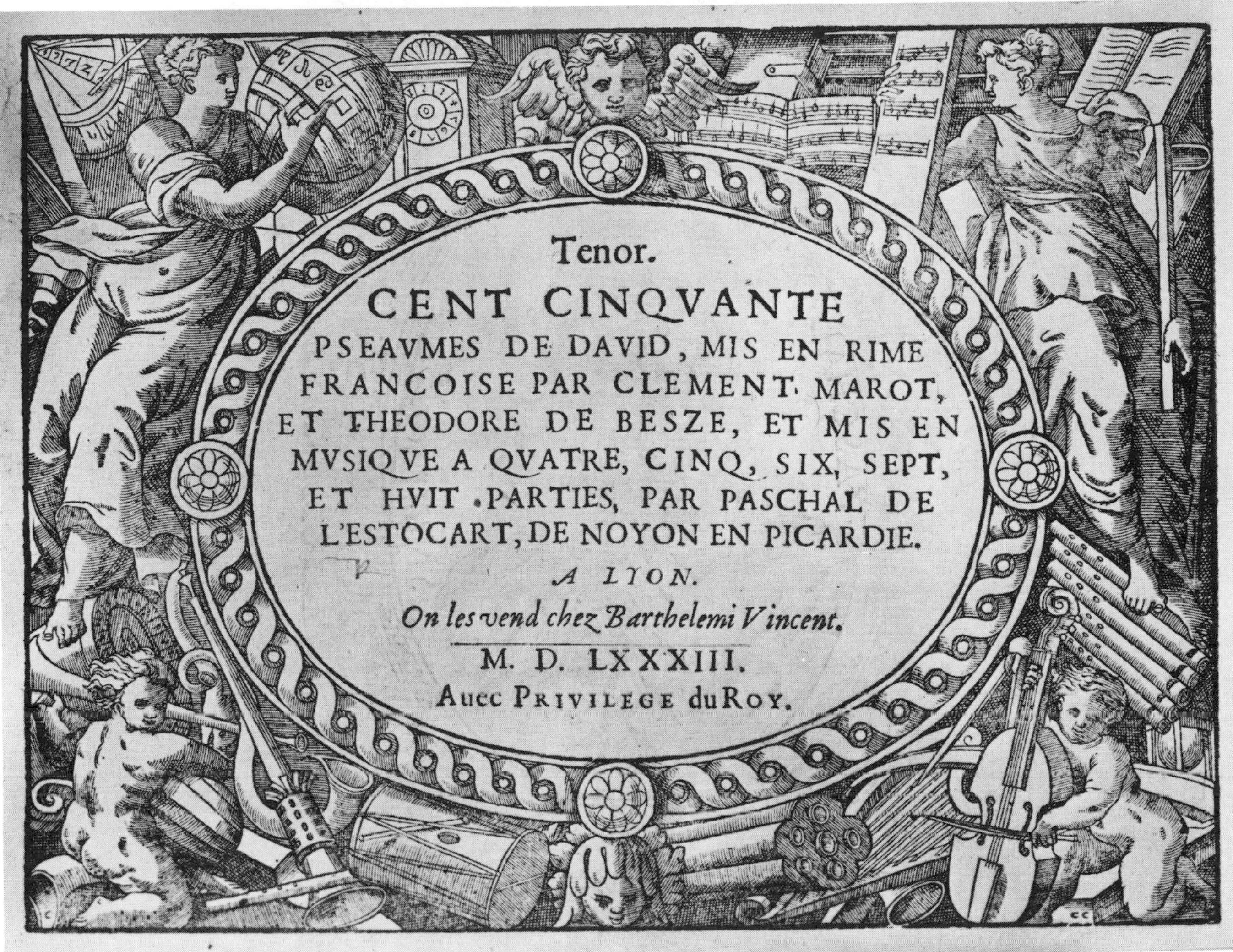

PASCAL DE L'ESTOCART

37 *Cent cinquante Pseaumes de David*. Barthélemy Vincent, Lyons, 1583.
British Museum, London.

L'Estocart (before 1540–?) was a French composer who furnished sacred music for both Catholic and Calvinistic circles. This is a setting of the Psalms, as translated by the eminent poet Clément Marot (1496–1544) and Théodore de Bèze (1519–1605), the successor of Calvin in Geneva. Lyons was an important center of printing in the sixteenth century.

QVATVOR

MISSAE

SVAVISSIMIS MODV-
LATIONIBVS REFERTÆ,
QVARVM VNA QVATVOR,
RELIQVÆ VERO QVINQVE
VOCIBVS CONCINENDÆ:

ADIVNCTO IN FINE Te Deum laudamus.

Auctore
IACOBO DE KERLE FLANDRO
IPRENSI, METROPOLITANÆ CA-
MERACENSIS ECCLESIÆ
CANONICO.

ANTVERPIÆ,
EX OFFICINA CHRISTOPHORI
PLANTINI.
M. D. LXXXIII.

LABORE, ET CONSTANTIA.

JACOBUS DE KERLE

38 *Quatuor Missae*. Christophe Plantin, Antwerp, 1583.
Bayerische Staatsbibliothek, Munich.

An eminent writer of Catholic liturgical music, Jacobus de Kerle (1531/2–1591) of Ypres was active as composer and organist in many cities of central Europe, especially at the cathedrals of Augsburg and Prague and in the service of the Holy Roman Emperor Rudolf II in the latter city. The title of this magnificent folio by the celebrated French-born printer Plantin (*c.* 1514–1588) shows various musical episodes from the Bible, including David playing for Saul, David's dance before the ark and Miriam's song after the destruction of the Egyptian host. Below is Plantin's famous printer's sign, a compass with the motto *Labore, et constantia*. For another work by de Kerle, see Plate 43.

PHILIPP GALLE

39 *Encomium Musices.* Antwerp, *c.* 1590.
Bibliothèque Nationale, Paris.

This is the title page of a collection of 18 full-page copperplate engravings of Biblical scenes featuring musical instruments. The printer-publisher was Philipp Galle (1537–1612); the illustrations were drawn by Jan van der Straet (Johannes Stradanus; 1523–1605) and engraved by Galle's son-in-law, Adriaen Collaert (*c.* 1560–1618). The book held by Musica is open to a six-part song on the power of music by the Flemish composer Andreas Pevernage (1543–1591).

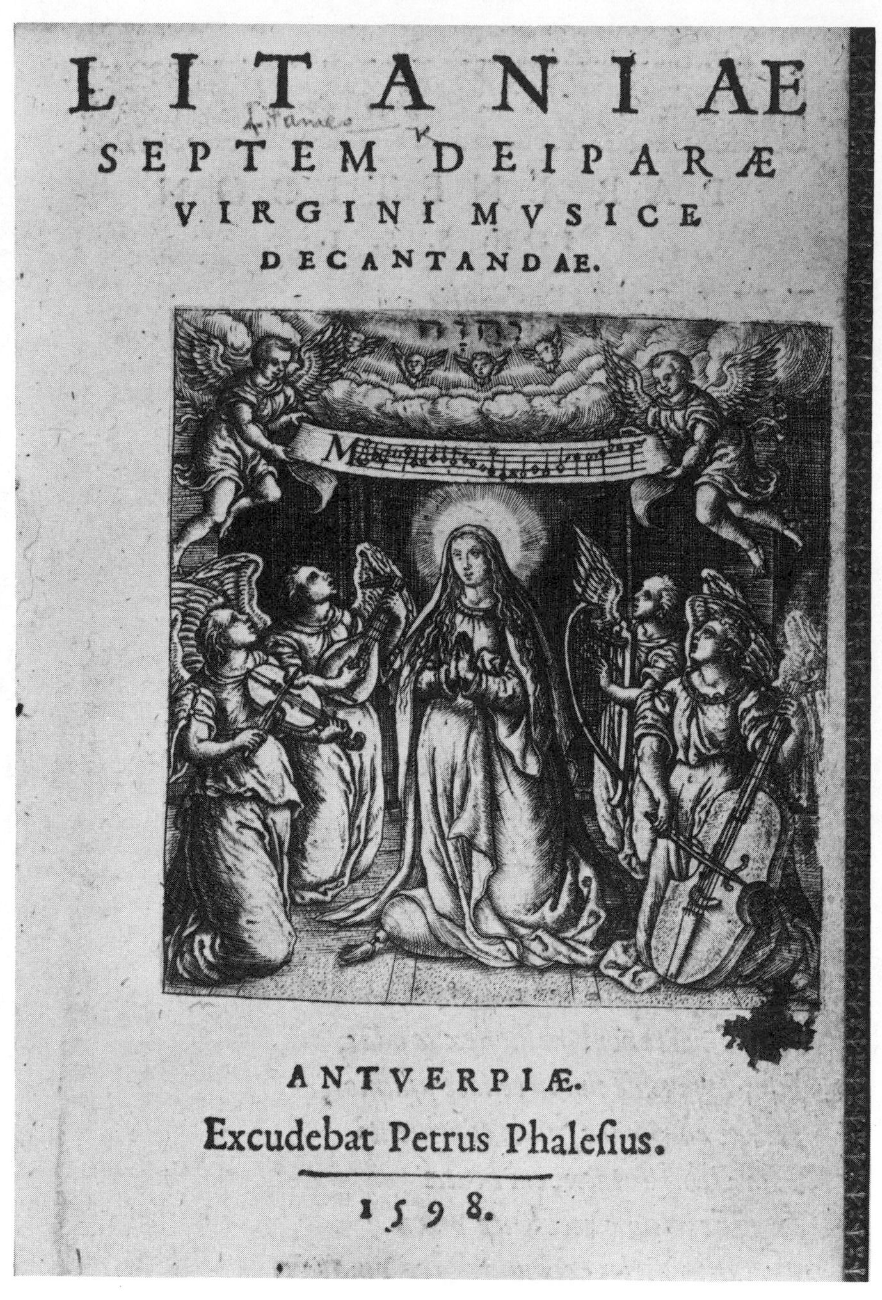

LITANIAE
SEPTEM DEIPARÆ
VIRGINI MVSICE
DECANTANDAE.

ANTVERPIÆ.
Excudebat Petrus Phaleſius.
1598.

40 *Litaniae septem Deiparae Virgini musice decantandae.* Pierre Phalèse the Younger, Antwerp, 1598.
British Museum, London.

This is one of the numerous books of litanies (prayers in honor of God, the Virgin—as here—or saints) issued by Phalèse. Pierre Phalèse the Elder (*c.* 1510–*c.* 1573) founded the house in Louvain. This publication is by his son Pierre in Antwerp.

PARS
HIEMALIS
ANTIPHONARII
ROMANI
SECVNDVM NOVVM
BREVIARIVM
RECOGNITI.
ANTVERPIÆ
APVD IOACH. TROGNÆSIVM
M.DCXI

41 *Pars Hiemalis Antiphonarii Romani.* Joachim Trognaesius, Antwerp, 1611. Uppsala University Library.

The typical early Baroque title of this antiphonary, a copperplate engraving, depicts St. Paul and St. Peter. Below, two putti hold the coat-of-arms of the Archbishop of Mechelen (Malines).

GIOVANNI GIACOMO GASTOLDI

42 *Balletti a tre voci*. Pierre Phalèse the Younger, Antwerp, 1602. Uppsala University Library.

Music director at the ducal church of St. Barbara in Mantua, Gastoldi (?–1622) is best known today for his *balletti*, characteristic dance songs of the period. This is a reprint of some of them. The border is made up of printer's flowers.

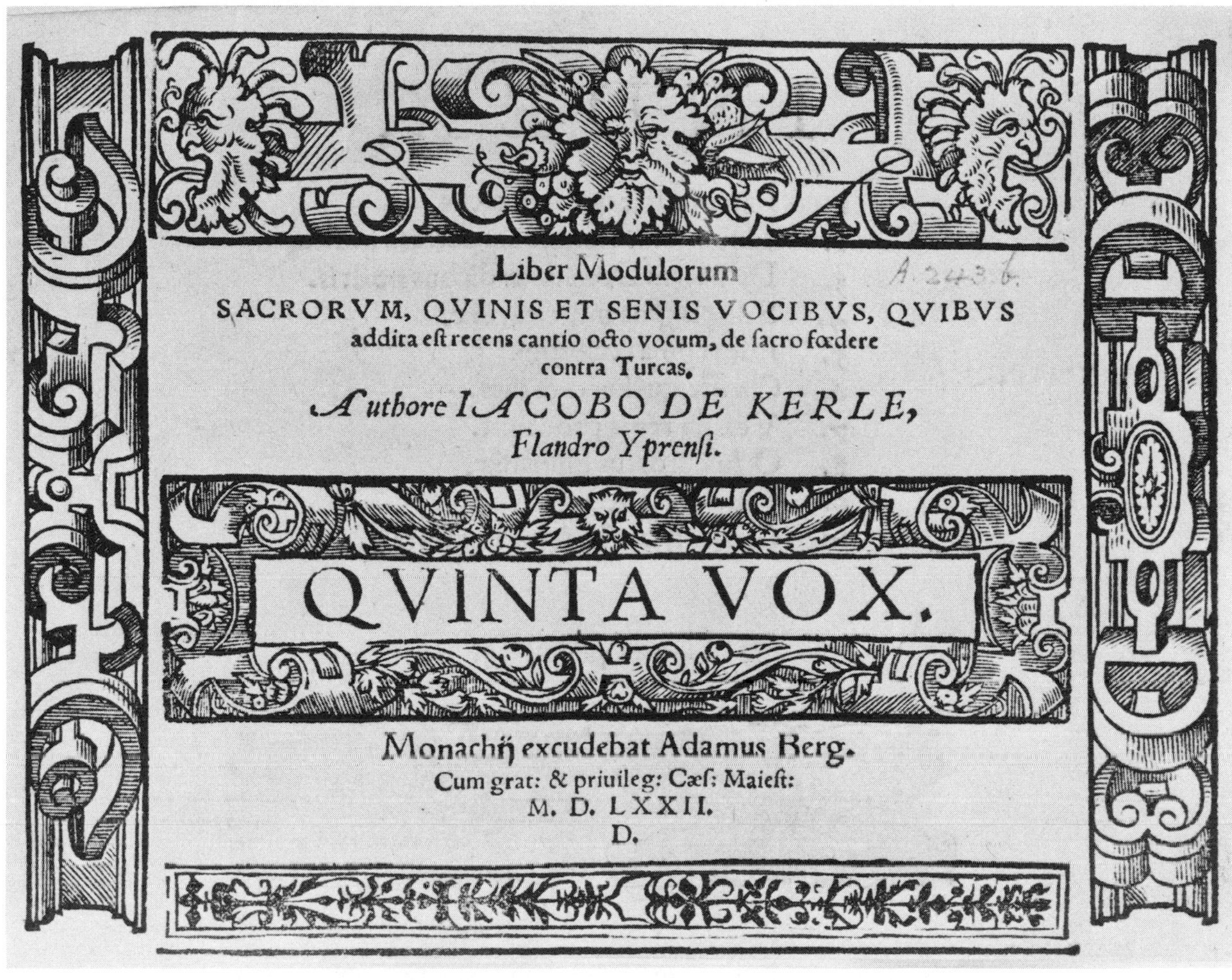

Liber Modulorum
SACRORVM, QVINIS ET SENIS VOCIBVS, QVIBVS
addita eſt recens cantio octo vocum, de ſacro fœdere
contra Turcas.
Authore IACOBO DE KERLE,
Flandro Yprenſi.

QVINTA VOX.

Monachĳ excudebat Adamus Berg.
Cum grat: & priuileg: Cæſ: Maieſt:
M. D. LXXII.
D.

JACOBUS DE KERLE

43 *Liber Modulorum sacrorum*. Adam Berg, Munich, 1572.
British Museum, London.

This is a book of motets by de Kerle (see Plate 38). Adam Berg (d. 1610) was an important music printer in Munich, especially noted for his Lasso publications (see the next two plates).

PATROCINIVM MVSICES.

LAVDATE DOMINVM. OMNES GENTES

ORLANDI DE LASSO,
Illustriss. Ducis Bauariæ, Chori Magistri,
CANTIONVM, QVAS MVTETAS
VOCANT, OPVS NOVVM.
PRIMA PARS.
Illustriss: Principis D. GVILHELMI Comitis Palatini Rheni, vtriusq; Bauariæ Ducis liberalitate in lucem editum.
Monachij excudebat Adamus Berg.
M. D. LXXIII.

ORLANDO DI LASSO

44 *Patrocinium Musices, Prima Pars.* Adam Berg, Munich, 1573.
Bayerische Staatsbibliothek, Munich.

Lasso's chief activity (see Plate 32) was as conductor of the court chapel of the dukes of Bavaria in Munich. Many of his works first appeared in the series known as *Patrocinium Musices,* printed by Berg in Munich under the patronage of Duke Wilhelm V. The exuberant title page of this folio series—which is one of the most monumental and beautiful examples of music printing of all time—depicts, among its many allegorical figures and ornaments, the coats-of-arms of several contemporary rulers and—below, center—the famous ducal chapel. The monogram at the bottom is believed to be that of Hans (Johannes) Nelt, a noted wood engraver in Munich.

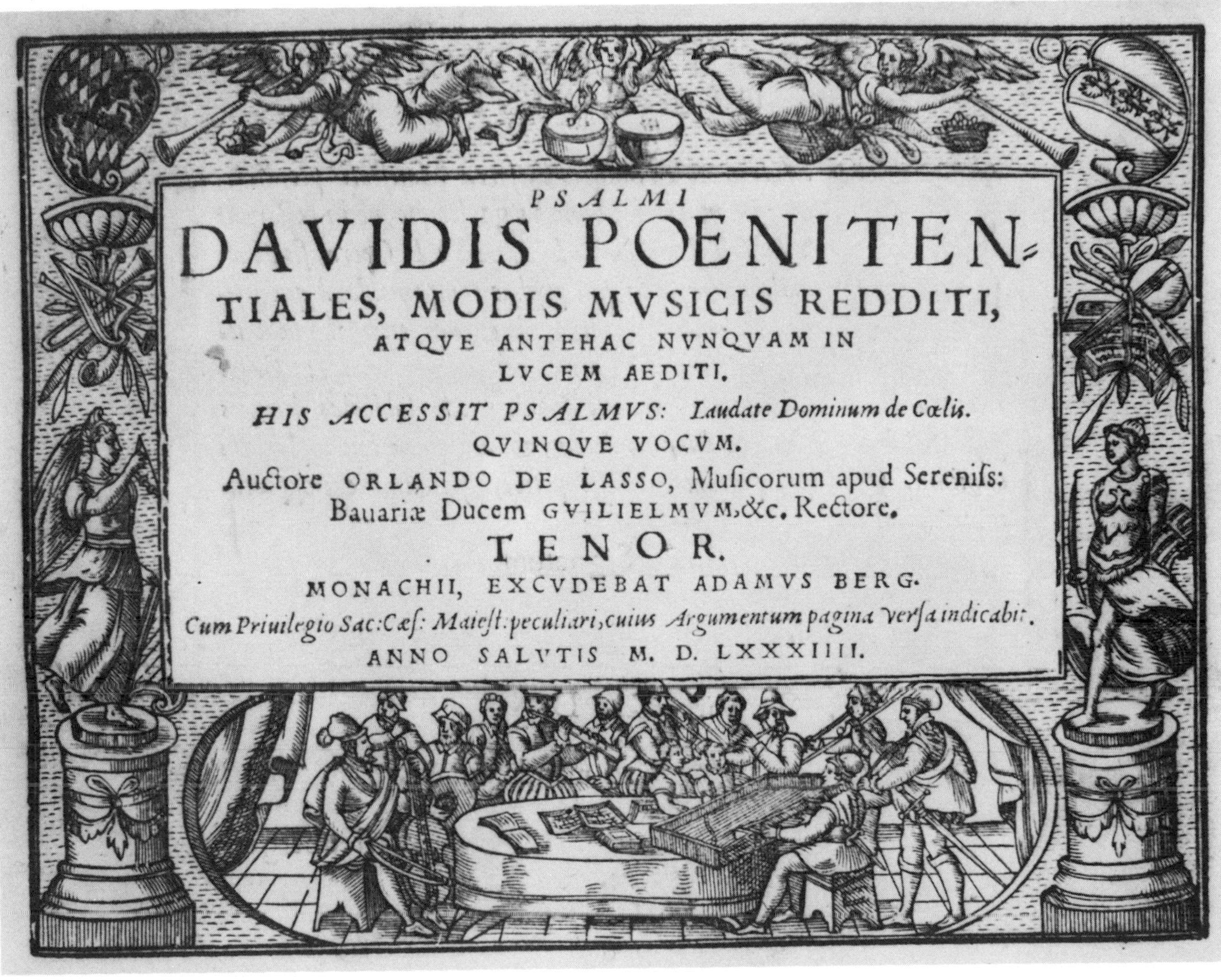

PSALMI

DAVIDIS POENITEN-
TIALES, MODIS MVSICIS REDDITI,
ATQVE ANTEHAC NVNQVAM IN
LVCEM AEDITI.

HIS ACCESSIT PSALMVS: Laudate Dominum de Cœlis.

QVINQVE VOCVM.

Auctore ORLANDO DE LASSO, Muſicorum apud Sereniſs:
Bauariæ Ducem GVILIELMVM,&c. Rectore.

TENOR.

MONACHII, EXCVDEBAT ADAMVS BERG.

Cum Priuilegio Sac: Cæſ: Maieſt. peculiari, cuius Argumentum pagina verſa indicabit.

ANNO SALVTIS M. D. LXXXIIII.

ORLANDO DI LASSO

45 *Psalmi Davidis Poenitentiales*. Adam Berg, Munich, 1584.
Uppsala University Library.

The ducal chapel is seen once more on the title page of the first edition of this celebrated collection.

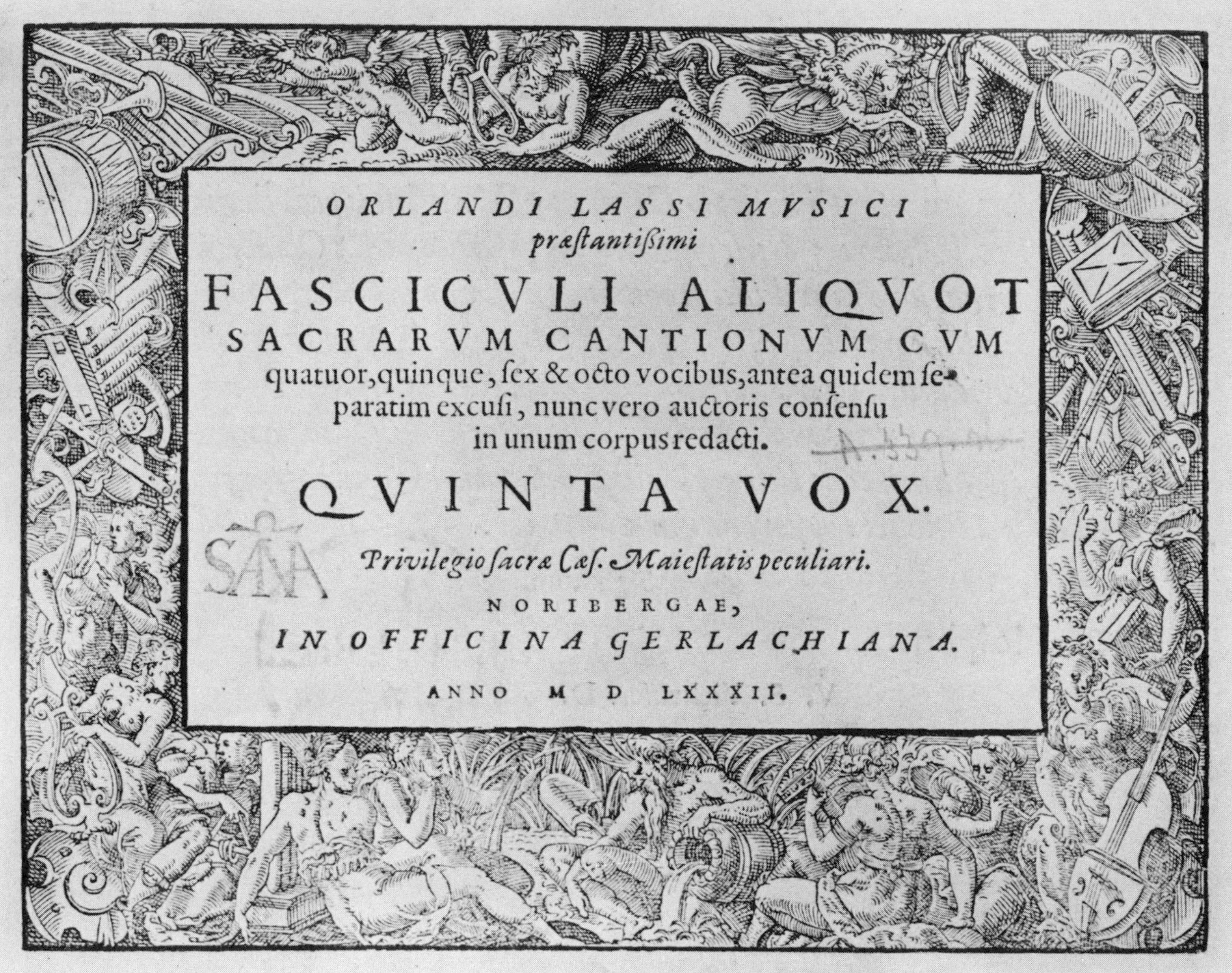

ORLANDI LASSI MVSICI
præſtantiſsimi
FASCICVLI ALIQVOT
SACRARVM CANTIONVM CVM
quatuor, quinque, ſex & octo vocibus, antea quidem ſe-
paratim excuſi, nunc vero auctoris conſenſu
in unum corpus redacti.
QVINTA VOX.
Privilegio ſacræ Cæſ. Maieſtatis peculiari.
NORIBERGAE,
IN OFFICINA GERLACHIANA.
ANNO M D LXXXII.

ORLANDO DI LASSO

46 *Fasciculi aliquot sacrarum cantionum.* Gerlach, Nuremberg, 1582.
British Museum, London.

Dietrich Gerlach (d. 1575) and his successors were noted publishers and music printers in Nuremberg from 1565 to 1591. The sacred pieces in this collection had already been printed separately.

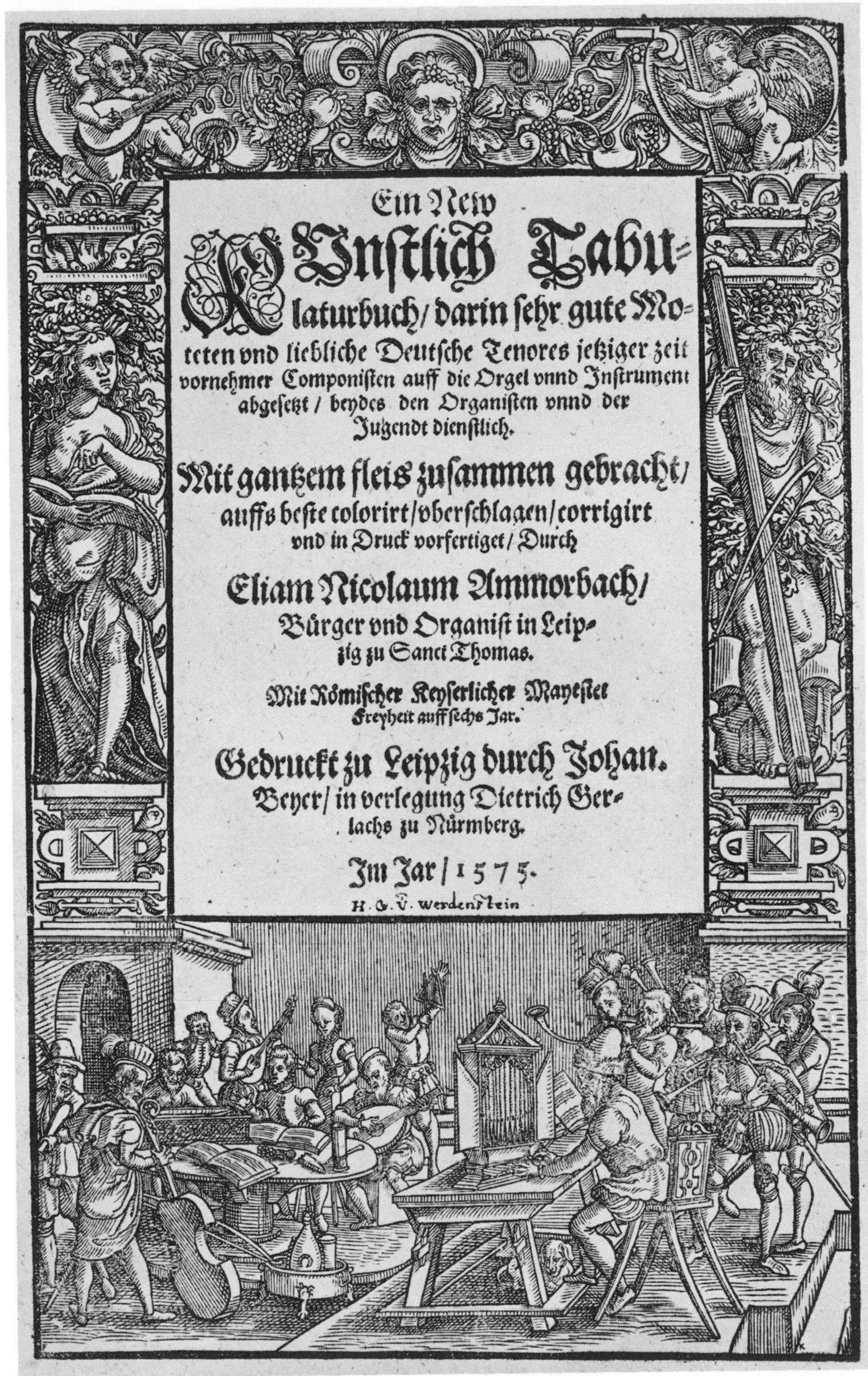

Ein New
Kunstlich Tabu-
laturbuch / darin sehr gute Mo-
teten vnd liebliche Deutsche Tenores jetziger zeit
vornehmer Componisten auff die Orgel vnnd Instrument
abgesetzt / beydes den Organisten vnnd der
Jugendt dienstlich.

Mit gantzem fleis zusammen gebracht /
auffs beste colorirt / vberschlagen / corrigirt
vnd in Druck vorfertiget / Durch

Eliam Nicolaum Ammorbach /
Bürger vnd Organist in Leipzig zu Sanct Thomas.

Mit Römischer Keyserlicher Mayestet
Freyheit auff sechs Jar.

Gedruckt zu Leipzig durch Johan.
Beyer / in verlegung Dietrich Ger-
lachs zu Nürmberg.

Im Jar / 1575.

H. G. V. Werdenstein

ELIAS NIKOLAUS AMMERBACH

47 *Ein New Kunstlich Tabulaturbuch.* Dietrich Gerlach (printed by Johannes Beyer), Nuremberg, 1575. Bayerische Staatsbibliothek, Munich.

Ammerbach (*c.* 1530–1597) was organist at St. Thomas' in Leipzig from 1560 on. His writings furnish valuable information on the methods of keyboard playing in Germany at the time. The present work, which contains instrumental transcriptions of vocal works, is an important source of contemporary songs. The title illustration, too, is historically significant, since it suggests that strings and melody instruments were used together with the organ in the instrumental ensembles of the period. It is signed H. G. V. Werdenstein.

KirchenGesäng/
So bey der predigt
deß Göttlichen Worts vnd auß-
spendung der H. Sacrament in den Kirchen
Augspurgischer Confession / gebraucht werden / Auß
dem Wittenbergischen vnd andern den besten Gesang-
büchern gesamlet / in eine richtige gute Ordnung
gebracht / vnd zum fleissigsten corri-
gieret vnd gebessert /
Durch den wolgelehrten Herrn
M. Eucharium Zinckeisen / Pfar-
herrn zu Langen.
Fürnemlich den Kirchen vnd Schuldie-
nern so sich mit jhren Kirchen zur gemel-
ten Confession bekennen / vnd bey den-
selben vorsingen müssen / zu dienst
vnd zum besten.
Getruckt zu Franckfort am Mayn / In verlegung
Sigmund Feyrabend.
M. D. LXXXIIII.

EUCHARIUS ZINCKEISEN

48 *Kirchen Gesäng*. Sigmund Feyerabend, Frankfurt am Main, 1584.
British Museum, London.

This collection of Protestant church songs was compiled and edited by the pastor Zinckeisen. The woodcut title, with scenes from the life of David, is by the eminent German Swiss artist Jost Amman (1539–1591). Feyerabend was an important Frankfurt publisher.

Teütsch Lauten-
büch

Darinnen
kunstliche Mutetē/lieb-
liche Italianische/Frantzösische/Teüt-
sche Stuck/fröliche Teütsche Täntz/Passo e
mezo/Saltarelle/vnd drei Fantaseien Alles mit
fleiß außgesetzt/auch artlich vnd
zierlich Coloriert/
durch

Melchior Newsidler/Bur-
ger vnd Lautenist in
Augspurg.

Getruckt zü Straßburg/durch
Bernhart Jobin/Im Jar.
1574.

Mit Röm. Key. May. Freyheit/
auff zehen Jar.

MELCHIOR NEUSIDLER

49 *Teutsch Lautenbuch*. Bernhard Jobin, Strassburg, 1574.
Bayerische Staatsbibliothek, Munich.

This is a collection of lute compositions by Neusidler (1531–1590/1), lutenist and composer in Nuremberg, Augsburg, Innsbruck and Italy. The title design is almost certainly by the eminent Tobias Stimmer (1539–1584), who at the time worked for the publisher Jobin (d. before 1597) in Strassburg.

CANTO.
MADRIGALI
à 5. 6. 7. & 8. voci. di Giouanne Leone Haſ-
ler, Organiſta dell Illuſtriſs: ſignor Octauiano ſe-
condo Fugger, Barone di Kirchberg & Weiſ-
ſenhorn, &c. Conſigliero della
S. M. Ceſarea.
Nouamente compoſti & dati in luce.
Con gratia & priuilegio della S. C. Maeſtà.
In Auguſta, appreſſo Valentin Schönigk.
M. D. X C V I.

HANS LEO HASSLER

50 *Madrigali à 5. 6. 7. & 8. voci.* Valentin Schönig, Augsburg, 1596.
Uppsala University Library.

Hassler (1564–1612), organist of the Fuggers in Augsburg, was one of the most noted German composers of graceful songs and madrigals, as well as church music. He was also the first of the important German composers who spent several years of their youth studying in Italy (where Hassler knew Giovanni Gabrieli). The coat-of-arms on this title is that of Count Moritz of Hesse. The publisher is Valentin Schönig (Schönigh; 1544–1614).

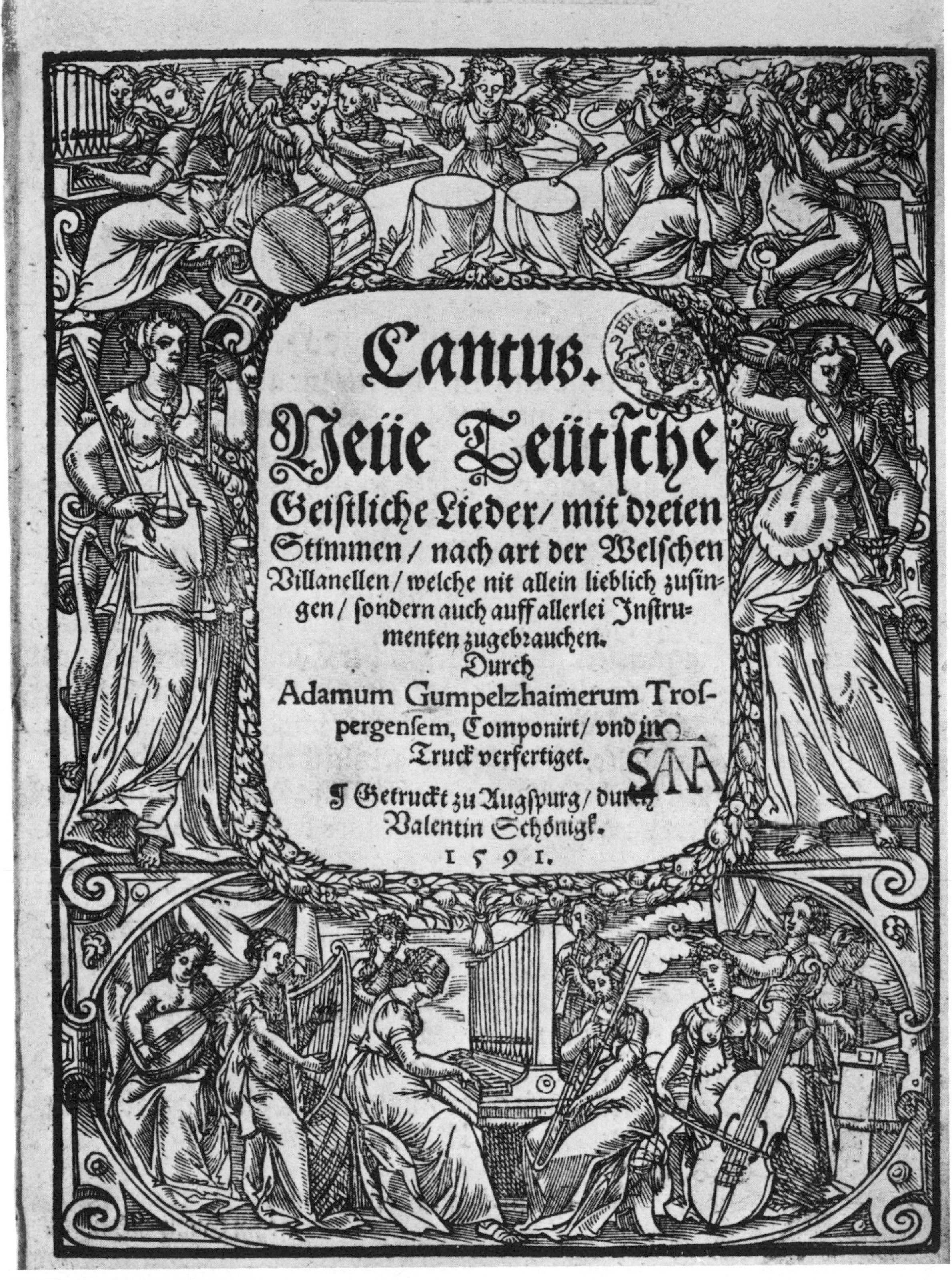
Cantus.

Neüe Teütsche

Geistliche Lieder/ mit dreien Stimmen/ nach art der Welschen Villanellen/ welche nit allein lieblich zusingen/ sondern auch auff allerlei Instrumenten zugebrauchen.

Durch

Adamum Gumpelzhaimerum Trospergensem, Componirt/ vnd in Truck verfertiget.

Getruckt zu Augspurg/ durch Valentin Schönigk.

1591.

ADAM GUMPELZHEIMER

51 *Neue Teutsche Geistliche Lieder*. Valentin Schönig, Augsburg, 1591.
British Museum, London.

Gumpelzheimer (1559–1625), from 1581 Cantor at the Gymnasium St. Anna in Augsburg, is known especially for his sacred songs to German texts.

Oſtergeſenge
Lateiniſch vnd Teutſch/mit
vier/fünff/ſechs vnd acht Stim-
men Componiret
Durch
LEONHARTVM SCHROTERVM,
Torgenſem, der Magdeburgiſchen Schulen/jtzi-
ger zeit Muſicum.
TENOR.
Gedruckt zu Magdeburgk. M. D. XC.

LEONHART SCHRÖTER
52 *Ostergesenge.* Magdeburg, 1590.
Uppsala University Library.

Schröter (*c.* 1532–*c.* 1600) was a German composer of sacred music at Wolfenbüttel and Magdeburg.

This collection of polyphonic Easter songs has Latin and German texts.

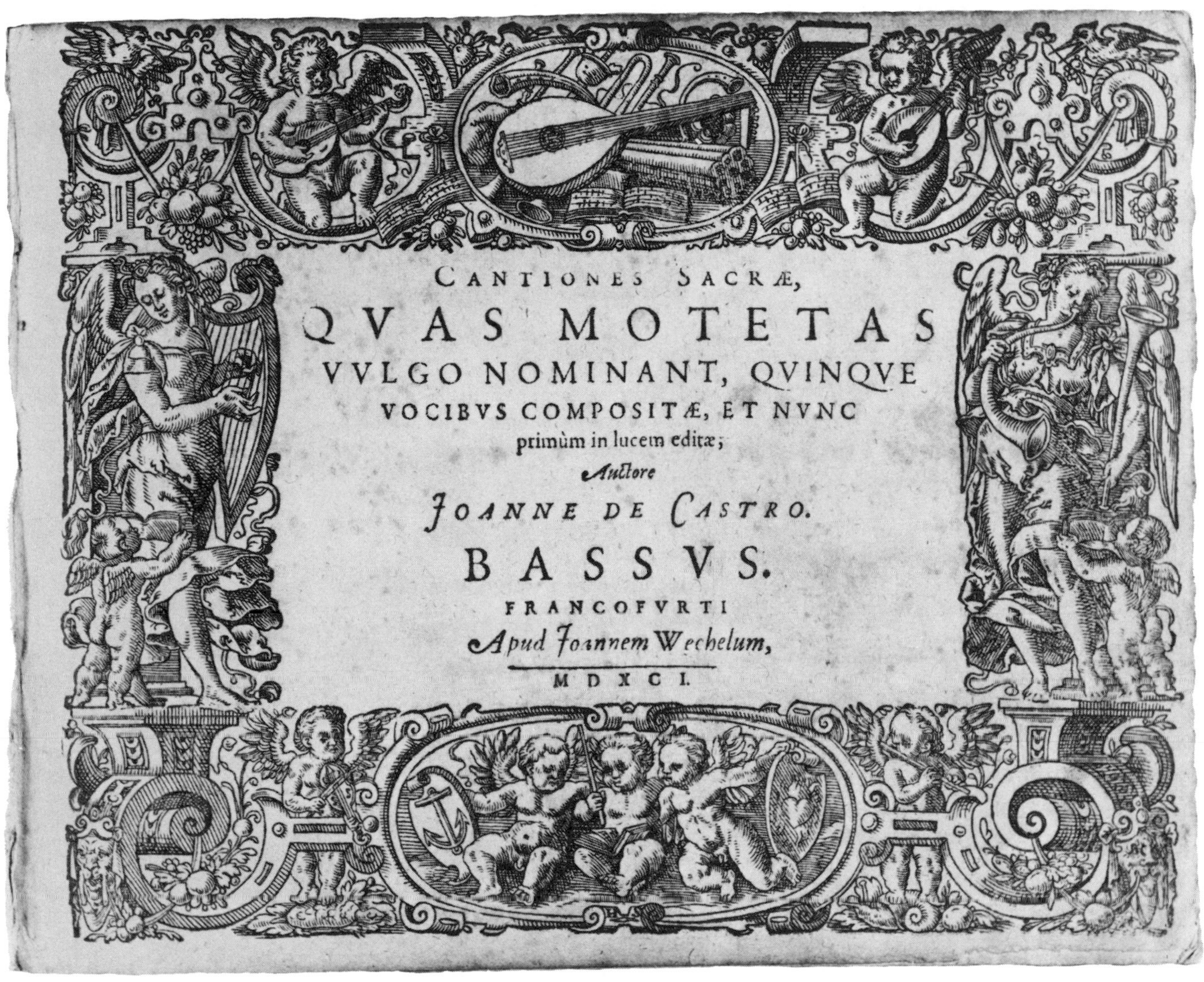

JOHANN DE CASTRO

53 *Cantiones Sacrae*. Johann Wechel, Frankfurt am Main, 1591.
Kungliga Musikaliska Akademiens Bibliotek, Stockholm.

Little is known about the origins and life of de Castro, who is presumed to have lived in Belgium and at Lyons and Cologne. He was a popular composer of church music and chansons. The publisher, Johann Wechel, son of a Parisian printer, fled France as a Huguenot and became established in Frankfurt.

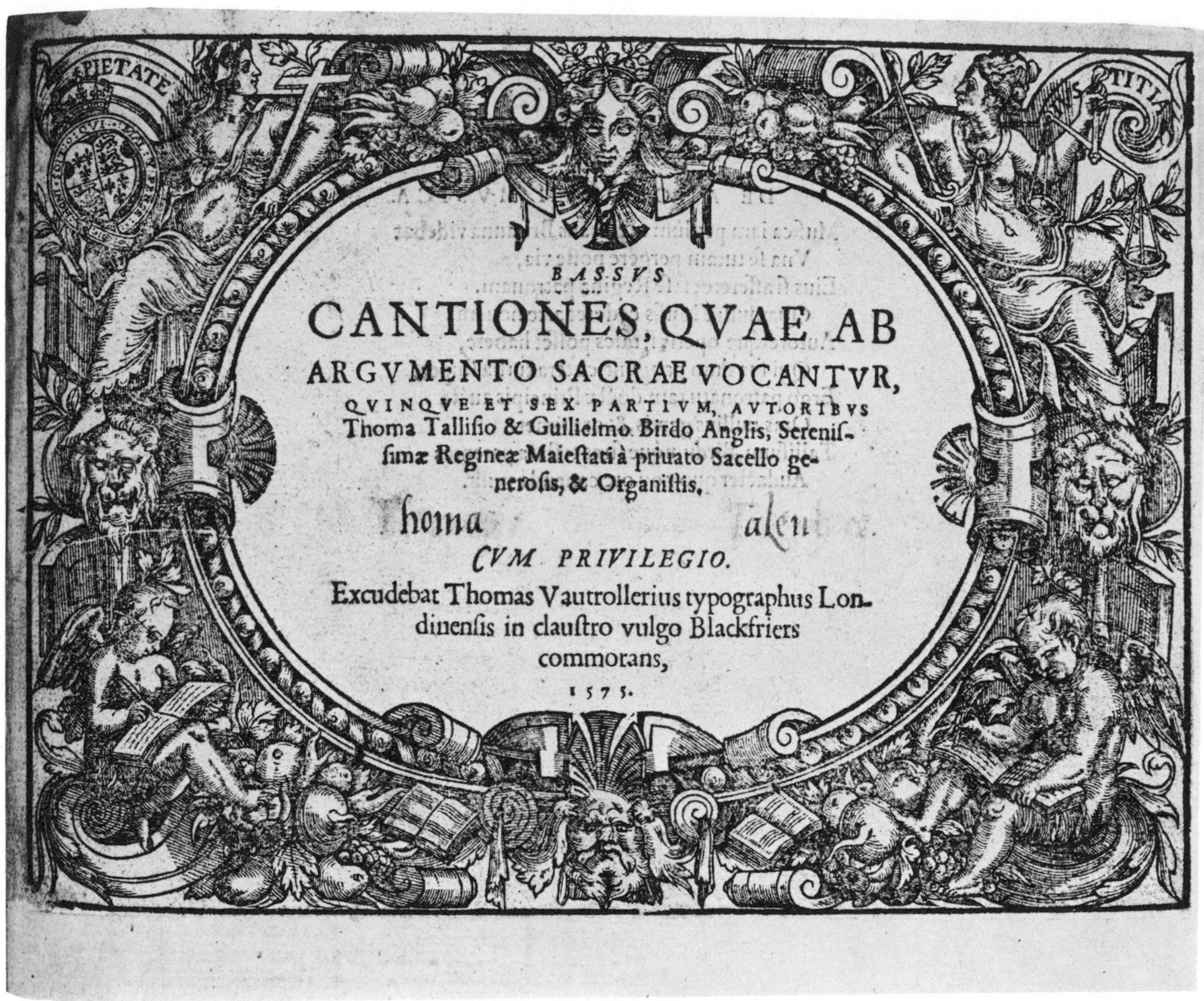

PIETATE

BASSVS

CANTIONES, QVAE AB
ARGVMENTO SACRAE VOCANTVR,
QVINQVE ET SEX PARTIVM, AVTORIBVS
Thoma Tallisio & Guilielmo Birdo Anglis, Serenissimæ Reginæ Maiestati à priuato Sacello generosis, & Organistis,

CVM PRIVILEGIO.

Excudebat Thomas Vautrollerius typographus Londinensis in claustro vulgo Blackfriers commorans,

1575.

THOMAS TALLIS AND WILLIAM BYRD

54 *Cantiones, quae ab argumento sacrae vocantur*. Published by the composers (printed by Thomas Vautrollier), London, 1575.
British Museum, London.

This was the first publication by the great English composers Tallis (*c.* 1505–1585) and Byrd (1543–1623) after they received a twenty-five-year music printing monopoly from Queen Elizabeth. At the time they were both organists in the Chapel Royal. The book contains 18 pieces by Byrd and 16 by Tallis—the only compositions of Tallis published in his lifetime, aside from five English anthems included in John Day's *Certaine Notes* (1560–5). The title design is copied from a compartment used often by Le Roy and Ballard, Paris, about that time (see Plate 32); the slight alterations include the addition of the royal arms. For another work by Byrd, see Plate 62.

THE PSALMES
OF DAVID IN ENGLISH
meter, with Notes of foure partes ſet vnto them,
by *Guilielmo Daman*, for *Iohn Bull*, to the vſe of the godly Chriſtians for recreatyng them ſelues, in ſtede of fond and vnſeemely Ballades.

Anno. 1579.

TENOR.

¶AT LONDON
Printed by Iohn Daye.

¶*Cum Priuilegio.*

ARISE · I · SAY · FOR · IT · IS · DAY ·

WILLIAM DAMAN

55 *The Psalmes of David in English meter*. John Day, London, 1579.
British Museum, London.

The year of publication of this harmonization of the Psalm tunes then in common use also saw the appointment of the composer (*c*. 1540–1591), a Walloon living in England, to the court. The work was revised in 1591. John Day (1522–1584) published numerous English Psalm settings. In other copies of this book, the blank area beneath "Arise I say" contains a pretty design of a person sleeping on the ground being awakened by someone standing (see McKerrow & Ferguson, No. 164).

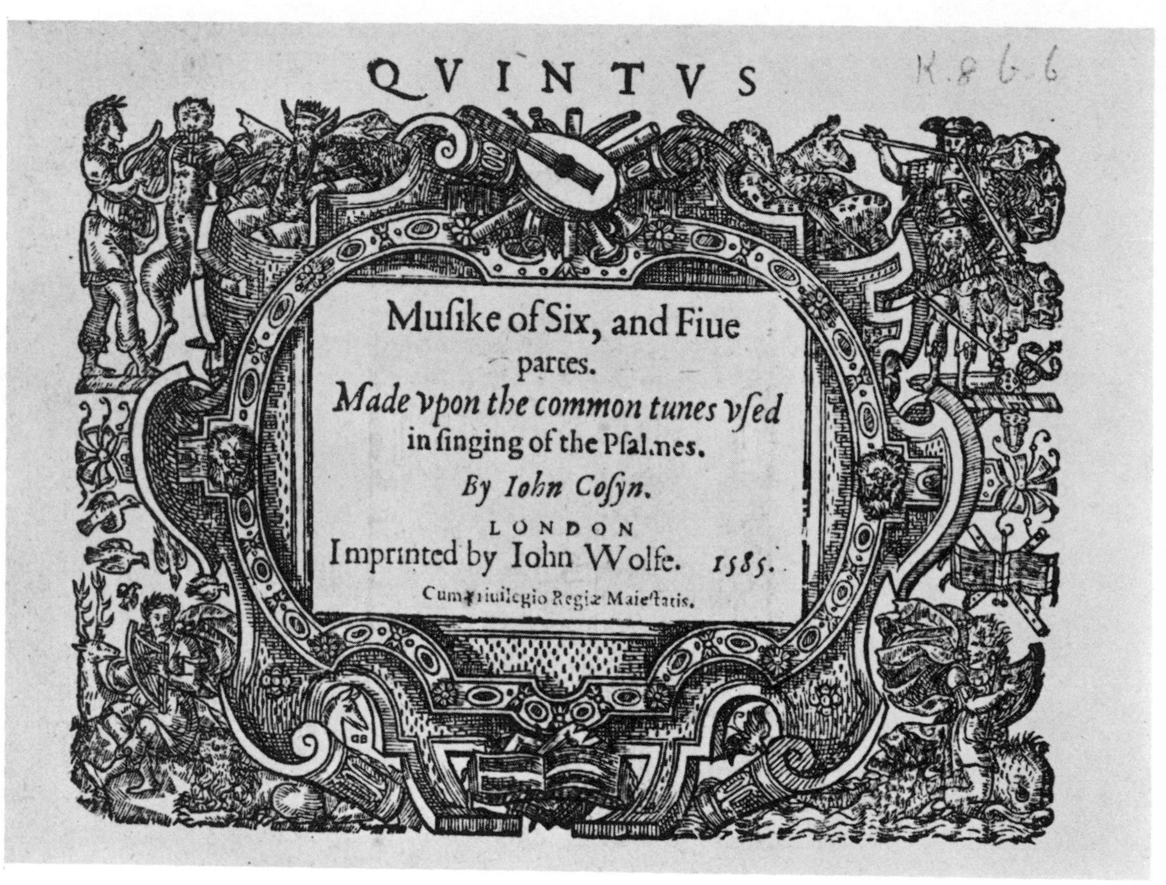

JOHN COSYN

56 *Musike of Six, and Five partes.* John Wolfe, London, 1585.
British Museum, London.

Nothing is known about the composer of these plain counterpoint arrangements of 60 Psalm tunes. The title page bears the initials GB below, left.

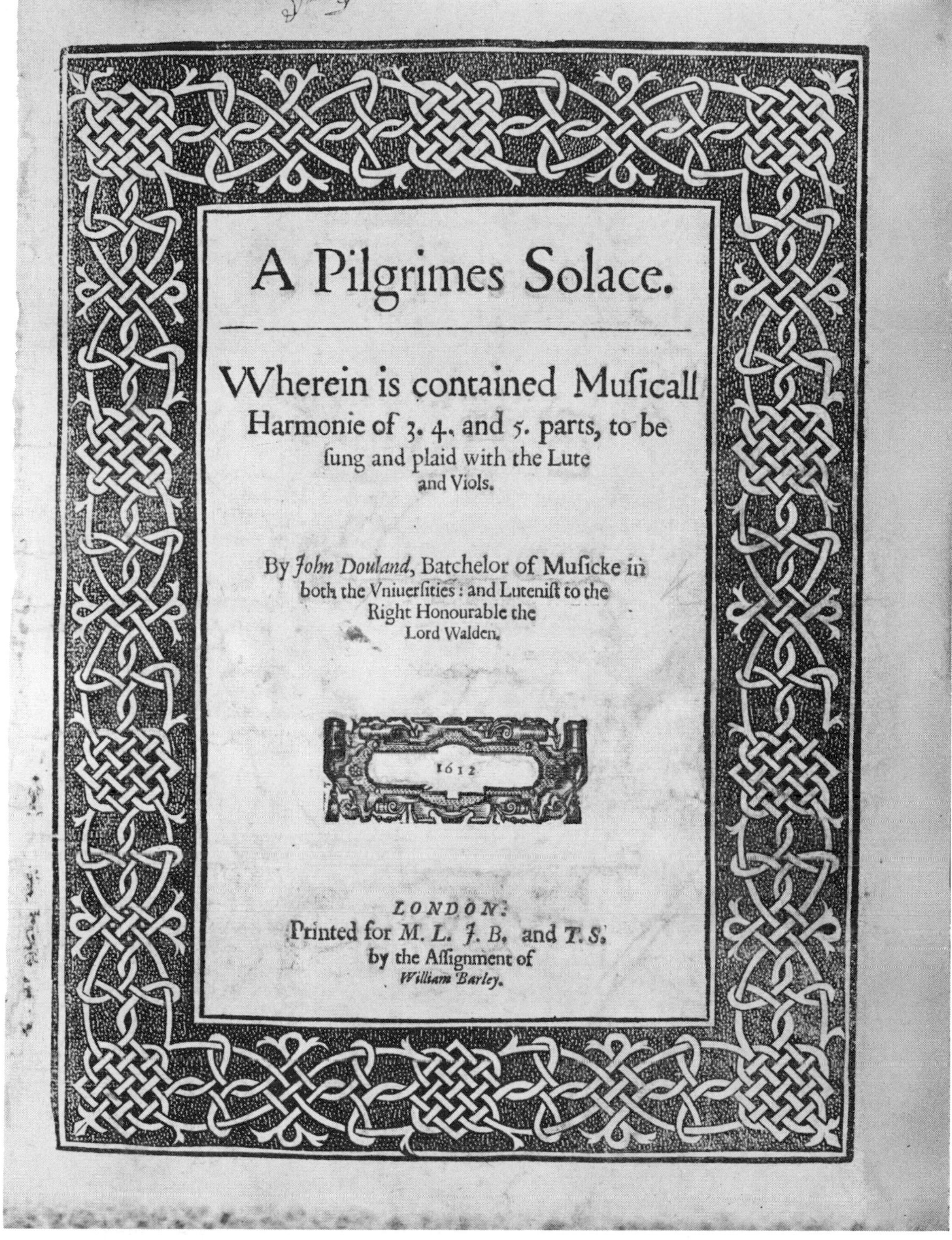

A Pilgrimes Solace.

Wherein is contained Muſicall Harmonie of 3. 4. and 5. parts, to be ſung and plaid with the Lute and Viols.

By *John Douland*, Batchelor of Muſicke in both the Vniuerſities: and Luteniſt to the Right Honourable the Lord Walden.

1612

LONDON:
Printed for *M. L. J. B.* and *T. S.*
by the Aſſignment of
William Barley.

JOHN DOWLAND

57 *A Pilgrimes Solace.* Matthew Lownes, John Browne & Thomas Snodham, London, 1612.
British Museum, London.

This was the last work of the illustrious lutenist and song composer Dowland (1562–1625/6), published in the same year that his appointment as court lutenist rescued him from the neglect he had been suffering in England. The border of this title was copied from a Parisian book published by Simon de Colines in 1544 (probably designed by Oronce Fine; see Nesbitt, *200 Decorative Title-Pages*, Plate 45). The design goes back to patterns like those on a 1523 Dürer title (publisher: Friedrich Peypus, Nuremberg; Nesbitt, Plate 24) and even earlier Italian models (for instance, Nesbitt, Plate 6; publisher: Alessandro Paganino, Toscolano, early sixteenth century).

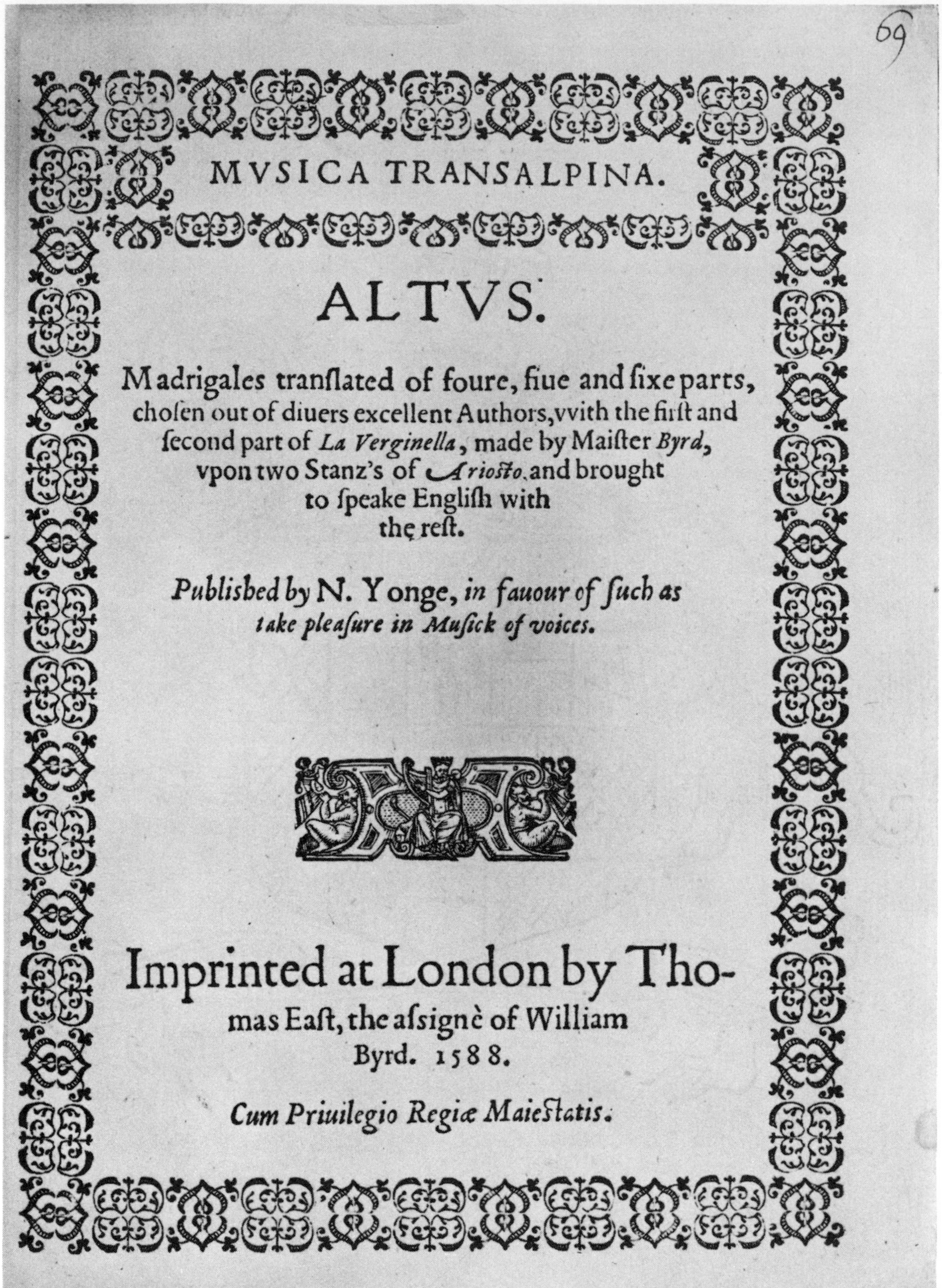

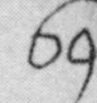

MVSICA TRANSALPINA.

ALTVS.

Madrigales tranſlated of foure, fiue and ſixe parts, choſen out of diuers excellent Authors, vvith the firſt and ſecond part of *La Verginella*, made by Maiſter *Byrd*, vpon two Stanz's of *Arioſto*, and brought to ſpeake Engliſh with the reſt.

Publiſhed by N. Yonge, *in fauour of ſuch as take pleaſure in Muſick of voices.*

Imprinted at London by Thomas Eaſt, the aſsignè of William Byrd. 1588.

Cum Priuilegio Regiæ Maieſtatis.

NICHOLAS YONGE

58 *Musica Transalpina.* Thomas East, London, 1588.
British Museum, London.

Yonge (?–1619; probably once a chorister at St. Paul's) edited this collection of 57 madrigals which greatly influenced the development of music in England. Represented are such masters as Baldissera Donato (*c.* 1530–1603), Alfonso (I) Ferrabosco (1543–1588), Luca Marenzio (1553/4–1599), Philipp de Monte (1521–1603), Palestrina (see Plate 18) and Giovanni Battista Pinello di Ghirardi (*c.* 1544–1587), as well as Lasso (see Plates 32, 33 and 44–46) and Byrd (see Plate 54). The decorative border of printer's flowers is typical of many English madrigal publications of the time, especially those of Thomas East (Este; *c.* 1540–*c.* 1608).

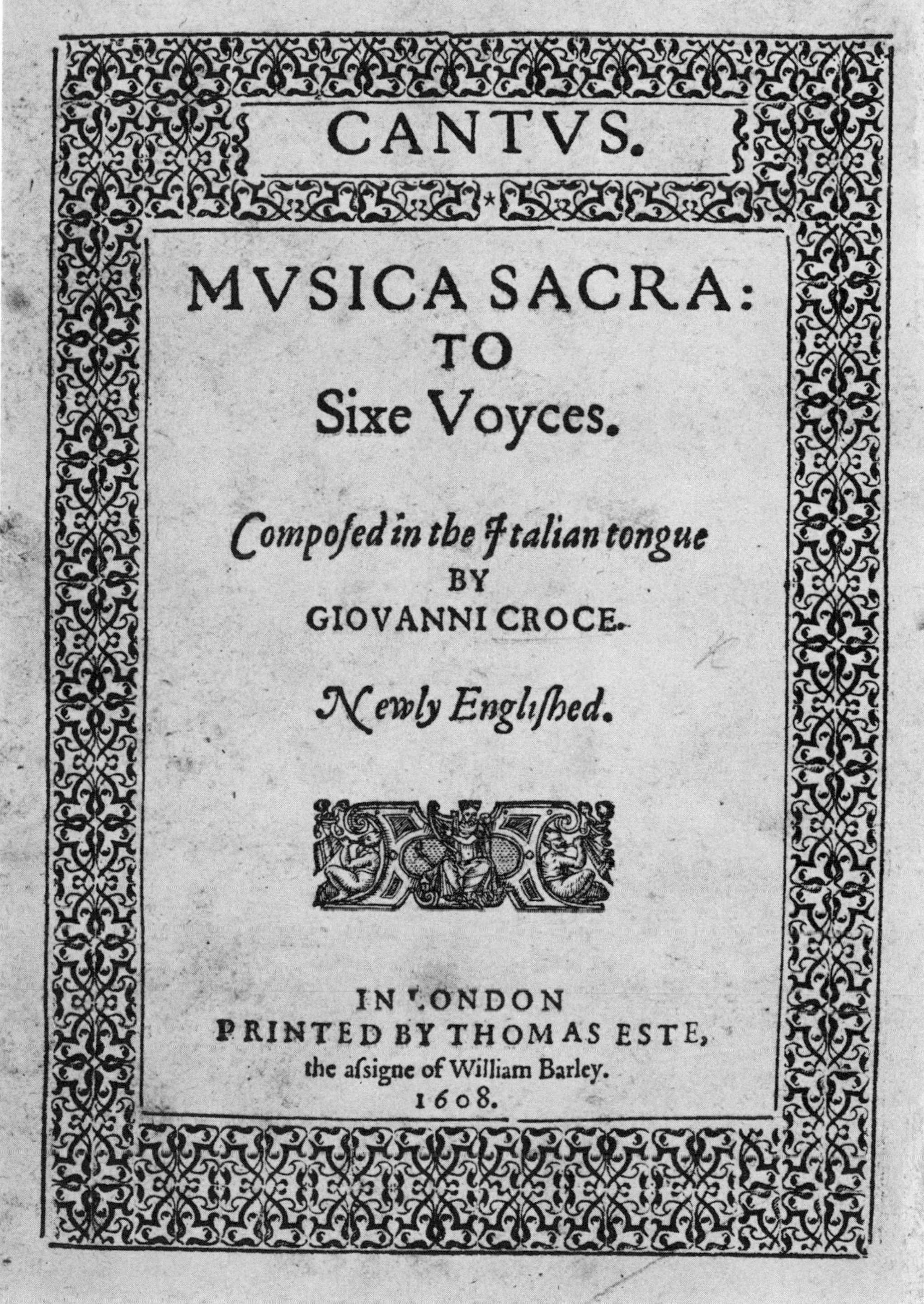

CANTVS.

MVSICA SACRA:
TO
Sixe Voyces.

Compoſed in the Italian tongue
BY
GIOVANNI CROCE.

Newly Engliſhed.

IN LONDON
PRINTED BY THOMAS ESTE,
the aſsigne of William Barley.
1608.

GIOVANNI CROCE

59 *Musica Sacra.* Thomas East, London, 1608.
British Museum, London.

For details on Croce, see Plate 24. This is an English-language version of *Li sette Sonetti penitentiali a sei voci* (published by G. Vincenti, Venice, 1603). Again we have a border of printer's flowers.

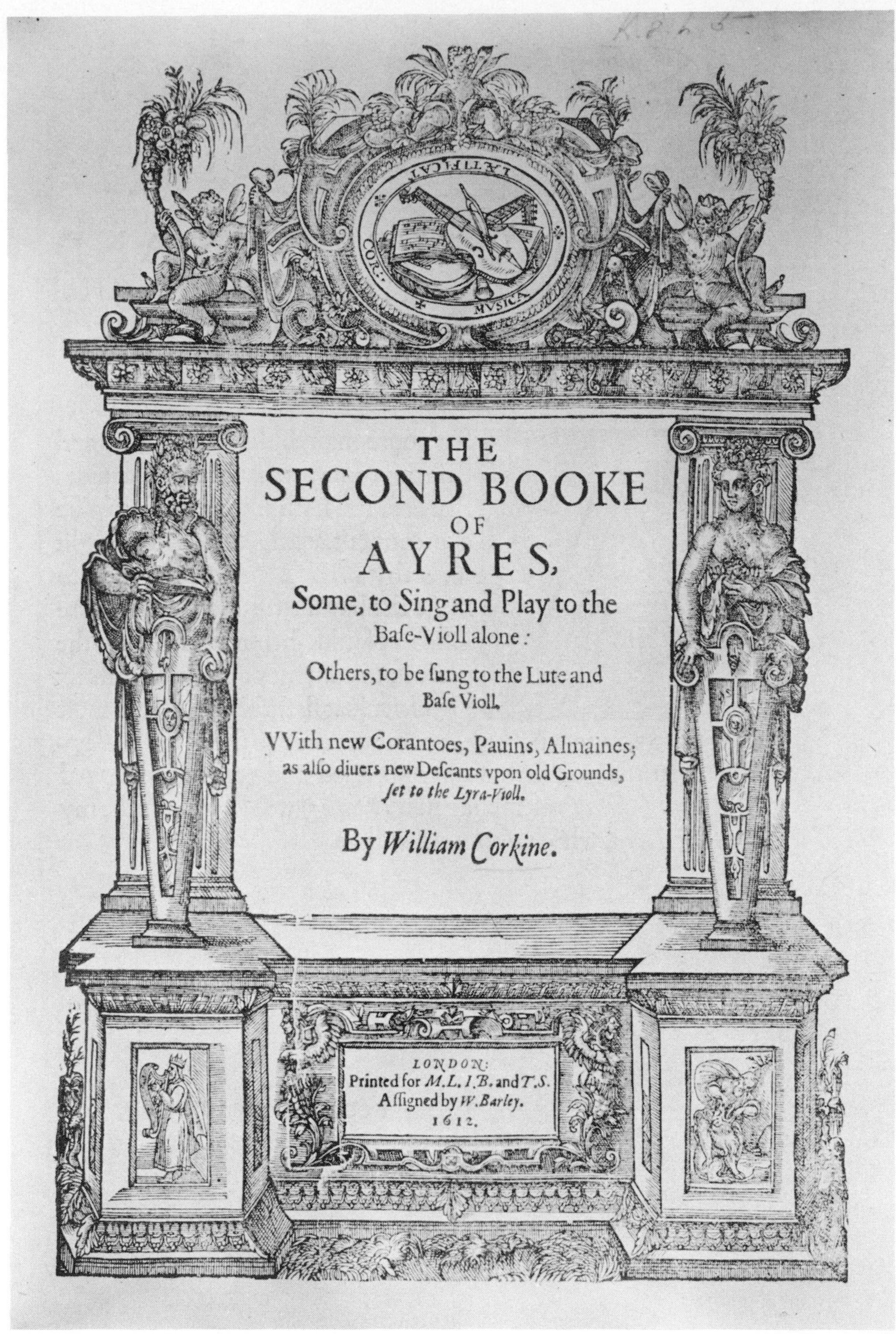

THE
SECOND BOOKE
OF
AYRES,
Some, to Sing and Play to the
Base-Violl alone:
Others, to be sung to the Lute and
Base Violl.
VVith new Corantoes, Pauins, Almaines;
as also diuers new Descants vpon old Grounds,
set to the Lyra-Violl.

By *William Corkine.*

LONDON:
Printed for *M.L. I.B.* and *T.S.*
Assigned by *W. Barley.*
1612.

WILLIAM CORKINE

60 *The Second Booke of Ayres.* Matthew Lownes, John Browne & Thomas Snodham, London, 1612. British Museum, London.

Corkine was a lutenist, gambist and composer in the late sixteenth and early seventeenth centuries. This title design, first used by Plantin in Antwerp in 1566, was adapted by East and Snodham for about ten music publications between 1600 and 1618.

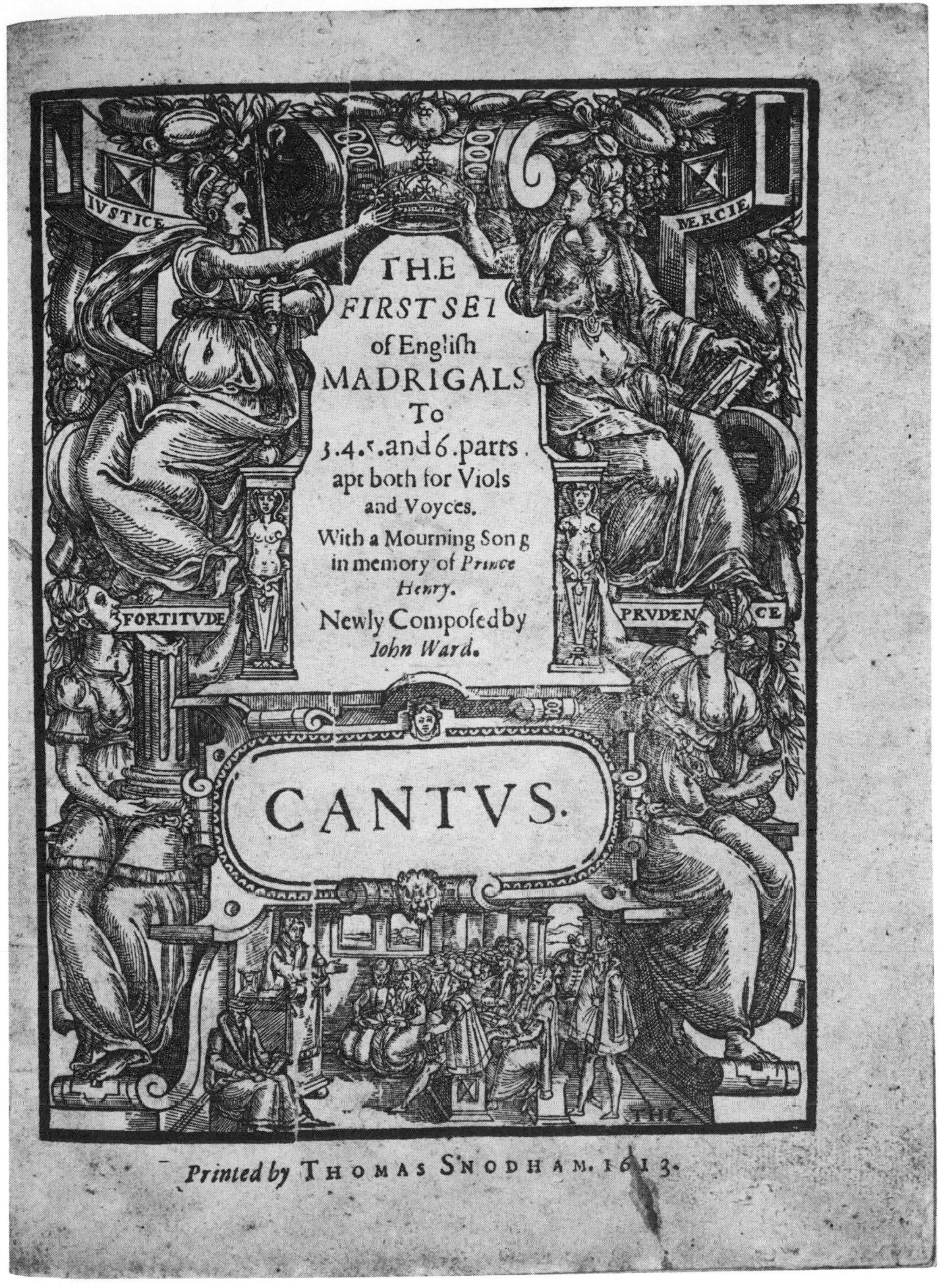
IVSTICE
MERCIE
THE
FIRST SET
of English
MADRIGALS
To
3.4.5.and 6.parts
apt both for Viols
and Voyces.
With a Mourning Song
in memory of Prince
Henry.
Newly Composed by
Iohn Ward.
FORTITVDE
PRVDEN CE
CANTVS.
THC
Printed by THOMAS SNODHAM. 1613.

JOHN WARD

61 *The First Set of English Madrigals.* Thomas Snodham, London, 1613. British Museum, London.

Almost nothing is known about Ward (?–*c.* 1641), an English composer of madrigals and music for viols. This, his only publication in his lifetime, contains some of the most exquisite madrigals written to English words. The title design was first used by the printer R. Jugge in 1569 for *The holi bible*; Queen Elizabeth was depicted on her throne, being crowned by Justice and Mercy. In this edition the Queen has been deleted and replaced by the lettering of the title, leaving the crown in mid-air and Fortitude and Prudence below holding up a non-existent throne. The word "the" at the lower right is all that remains of the original motto "God save the queene."

CONTRATENOR.

Pſalmes, Sonets, & ſongs of ſadnes and pietie, made into Muſicke of fiue parts: whereof, ſome of them going abroad among diuers, in vntrue coppies, are heere truely corrected, and th'other being Songs very rare & newly compoſed, are heere publiſhed, for the recreation of all ſuch as delight in Muſick: By *William Byrd*, one of the Gent. of the Queenes Maieſties honorable Chappell.

Printed by Thomas Eaſt, the aſsigne of W. Byrd, and are to be ſold at the dwelling houſe of the ſaid T. Eaſt, by Paules wharſe. 1588.

Cum priuilegio Regiæ Maieſtatis.

WILLIAM BYRD

62 *Psalmes, Sonets, & songs of sadnes and pietie.* Thomas East, London, 1588. British Museum, London.

After the death of his co-publisher Tallis (see Plate 54), Byrd, the famous composer of sacred works, madrigals and virginal music, became associated with the printer East. Of this collection of five-part vocal music, No. 1–10 are Psalms, 11–26 are madrigals (called Sonnets and Pastorals) and 27–33 are "songs of sadnes and pietie."

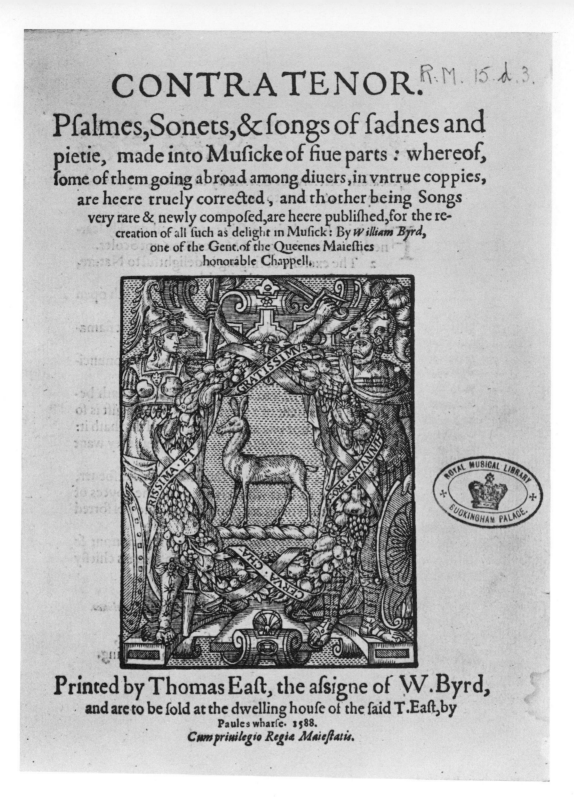

A
PLAINE AND
EASIE INTRODVCTI-
ON TO PRACTICALL
MVSICKE,
Set downe in forme of a dialogue:
Deuided into three partes,
The firſt teacheth to ſing with all
things neceſſary for the knowledge of
prickſong.
The ſecond treateth of deſcante
and to ſing two parts in one vpon a plainſong or
ground, with other things neceſſary
for a deſcanter.
The third and laſt part entreateth of com
poſition of three, foure, fiue or more parts with
many profitable rules to that effect.
With new ſongs of.2.3.4. and.5 parts.

By Thomas Morley, Batcheler of muſick, &
one of the gent. of hir Maieſties Royall Chappell.
Imprinted at London by Peter Short dwelling on
Breedſtreet hill at the ſigne of the Starre. 1597.

THOMAS MORLEY

63 *A Plaine and Easie Introduction to Practicall Musicke.* Peter Short (printer), London, 1597.
British Museum, London.

Morley (1557–1602?) a pupil of Byrd, was one of the foremost representatives of the Elizabethan madrigal school. This elementary textbook of music theory, which remained popular for almost 200 years, contains many examples of part songs. The astronomical title design was first used for a book by William Cuningham, The *Cosmographical Glasse*, published by John Day in 1559, and figured in many later books. Starting in 1597 it was employed in several editions of music by Dowland (see Plate 57) and Philip Rosseter (1568–1623), as well as this book by Morley. The design is possibly by John Bettes (*c.* 1530–not later than 1580).

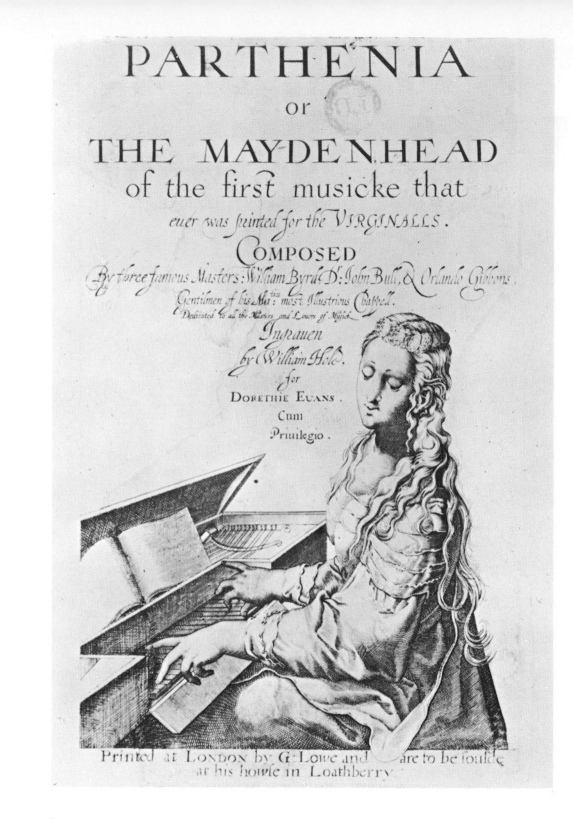

64 *Parthenia.* Printed by G. Lowe, London, 1612/3.
British Museum, London.

This is the earliest and most important printed collection of English virginal music. The composers represented are William Byrd (see Plates 54 and 62), John Bull (1543–1628), organist of the Chapel Royal, and Orlando Gibbons (1583–1625), virginalist to King James I. *Parthenia* was one of the first English music books printed throughout from engraved plates; the engraver was the well-known William Hole, active between 1607 and 1624 (see also next plate).

ANGELO NOTARI

65 *Prime musiche nuove*. London, 1613.
British Museum, London.

Notari (d. before 1664) was an Italian composer in the service of the King of England from 1625 on. According to *Grove's*, "His 'Prime musiche nuove' (1613), engraved by W. Hole, is a curious miscellany of music *a* 1, 2, and 3, partly in the new monodic style for voice(s) and theorbo, partly in the informal scherzo style of Monteverdi's lighter concerted music." The book was engraved throughout, as noted above, by Hole (see preceding plate).

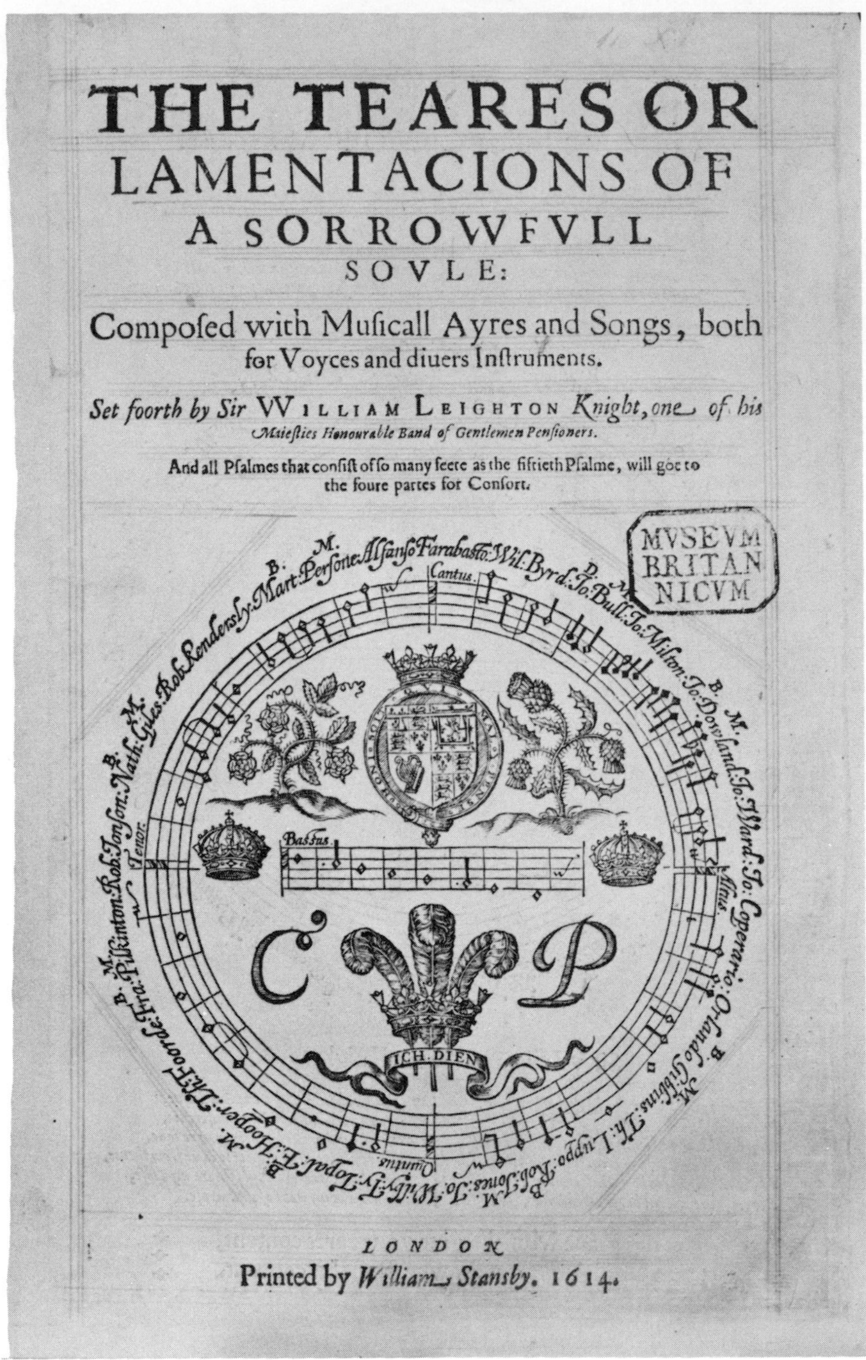

THE TEARES OR LAMENTACIONS OF A SORROWFVLL SOVLE:

Composed with Musicall Ayres and Songs, both for Voyces and diuers Instruments.

Set foorth by Sir WILLIAM LEIGHTON *Knight, one of his Maiesties Honourable Band of Gentlemen Pensioners.*

And all Psalmes that consist of so many feete as the fiftieth Psalme, will goe to the foure partes for Consort.

LONDON.
Printed by *William Stansby.* 1614.

SIR WILLIAM LEIGHTON

66 *The Teares or Lamentacions of a Sorrowfull Soule.* Printed by William Stansby, London, 1614. British Museum, London.

This is a collection of 54 Psalms and hymns, mostly in four or five parts. The texts are by Leighton (?–1616), a music editor and minor composer. The music was furnished by some of the most celebrated English composers of the time, including Bull (see Plate 64), Byrd (see Plate 54), Dowland (see Plate 57), Gibbons (see Plate 64), Thomas Weelkes (d. 1623), John Wilby (1574–1638) and Leighton himself. The composers' names are written in a decorative ring around a circular arrangement of the beginning of a five-part hymn. Leighton was in debtors' prison while compiling this collection.

WILLIAM SLATYER

67 *The Psalmes of David*. George Thomason & Octavian Pullen (printed by Thomas Harper), London, 1643.
British Museum, London.

The texts in all "4 Languages" mentioned in the title (Greek, Hebrew, Latin and English) are arranged to be sung to the same music. Among the composers named in the book are Thomas Campion (1567–1620) and John Milton (1563–1647), father of the poet. A shorter, "corrected" edition of this book appeared in 1652.

GIULIO CACCINI

68 *L'Euridice*. Giorgio Marescotti, Florence, 1600. Boston Public Library.

For the wedding celebration of Henry IV of France and Maria de' Medici in 1600, the eminent poet Ottavio Rinuccini (d. 1621) wrote the libretto of one of the earliest operas, *Euridice*, which was set to music by Jacopo Peri (1561–1633). Caccini (*c.* 1550–1610), a singer and composer in the service of the Medici in Florence whose name is inseparably linked with the new monody of the early Baroque, wrote and published an opera to the same text in the same year (it was not performed until 1602). The title design was first used by Torrentino in Florence in 1550/1, and is better suited to the original publication: an edition of the Greek geographical writer Pausanias. Below left is the Medici arms.

CANTO
IL METAMORFOSI
MVSICALE
QVARTO LIBRO DELLE CANZO-
NETTE A TRE VOCI,
Di Adriano Banchieri Bolognese
Nuouamente, con spassevoli trattenimenti, diuiso in
Epilogati, & vaghi discorsi.
IN VENETIA MDCI.
Appresso Ricciardo Amadino.

ADRIANO BANCHIERI

69 *Il Metamorfosi musicale.* Ricciardo Amadino, Venice, 1601.
British Museum, London.

Banchieri (1567–1634) was an eminent organist, music theorist and composer in Bologna, who wrote both sacred and theatrical music, introducing major innovations in the latter. This set of "three-part canzonette" is actually a madrigal-opera (see also Plate 24). The illustrations inside the book are the earliest depictions of opera sets that we possess.

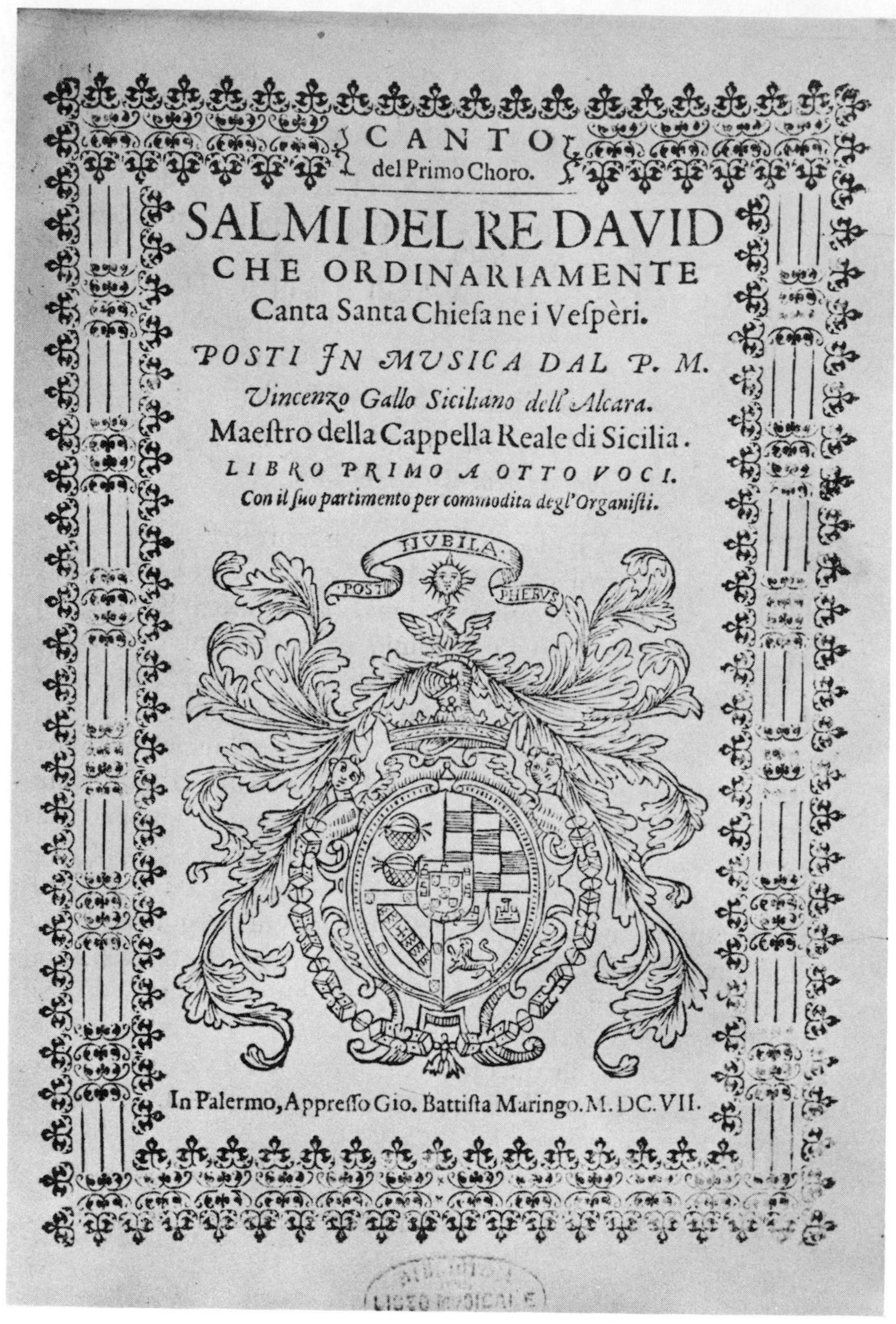

CANTO
del Primo Choro.
SALMI DEL RE DAVID
CHE ORDINARIAMENTE
Canta Santa Chiesa ne i Vespèri.
POSTI IN MUSICA DAL P. M.
Vincenzo Gallo Siciliano dell'Alcara.
Maestro della Cappella Reale di Sicilia.
LIBRO PRIMO A OTTO VOCI.
Con il suo partimento per commodita degl'Organisti.
IVBILA
POST
PHEBVS
In Palermo, Appresso Gio. Battista Maringo. M. DC. VII.

VINCENZO GALLO

70 *Salmi del Re David*. Giovanni Battista Maringo, Palermo, 1607.
Civico Museo Bibliografico Musicale, Bologna.

These Psalm settings in traditional post-Palestrina counterpoint are by Vincenzo Gallo (b. between 1560 and 1570, d. 1624), music director at the court and cathedral of Palermo. The coat-of-arms is probably that of one of the Spanish families then governing Sicily.

אלטו
השירים
אשר לשלמה
מזמורים ושירות ותשבחות אשר
הביא בחכמת הנגון והמוסיקה
לשלשה ד׳ ה׳ ו׳ ז׳ ח׳ קולות
כמר שלמה מהאדומים יצו
מדרי קק מאנטובה
להודות לה׳ ולזמר לשמו עליון בכל
דבר שבקדושה · חדשה
בארץ:
פה ויניציאה שפג
במצות השרים
פייטרו ולורינצו בראגאדיני ·
בבית ייואני קאליאוני
Appreſſo gli Illuſt. Sig.
Pietro e Lorenzo Brag.

SALOMONE ROSSI

71 *Ha-Shirim asher li-Shlomo* (*Salmi e cantici ebraici*). Pietro & Lorenzo Bragadino, Venice, 1622. British Museum, London.

Salomone Rossi (*c.* 1570–*c.* 1630) was a violinist at the court of Mantua and a celebrated composer of madrigals and instrumental music. On the Italian title pages of his works he is generally identified as "Ebreo"; on this volume of synagogue music (which contains 28 settings of Psalms and other sacred texts in contemporary madrigal style), he refers to himself as "Shlomo me-ha-Adumim" (= Solomon of the Red = Salomone [dei] Rossi). This is the only music print by the Bragadini.

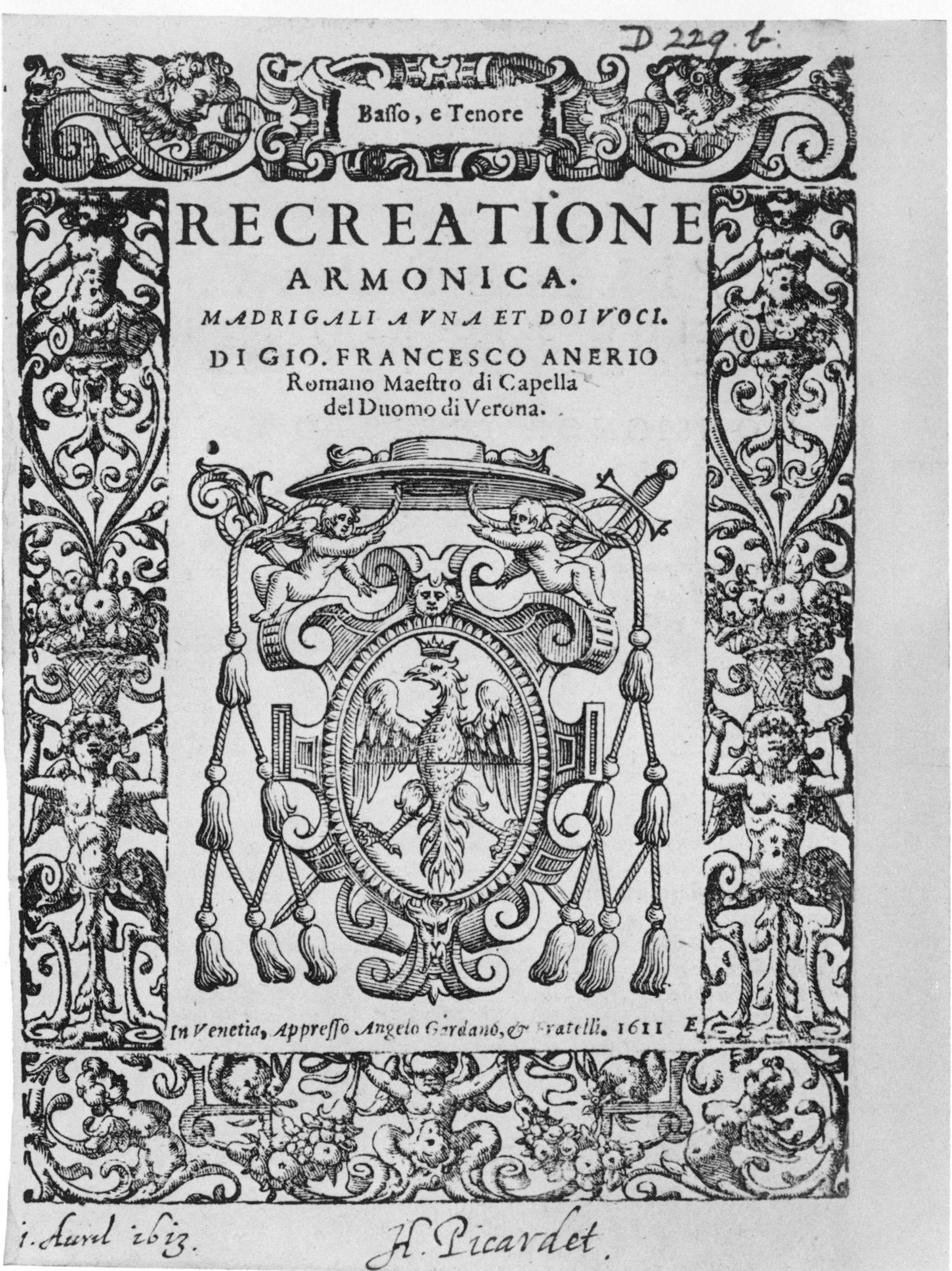

GIOVANNI FRANCESCO ANERIO

72 *Recreatione armonica.* Angelo Gardano & Brothers, Venice, 1611.
British Museum, London.

Brother of Felice Anerio (see Plate 23), G. F. Anerio (*c.* 1567–*c.* 1621), who lived most of his life in Rome, is best known for his secular vocal music in the style of Palestrina. This book of one- and two-part madrigals was published while he was music director at the Duomo of Verona. The coat-of-arms is probably that of the bishop of that city.

MADRIGALI
Di Luzzasco Luzzaschi per cantare, et sonare
A uno, e doi, e tre Soprani, fatti
per la Musica del gia Ser.mo
Duca Alfonso
d'Este.
Stampati
In Roma appresso Simone Verovio
1601
C.A.
C.A.
Con Licenza de' Superiori

LUZZASCO LUZZASCHI

73 *Madrigali*. Simone Verovio, Rome, 1601.
Library of Congress, Washington.

Luzzaschi (1545–1607), one of the major harbingers of the monodists and teacher of Frescobaldi (see Plates 78–80), was organist and composer to the Estes in Ferrara. His printed compositions are chiefly madrigals. The present work is one of the most successful engraved productions of Verovio (see Plate 28). The coat-of-arms is that of the Aldobrandini family.

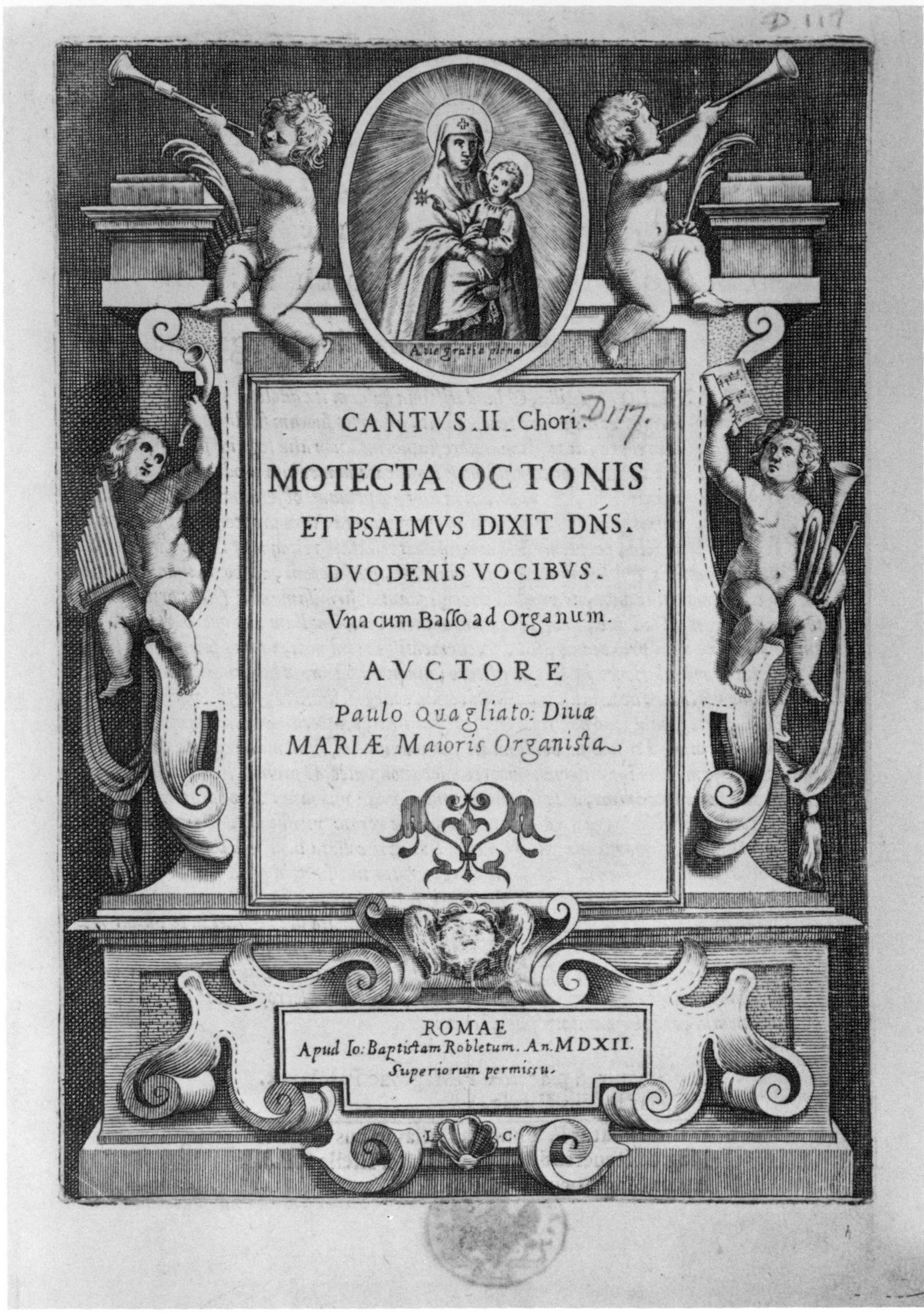
CANTVS.II.Chori.
MOTECTA OCTONIS
ET PSALMVS DIXIT DNS.
DVODENIS VOCIBVS.
Vna cum Basso ad Organum.
AVCTORE
Paulo Quagliato: Diuæ
MARIÆ Maioris Organista
ROMAE
Apud Io: Baptistam Robletum. An. MDXII.
Superiorum permissu.

PAOLO QUAGLIATI

74 *Motecta octonis . . . vocibus*. Giovanni Battista Robletti, Rome, 1612. British Museum, London.

Quagliati (*c.* 1555–1628) was the organist of Santa Maria Maggiore in Rome from 1609 on. Writing partially in the new monodic style, he composed madrigals, motets and sacred songs. All his keyboard works have been lost. Note the misprint "MDXII" instead of "MDCXII."

SIGISMONDO D'INDIA

75 *Le Musiche.* Heir of Simon Tini & Filippo Lomazzo, Milan, 1609. Bibliothèque Nationale, Paris.

D'India (*c.* 1580–1629) was an Italian composer of madrigals, villanellas and arias active at Mantua, Florence, Rome, Piacenza, Turin and Modena. This is a collection of chamber arias in D'India's new, experimental, expressive lyric style. The composer wrote some of his own texts.

DEL SONARE
SOPRA'L BASSO
CON TVTTI LI
STROMENTI
E dell'vſo loro nel Conſerto
Dell'Ill.re Sig.
AGOSTINO AGAZZARI
SANESE
Armonico Intronato

EX MOTV ARMONIA
NEC TAMEN INFICIVNT

IN SIENA
Appreſſo Domenico Falcini
Con Priuilegio di S. A. Ser.ma
Anno 1607.

AGOSTINO AGAZZARI

76 *Del sonare sopra'l basso.* Domenico Falcini, Siena, 1607.
Civico Museo Bibliografico Musicale, Bologna.

This is one of the earliest and most celebrated instruction books for the realization of the figured bass, with many musical examples. Agazzari (1578–1640), a Sienese musician and composer who taught for some time at the Collegium Germanicum in Rome, was a champion of the *stile nuovo* of his pioneering contemporaries. The epithet "Armonico Intronato" after Agazzari's name in the title refers to his membership in the Sienese learned academy of the Intronati (the "Dazed").

LIBRO PRIMO
DI ARIE Passeggiate à Vna Voce
Con l'intauolatura del Chitarone
Del Sig.r
GIO: GIROLAMO KAPSPERGER
Nobile Alemano.
RACCOLTO
Dal Sig.r Cau.r fra Iacomo
Christoforo Ab Andlaw del
Ordine di S.to Gio: Battista
In Roma 1612
Con Priuilegio

JOHANN HIERONYMUS [GIOVANNI GIROLAMO] KAPSBERGER

77 *Libro Primo Di Arie.* Rome, 1612.
British Museum, London.

Kapsberger (*c.* 1575–*c.* 1650), a German, lived in Italy as a composer and virtuoso on the theorbo, lute, chitarrone and trumpet. He is a representative of early monody.

TOCCATE D'INTAVOLATVRA
DI CIMBALO ET ORGANO
PARTITE DI DIVERSE ARIE E COR-
RENTE, BALLETTI, CIAC-
CONE, PASSACHAGLI.
DI
GIROLAMO FRESCOBALDI
ORGANISTA IN S. PIETRO DI ROMA.
Libro P.°

STAMPATO L'ANNO M·D·CXXXVII
Per Nicolo Borbone in Roma Con licenza de' Superiori.

GIROLAMO FRESCOBALDI

78 *Toccate d'intavolatura di cimbalo et organo.* Nicolò Borbone (Borboni), Rome, 1637. Library of Congress, Washington.

Pupil of Luzzaschi (see Plate 73) and teacher of Froberger (and thus extraordinarily influential in the development of German keyboard music), world-famous in his own day, Frescobaldi (1583–1643) was the greatest seventeenth-century Italian organist, active at St. Peter's in Rome from 1608 on. He is considered as the composer who consolidated and perfected the instrumental trends of the first phase of the Baroque. This is the title page of the fifth edition (the first appeared in 1615) of his first collection of keyboard pieces. The coat-of-arms is that of the Barberinis (the family of Urban VIII, who was Pope from 1623 to 1644).

IL SECONDO LIBRO
DI TOCCATE·CANZONE
VERSI D·HINNI MAGNIFICAT
GAGLIARDE·CORRENTI
ET ALTRE PARTITE
D·INTAVOLATVRA
DI CIMBALO ET ORGANO
DI GIROLAMO FRESCOBALDI
ORGANISTA
IN S·PIETRO DI ROMA
Con priuilegio.

In Roma con licenza de Superiori 1637 Da Nicolò Borbone.

GIROLAMO FRESCOBALDI

79 *Il secondo libro di toccate*. Nicolò Borbone, Rome, 1637.
Library of Congress, Washington.

1637 also saw this second edition (in a format matching that of Plate 78) of Frescobaldi's second keyboard collection (first edition 1627). The coat-of-arms is that of Luigi Gallo, to whom the book is dedicated.

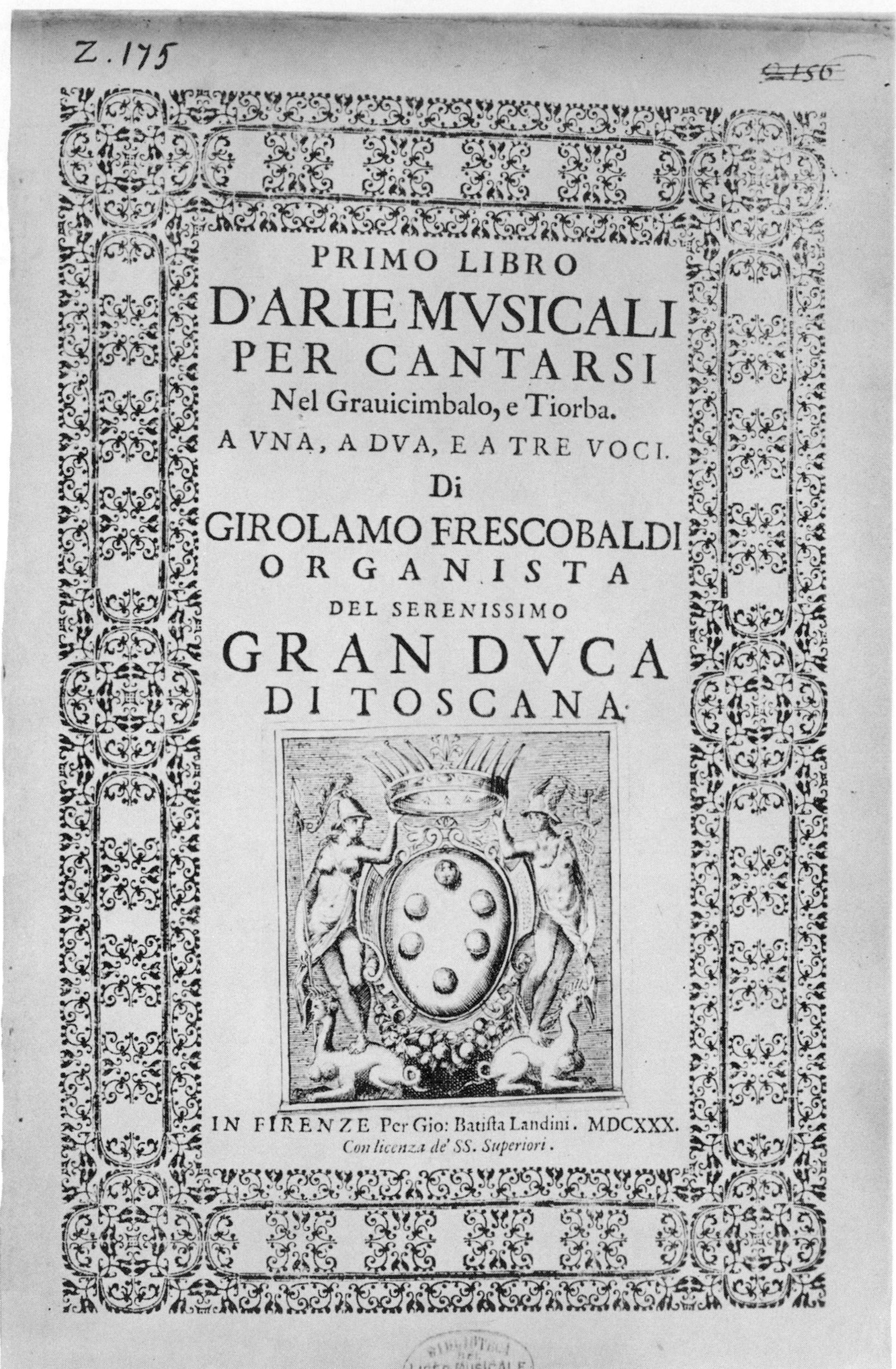
PRIMO LIBRO
D'ARIE MVSICALI
PER CANTARSI
Nel Grauicimbalo, e Tiorba.
A VNA, A DVA, E A TRE VOCI.
Di
GIROLAMO FRESCOBALDI
ORGANISTA
DEL SERENISSIMO
GRAN DVCA
DI TOSCANA.

IN FIRENZE Per Gio: Batista Landini. MDCXXX.
Con licenza de' SS. Superiori.

GIROLAMO FRESCOBALDI

80 *Primo libro d'arie musicali.* Giovanni Battista Landini, Florence, 1630.
Civico Museo Bibliografico Musicale, Bologna.

This set of "arias" for one, two and three voices was composed while Frescobaldi was organist to the Grand Duke of Tuscany, Ferdinand II, to whom the work is dedicated. The title bears the armorial shield of the Medici. A second book of Frescobaldi's *arie musicali* appeared the same year, 1630.

IL

TRANSILVANO

DIALOGO

SOPRA IL VERO MODO DI SONAR

Organi, & Iſtromenti da penna.

DEL R. P. GIROLAMO DIRVTA

PERVGINO,

Dell'Ordine de' Frati Minori Conu. di S. Franceſco.

ORGANISTA DEL DVOMO

DI CHIOGGIA.

Nel quale facilmente, & preſto s'impara di conoſcere ſopra la Taſtatura il luogo di ciaſcuna parte, & come nel Diminuire ſi deueno portar le mani, & il modo d'intendere la Intauolatura; prouando la verità, & neceſſità delle ſue Regole, con le Toccate de diuerſi Eccellenti Organiſti, poſte nel fine del Libro.

Opera nuouamente ritrouata, vtiliſſima, & neceſſaria a Profeſsori d'Organo.

AL SERENISSIMO PRENCIPE di Tranſiluania.

CON PRIVILEGIO.

IN VENETIA, Appreſſo Aleſſandro Vincenti. MDCXXV.

GIROLAMO DIRUTA

81 *Il Transilvano.* Alessandro Vincenti, Venice, 1625.
Library of Congress, Washington.

Diruta (1561–?), a Franciscan monk, organist, theorist and composer, was active at the cathedrals of Chioggia and Gubbio. *Il Transilvano,* written in dialogue form and dedicated to Sigismund Bathory, a Transylvanian prince who freed his territory from the dominion of the Turks, was, strictly speaking, the first instruction book for the organ and cembalo. It appeared first in 1593; this is the title of the fifth edition. The pine cone was the emblem of the music publisher Vincenti. The book contains musical examples by Luzzaschi, Diruta himself, and other contemporaries.

DOMENICO MAZZOCCHI

82 *Musiche sacre e morali*. Lodovico Grignani, Rome, 1640.
British Museum, London.

Mazzocchi (1592–1665) was an important Roman composer of secular and sacred vocal music, a pioneer in the opera of the Roman style and one of the last important Italian madrigalists. The present work stands formally between the cantata and the oratorio. Mazzocchi was in the service of the Aldobrandini, and the *Musiche sacre* is dedicated to a member of that family who married a Borghese. On the title, the Borghese coat-of-arms appears on the left, the Aldobrandini arms on the right. The designer and engraver was Andrea Podestà (d. before 1674), a painter in Genoa known for his frequent use of graceful nudes and putti. His name appears on a tablet being inscribed by one of the putti.

PIETRO PAOLO SABBATINI [SABBATINO]
83 *Canzoni spirituali.* Lodovico Grignani, Rome, 1640.
British Museum, London.

A chapel director in Rome, Sabbatini (*c.* 1600–after 1657) was a composer of sacred songs. This work is dedicated to a princess of the Cesi Peretti. The Peretti lion and the Cesi tree are united on the shield in the title design.

BELLEROPHONTE CASTALDI

84 *Capricci a due stromenti*. Published by the composer, Modena, 1622. Bibliothèque Nationale, Paris.

Castaldi (*c*. 1581–1649) was a theorbo player in Modena. The eccentricities of his life, as well as the notion of caprice and fantasy, are reflected in this unusual title in which his first name is spelled backwards.

SISTO REINA

85 *La pace de numeri*. Francesco Magni, Venice, 1662.
British Museum, London.

Born in the first quarter of the seventeenth century, Reina was an organist at Saronno, Milan, Piacenza and Modena, and a composer of church music of no great merit. This is a collection of five-part vocal works. The title, which shows the tower of the cathedral of Modena, was designed by Alex. Fab. de Cas. (?) and engraved by the well-known painter and engraver Francesco Stringa in Modena (1635–1709).

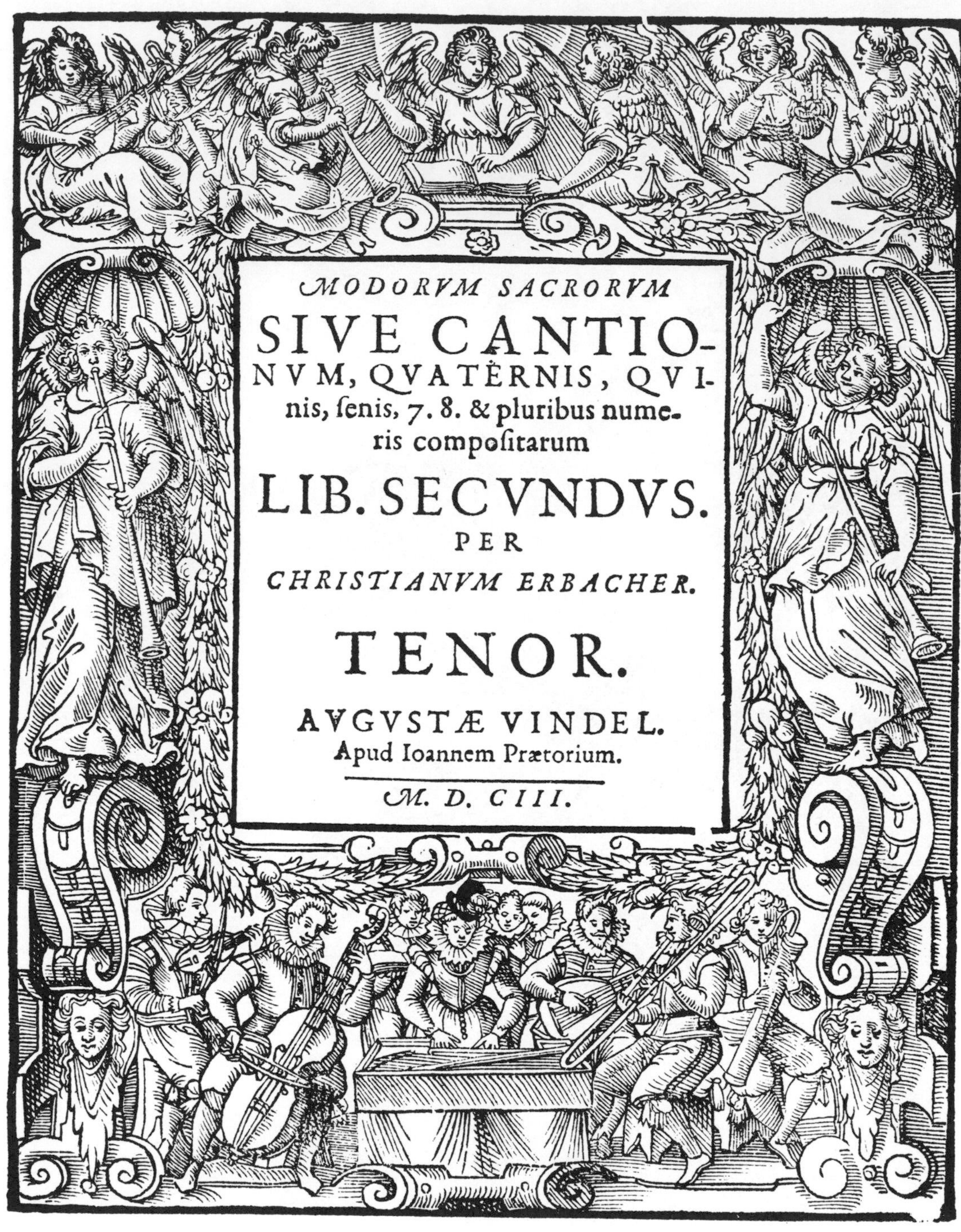

MODORVM SACRORVM
SIVE CANTIO-
NVM, QVATERNIS, QVI-
nis, ſenis, 7. 8. & pluribus nume-
ris compoſitarum
LIB. SECVNDVS.
PER
CHRISTIANVM ERBACHER.
TENOR.
AVGVSTÆ VINDEL.
Apud Ioannem Prætorium.
M. D. CIII.

CHRISTIAN ERBACH

86 *Modorum sacrorum . . . lib. secundus.* Johannes Praetorius, Augsburg, 1603.
Staats- und Stadtbibliothek, Augsburg.

This is the second book (Johannes Praetorius had published the first set in 1600) of motets for four to nine parts by Erbach (*c.* 1570–1635), Augsburg organist and composer of organ music and motets. Erbach is known especially as an influential keyboard teacher.

DELITIÆ

MVSICÆ,

SIVE

Cantiones, e quamplurimis præſtantiſſimorum noſtri æui Muſicorum Libris ſelectæ.

Ad TESTVDINIS uſum accommodatæ, *OPERA* atque induſtriâ

IOACHIMI VANDEN HOVE ANTVERPIANI.

Quarum omnium INDICEM proxima à Præfatione pagina repræſentat.

VLTRAIECTI,

Apud Salomonem de Roy, & veneunt apud Ioannem Gulielmi de Rhenen.

ANNO DOMINI, M.DC.XII.

JOACHIM VAN DEN HOVE

87 *Delitiae musicae*. Salomon de Roy, Utrecht, 1612.
British Museum, London.

Van den Hove (*c.* 1570–?), an eminent lute virtuoso in Leyden and The Hague, prepared many lute transcriptions of vocal music by such composers as Dowland, Giovanni Gabrieli, Lasso, Marenzio and Vecchi, and wrote original compositions. The title illustration of this collection of transcriptions, designed by an unknown L.L., was engraved by Joannes Barra (?–1634), a noted Amsterdam engraver of the time.

NVLLA SALUS MUNDO DULCIS MIHI PATRIA COELUM. RAPTUS AMORE CHELY, PATIENS DURISSIMA VINCO.

MVSAE
SIONIAE
Geistliche Concert Gesänge
uber die fürnembste
Deutsche Psalmen und Lieder / wie sie in der Christlichen Kirchen gesungen werden / mit VIII. Stimmen gesetzet /
Und in Druck verfertiget
Durch
Michaëlem Prætorium,
Fürstlichen Braunschweigischen
Capelmeister.

Vierdter Theil.

TENOR I. CHORI.

Helmstadt / 1607.

Mihi Patria Coelum

MICHAEL PRAETORIUS

88 *Musae Sioniae . . . Vierdter Theil.* Jacob Lucius, Helmstedt, 1607.
British Museum, London.

Praetorius (1571–1621), in the service of the Duke of Brunswick at Wolfenbüttel, was an eminent composer of instrumental and sacred polyphonic vocal music, as well as a great authority on music theory. The *Musae Sioniae* is a gigantic collection, issued in nine parts in various cities between 1605 and 1610; it comprises 1244 two- to twelve-part Psalms and songs to German and Latin texts, and a few organ compositions. This fourth part of the *Musae* (eight-part pieces for two choruses) was published by Jacob Lucius, the university printer in Helmstedt, who was a wood engraver in his own right.

Musarum Sioniar:
MOTECTAE ET PSALMI LATINI,
Michaëlis Prætorij C.
apud
Sereniss. principem
Henricum Julium
Ducem Brunsv. & Lunæb., Chori Musici Magistri,
IV. V. VI. VII. VIII. IX. X. XII. XVI.
vocum, Choro & Organis accommodatæ.
I. PARS.
QVINTA VOX.

MICHAEL PRAETORIUS

89 *Musarum Sioniar[um] motectae et psalmi latini*. Abraham Wagenmann, Nuremberg, 1607.
British Museum, London.

This set of 52 motets and Psalms for four to sixteen parts to Latin texts (some of the pieces are free motets, without *cantus firmus*) was first published by Francke in Magdeburg in 1606.

MICHAEL PRAETORIUS

90 *Polyhymnia panegyrica.* Elias Holwein, Wolfenbüttel, 1618. British Museum, London.

This is a collection of 40 choral pieces for one to twenty-one parts. The letters OR or UR on the organ at the lower right may be the engraver's initials. The publisher, himself a noted wood engraver, may have designed this title.

PARNASSVS MVSICVS

TERPSICHORE PRIMA.

Hoc eſt

Paduana, Galliarda,
Intrada, Alemanda, Maſcarada,
Aria, Couranta, Volta, quinq; Vocum,
cum Baſſo generali, ad uſum &
gratiam Muſicorum e-
miſſa,

ab

*Henrico Vtrecht Mindano, Organiſta
Aulæ Cellenſis,*

BASSUS GENERALIS

Impreſſa Gvelpherbyti, per Eliam
Holvvein, ſumptibus Authoris,
Anno
cIↃ. IↃc. XXIV.

HEINRICH UTRECHT

91 *Terpsichore prima.* Elias Holwein, Wolfenbüttel, 1624.
Uppsala University Library.

This is a collection of dances by Utrecht (dates unknown), who was court organist at Celle from 1611 on. About the publisher, see the preceding plate.

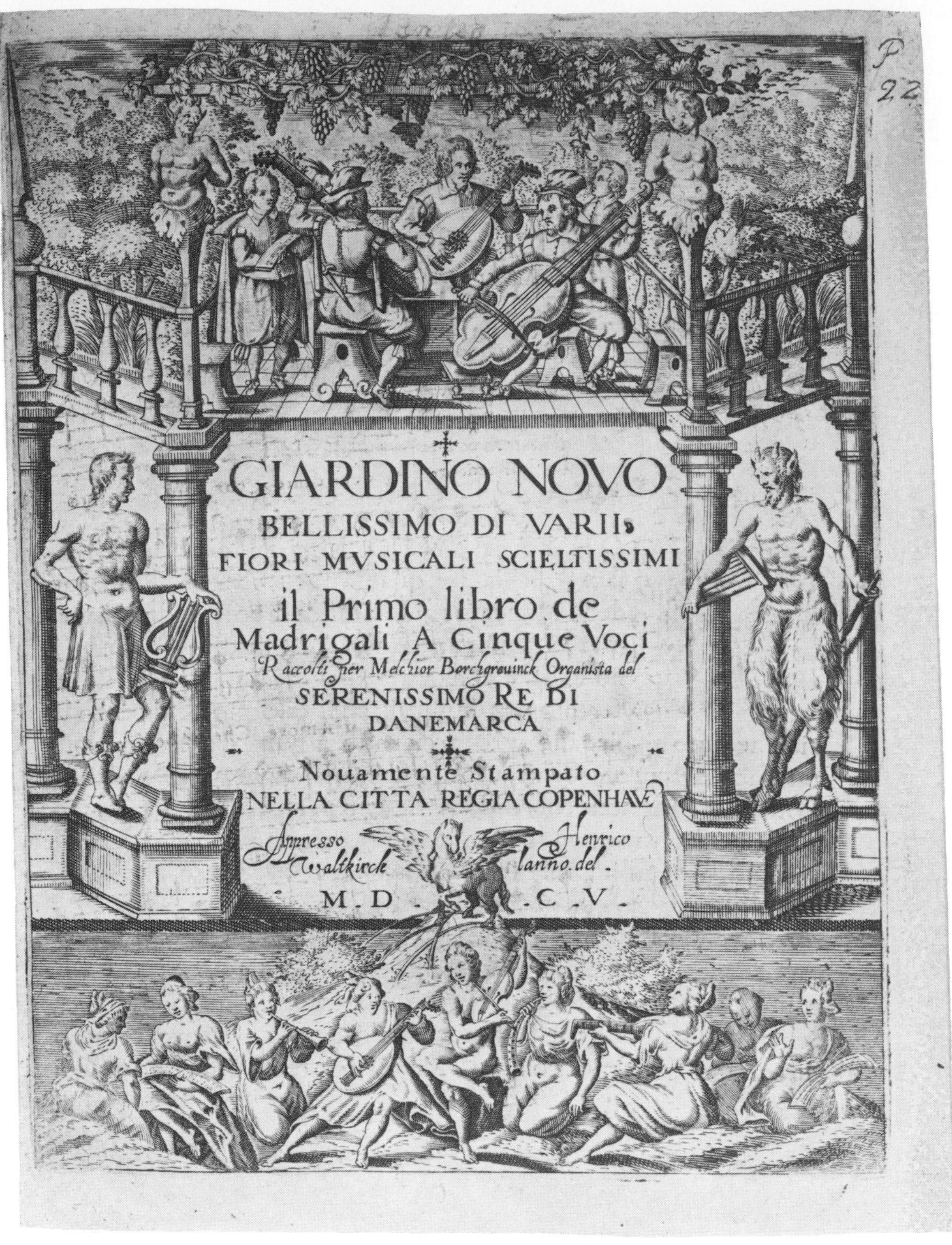

GIARDINO NOVO
BELLISSIMO DI VARII,
FIORI MVSICALI SCIELTISSIMI
il Primo libro de
Madrigali A Cinque Voci
Raccolti per Melchior Borchgreuinck Organista del
SERENISSIMO RE DI
DANEMARCA
Nouamente Stampato
NELLA CITTA REGIA COPENHAVE
Appresso Henrico
Waltkirch lanno. del.
M.D. .C.V.

MELCHIOR BORCHGREVINCK

92 *Giardino novo bellissimo.* Henricus Waltkirch, Copenhagen, 1605.
British Museum, London.

Borchgrevinck (?–1632), a Netherlander, was Danish court organist and conductor of the Copenhagen royal chapel. He contributed one or two of his own five-part madrigals to this compilation that includes specimens by Claudio Monteverdi (1567–1643), Rossi (see Plate 71), Croce (see Plate 24) and others.

IOAN. BAPT. BE-
SARDI VESONTINI
NOVVS PARTVS,
siue
CONCERTATIONES MV-
SICAE, DVODENA TRIVM, AC TOTIDEM
binarum Testudinum (quibus & notæ Musicæ adduntur)
singulari ordine modulamina continentes.
HIS ADDIDIT AVTHOR, LECTISSIMI STI-
li partes aliquot seorsim, tam proprias, quàm alienas; atque in gratiam
Philomusi, e tenebris in meliorem lucem liberaliter eduxit:
NECNON
Ad artem Testudinis breui, citraque magnum fastidium ca-
pescendam, facilem & methodicam insti-
tutionem hisce subiecit.
VT EMENDATISSIMVM PRODIRET
opus, Stephanus Michelspacherus Tirolensis, ex
authoris manuscripto, suis sumptibus to-
tum curauit incidi & excudi.
AVGVSTAE VINDELICORVM
per Dauidem Francum,
Anno Salutis Humanæ
M. DCXVII.
Cum gratiâ, & priuilegio
Cæs. Maiestatis.

L. Kilian. F. A. 1617.

JEAN-BAPTISTE BESARDUS

93 *Novus partus, sive concertationes musicae.* David Franck, Augsburg, 1617.
Bayerische Staatsbibliothek, Munich.

This work contains lute compositions by the French lutenist Besardus (*c.* 1567–*c.* 1625), who was active in Germany, and by other composers. The notation is partly in letter tablatures, partly in modern notes. Besardus was also a prominent jurist. The title page was engraved by Lucas Kilian (1579–1637), the most important member of a noted Augsburg family of engravers and publishers active from the sixteenth to the eighteenth centuries.

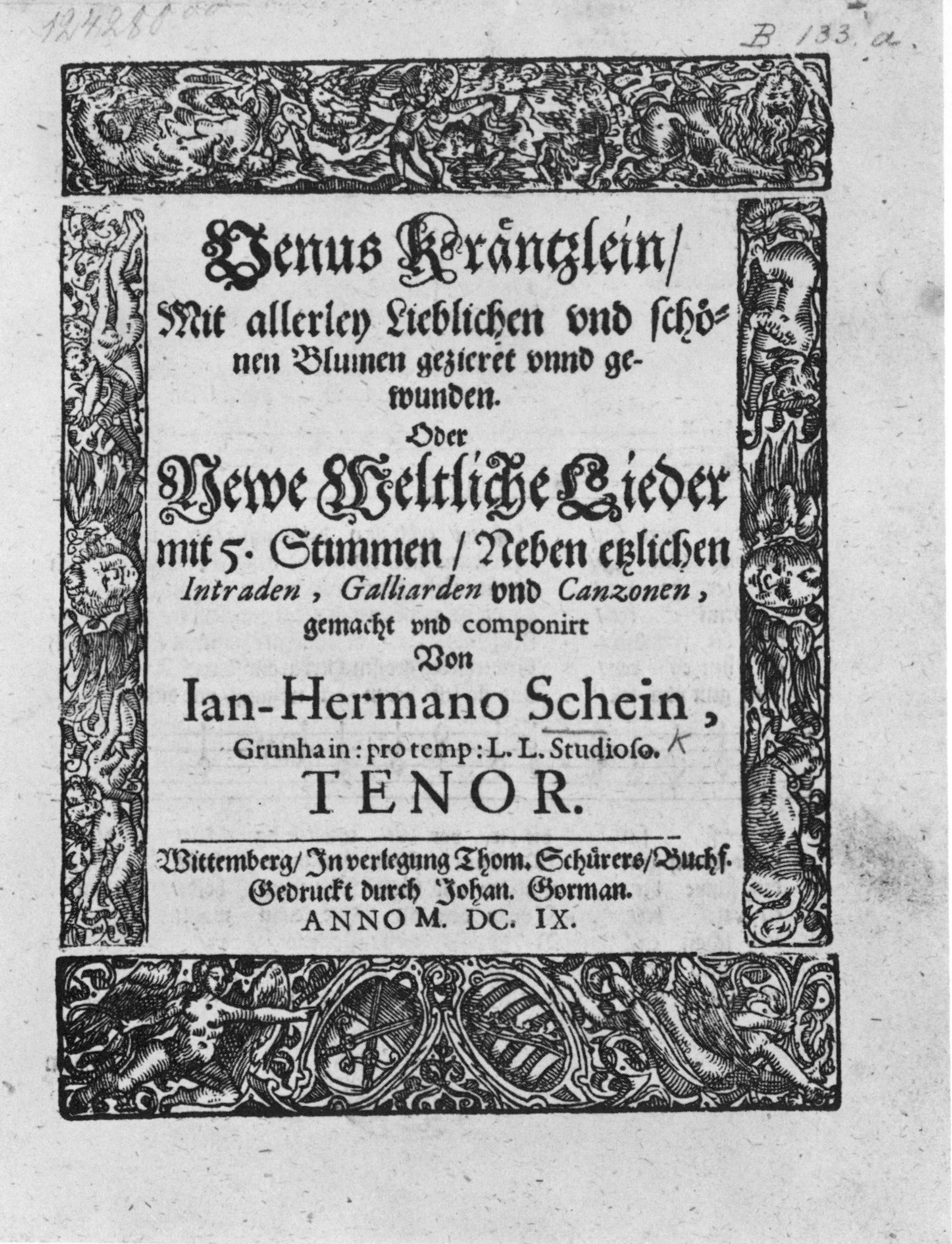

124286
B. 133. a.
Venus Kräntzlein/
Mit allerley Lieblichen vnd schö-
nen Blumen gezieret vnnd ge-
wunden.
Oder
Newe Weltliche Lieder
mit 5. Stimmen / Neben etzlichen
Intraden, Galliarden vnd Canzonen,
gemacht vnd componirt
Von
Ian-Hermano Schein,
Grunhain: pro temp: L. L. Studioso.
TENOR.
Wittemberg/ In verlegung Thom. Schürers/ Buchf.
Gedruckt durch Johan. Gorman.
ANNO M. DC. IX.

JOHANN HERMANN SCHEIN

94 *Venus Kräntzlein*. Thomas Schürer (printed by Johannes Gormann), Wittenberg, 1609. British Museum, London.

One of the major seventeenth-century German composers, Schein (1586–1630) was Cantor at St. Thomas' in Leipzig from 1616 on. A friend of Heinrich Schütz (1585–1672), he too built upon the style and manner of the new Italian school, writing madrigals, motets of great emotional power, and instrumental suites. *Venus Kräntzlein* is a collection of 24 secular pieces: 15 five-part songs, one eight-part song, four intradas, two galliards and two (instrumental) canzonas. It was Schein's first published work.

JOHANN HERMANN SCHEIN

95 *Fontana d'Israel* (*Israels Brünnlein*). Published by the composer (printed by J. Glück), Leipzig, 1623. Bayerische Staatsbibliothek, Munich.

The long title of this superb musical work explains that these motets are in the style of the Italian madrigalists. A second edition was published in 1651/2.

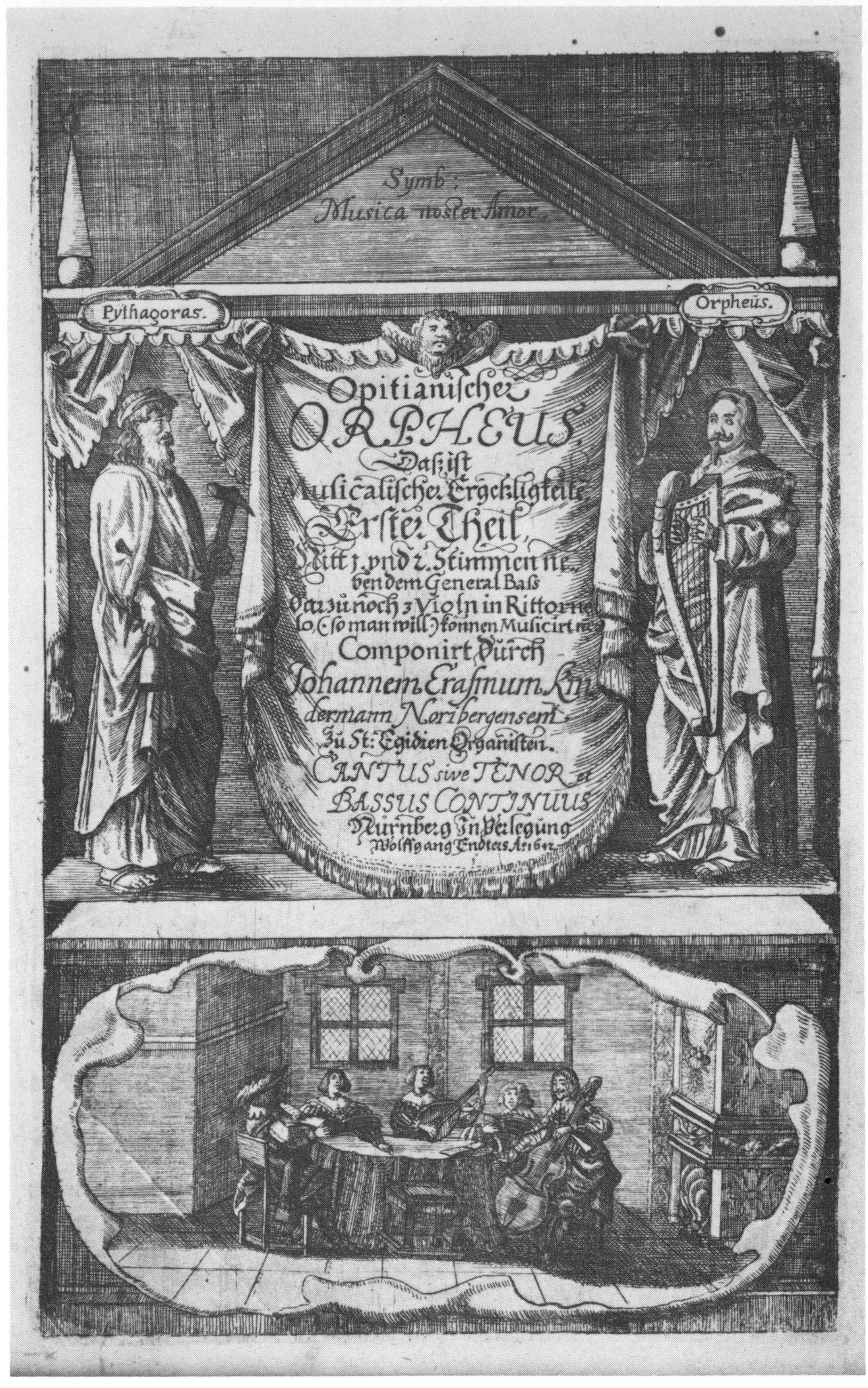

JOHANN ERASMUS KINDERMANN

96 *Opitianischer Orpheus*. Wolfgang Endter, Nuremberg, 1642.
British Museum, London.

This is a collection of songs with instrumental accompaniment in the style of Heinrich Albert (see next plate) by the Nuremberg organist and composer Kindermann (1616–1655). The poems are by the famed Martin Opitz (1597–1639): hence the title. The publisher Endter founded a family business of printing and bookselling in Nuremberg about 1615 that existed over a hundred years.

HEINRICH ALBERT

97 *Achter Theil der Arien*. Published by the composer, Königsberg, 1650.
British Museum, London.

A noted Königsberg organist, composer and poet who supplied some of his own song texts, Albert (1604–1651), a cousin of Schütz, developed the "orchestral" song and is best known for his eight volumes of sacred and secular songs (this is the eighth). The double character of this work is expressed in the design of the title page, with a funeral procession on the left and a merry singing party on the right. The three eagles probably symbolize the Holy Roman Empire, Poland and Brandenburg. The engraver's signature appears to be "H. Jamer."

ANDREAS HAMMERSCHMIDT

98 *Missae.* Christian Bergen (printed by Seyffert), Dresden, 1663. Uppsala University Library.

Hammerschmidt (1612–1675), organist at Zittau, was one of the chief composers for the Lutheran liturgy in his time. With Schütz as his model, he combined the new *concertante* style with the Protestant goal of transparency of textual setting. The Masses in this set consist of Kyrie and Gloria only: the Lutheran *missa brevis.* The title page, which features the portrait of the composer at age fifty-one, was designed by the Saxonian court painter Centurio Wiebel (1616–1684) and engraved by the court engraver Johann Caspar Höckner (1629–?), both from Dresden.

Andreas Hammer-schmiedts
Kirchen- vnd Tafel-Music
Darinnen
1.2.3. Vocal vnd 4.5.6
Instrumenta
enthalten
in
Verlegung des Autoris
Dritte Stimme.

Mit Chur-Sächß. special-Privilegio
Gedruckt bey Johann Caspar Dehnen. 1.6.6.2.

ANDREAS HAMMERSCHMIDT

99 *Kirchen- und Tafel-Music.* Published by the composer (printed by Johann Caspar Dehnen), Zittau, 1662.
British Museum, London.

This work contains 22 sacred songs, monodic and polyphonic, with instrumental accompaniment. The title illustration depicting the town of Zittau where the composer was active was engraved by Weishun, either Nicolas (1607–1687) or his brother Samuel (d. after 1676), both engravers in Dresden.

PHILIPP JAKOB BAUDREXEL

100 *Primitiae Deo et Agno . . . cantatae.* Published by the composer (printed by Michael Wagner), Innsbruck, 1664.
Bibliothèque Nationale, Paris.

A student of Carissimi (*c.* 1604–1674) in Rome, Baudrexel (1627–1691) directed chapels and composed Catholic church music in Fulda, Mainz and elsewhere. When this collection of sacred vocal pieces, his major work, was published, he was a parson in Kaufbeuren. The name of the collection is given differently in the various part books; this, the organ part, has a title by Mathäus Küsel (1629–1681), one of a well-known family of engravers in Augsburg.

ESAIAS REUSNER THE YOUNGER

101 *Neue Lauten-Früchte*. Published by the composer, Berlin, 1676. Österreichische Nationalbibliothek, Vienna.

Reusner (1636–1679), lute performer and composer, was active in Poland, Silesia and finally at the court of the Elector of Brandenburg. The copy of this book of lute pieces preserved in Berlin contains the handwritten solo part for a lute concerto, a very early example of this genre.

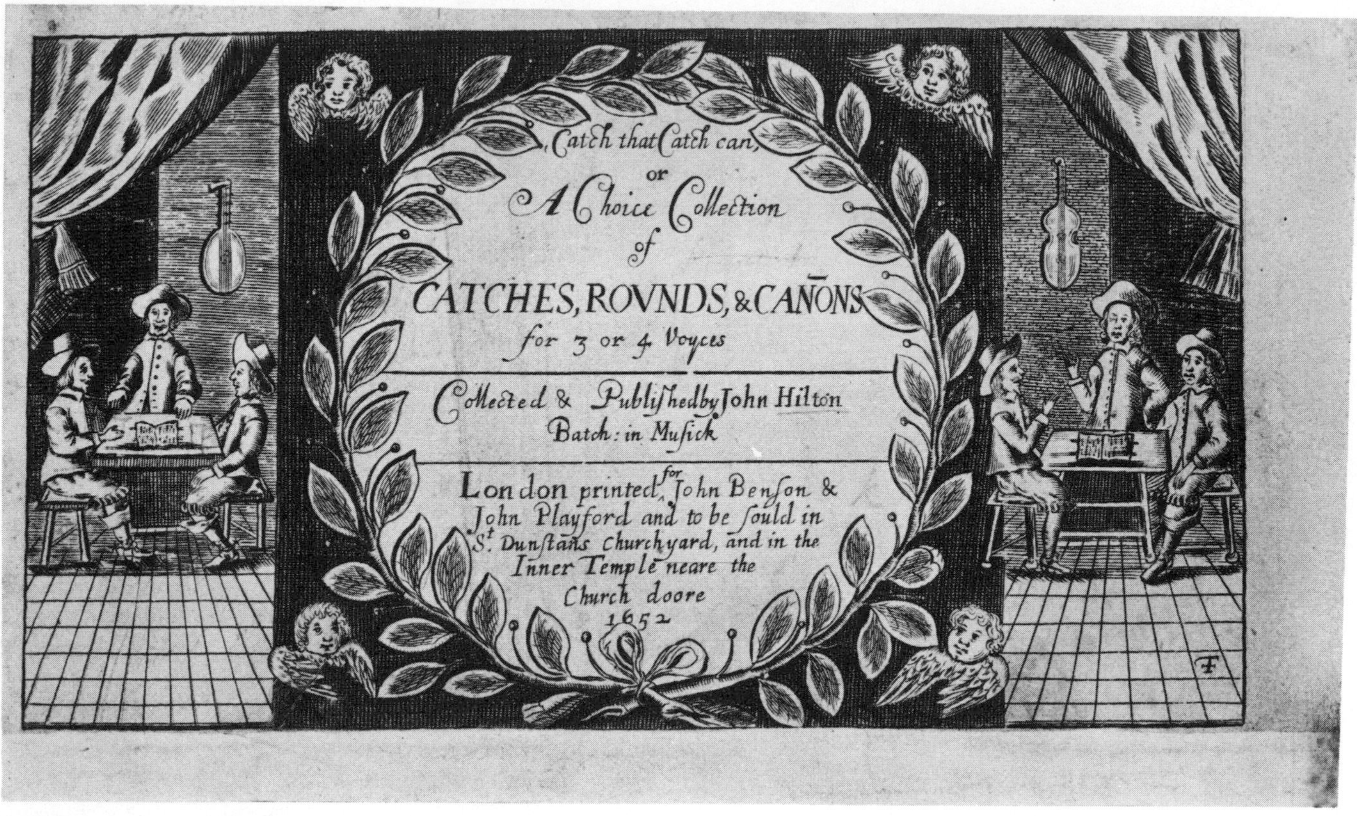

JOHN HILTON, JR.

102 *Catch that Catch can*. John Benson & John Playford, London, 1652.
British Museum, London.

This famous collection of English catches, rounds and canons by the Westminster organist Hilton (1599–1657) and many other composers was one of the earliest publications of John Playford (1623–1686), who was still associated with his master John Benson. Later editions of *Catch that Catch can* appeared in 1658, 1663 and 1667. It was continued in 1673 as *The Musical Companion*, under which name it appeared again and again into the eighteenth century (see next plate).

THE
Musical Companion,
In Two BOOKS.
The First Book containing CATCHES and ROUNDS for Three Voyces.
The Second Book containing DIALOGUES, GLEES, AYRES and SONGS for Two, Three and Four VOYCES.
Collected and Published By JOHN PLAYFORD Practitioner in MUSICK.
London, Printed by W. Godbid for John Playford, at his Shop in the Temple near the Church, 1673.
A 412 c

JOHN PLAYFORD

103 *The Musical Companion*. Printed by W. Godbid, London, 1673. British Museum, London.

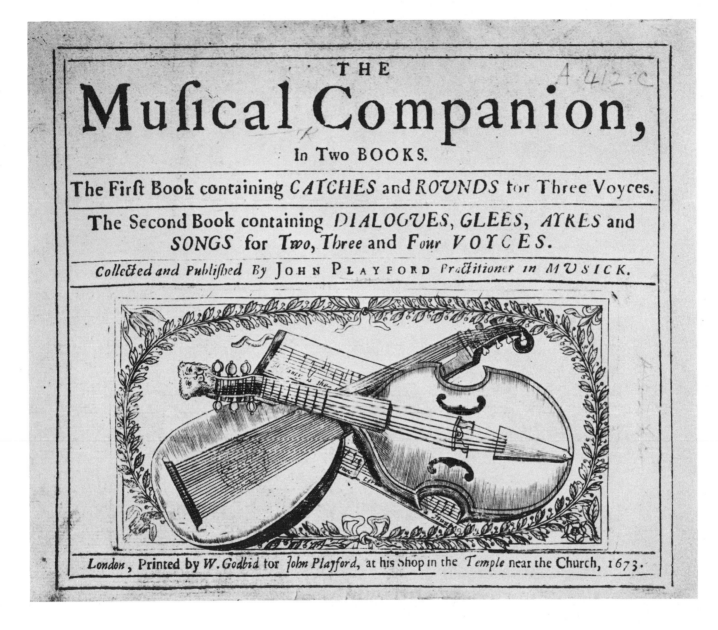

John Playford (Senior; see also Plates 102 and 104) was the most important English music publisher in the second half of the seventeenth century. Some of the eminent composers represented in this first edition of *The Musical Companion* are Purcell (see Plate 105), William Lawes (1602–1645), Matthew Locke (*c.* 1630–1677), Hilton (see Plate 102) and Playford himself.

JOHN PLAYFORD

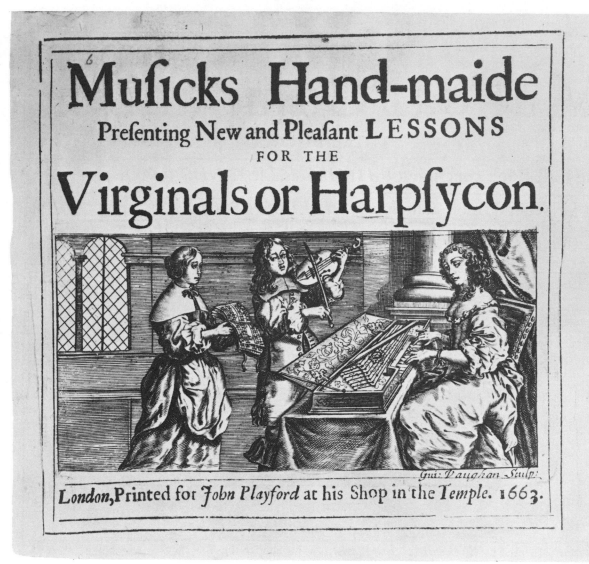

104 *Musicks Hand-maide*. London, 1663.
British Museum, London.

Like *Parthenia* (Plate 64), on which it is modeled, this book is engraved throughout. The composers named in the book are B. Sandley, William Lawes (1602–1645), Benjamin Rogers (1614–1698), Matthew Locke (*c.* 1630–1677) and John Moss (second half of the seventeenth century). The title vignette is by William Vaughan, an English engraver who worked chiefly for publishers.

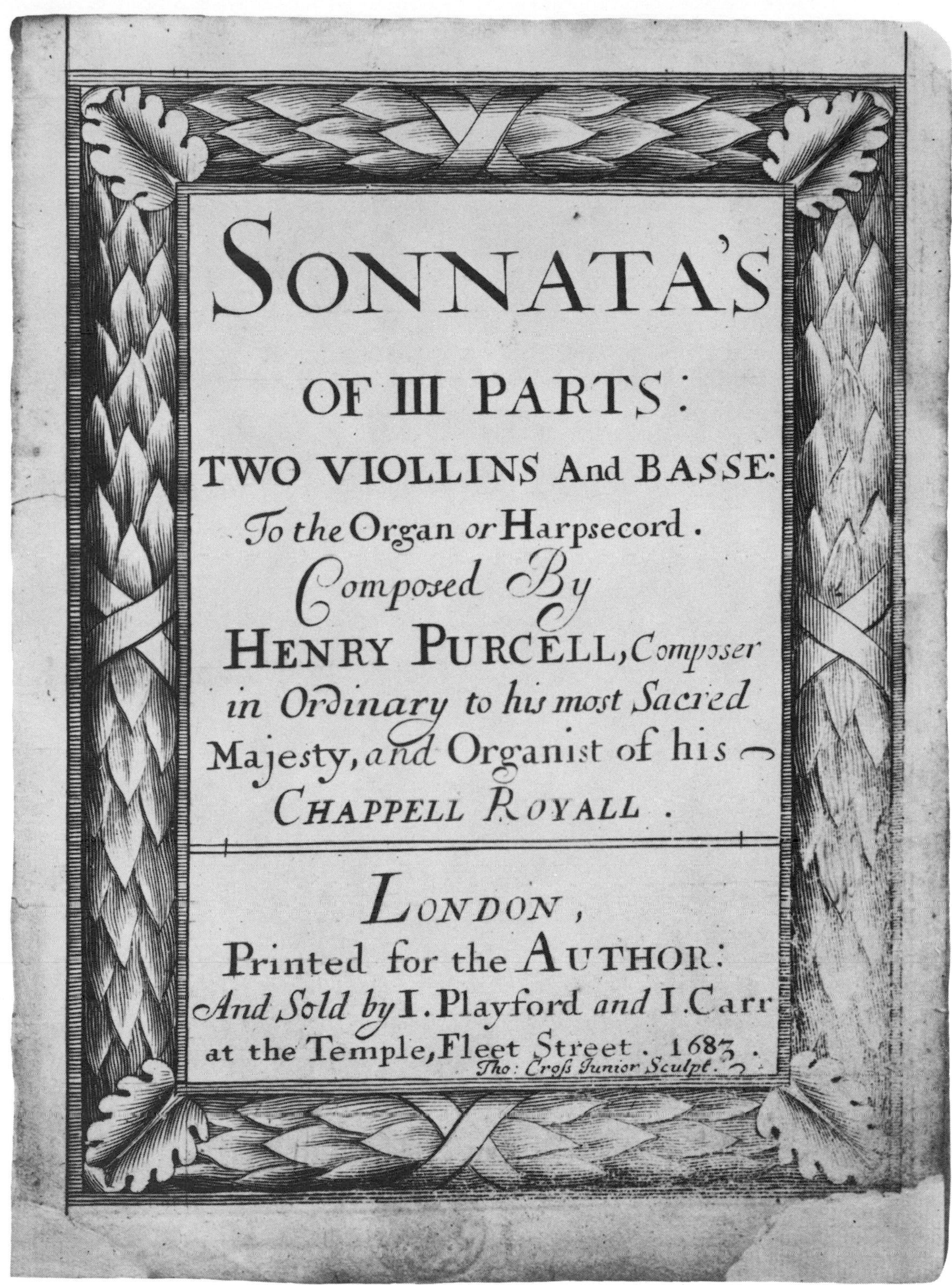
SONNATA'S
OF III PARTS:
TWO VIOLLINS And BASSE:
To the Organ or Harpsecord.
Composed By
HENRY PURCELL, Composer
in Ordinary to his most Sacred
Majesty, and Organist of his
CHAPPELL ROYALL.
LONDON,
Printed for the AUTHOR:
And Sold by I. Playford and I. Carr
at the Temple, Fleet Street. 1683.
Tho: Cross Junior Sculpt.

HENRY PURCELL

105 *Sonnata's of III Parts.* Published by the composer, London, 1683.
British Museum, London.

These trio sonatas, partly in the latest contemporary Italian instrumental style, are important youthful works of Purcell (1659–1695), the celebrated English composer of operas, church music and instrumental pieces. This title page was engraved by Thomas Cross, Jr.

ARCANGELO CORELLI

106 *Sonate A trè* (Op. 1). Mascardi, Rome, 1685.
Civico Museo Bibliografico Musicale, Bologna.

The most renowned composer of his time for the violin and string orchestra, whose works were widely printed and reprinted in Italy, France, England and the Netherlands, Corelli (1653–1713) lived most of his life in Rome. These trio sonatas, dedicated to the Queen of Sweden, were first published in Rome by Giovanni Angelo Mutii in 1681 and appeared many times afterwards.

posteri laudi
Organo
Sonate à tre, doi Violini, e Violone, ò Arcileuto
col Basso per l'Organo
Consecrate all'
MA
ALTEZZA SER. DI FRANCESCO II. DVCA
di Modena, Reggio &c.
da Arcangelo Corelli da Fusignano detto il Bolognese
Opera Terza
In Roma per Gio. Giacomo Komarek Boemo con licenza de sup. 1689
Nicolaus Dorigny
Inu. et sculp.

ARCANGELO CORELLI

107 *Sonata à tre* (Op. 3). Giovanni Giacomo Komarek (Boemo), Rome, 1689.
British Museum, London.

This is the first edition of Corelli's third set of trio sonatas. The title page, featuring the arms of Duke Francis II of Modena, to whom the collection is dedicated, was designed and engraved by the French artist Nicolas Dorigny (1658–1746), who was then active in Rome and later moved on to London.

PARTE PRIMA

SONATE A VIOLINO E VIOLONE O CIMBALO
DEDICATE ALL ALTEZZA SERENISSIMA ELETTORALE DI

SOFIA CARLOTTA

ELETTRICE DI BRANDENBVRGO
PRINCIPESSA DI BRVNSWICH ET LVNEBVRGO DVCHESSA DI PRVSSIA E DI MAGDEBVRGO CLEVES GIVLIERS BERGA STETINO POMERANIA CASSVBIA E DE VANDALI IN SILESIA CROSSEN BVRGRAVIA DI NORIMBERG PRINCIPESSA DI HALBERSTATT MINDEN E CAMIN CONTESSA DI HOHENZOLLERN E RAVENSPVRG RAVENSTAIN LAVENBVRG E BVTTAV

DA ARCANGELO CORELLI DA FVSIGNANO

OPERA QVINTA

Incisa da Gasparo Pietra Santa

SONATE
a Violino e Violone o Cimbalo
Da
ARCANGELO CORELLI
Da
Fusignano
OPERA QUINTA
Parte Prima
SECONDE EDITION
A Amsterdam
Chez ESTIENNE ROGER Marchand Libraire

ARCANGELO CORELLI

108 *Sonate a violino e violone o cimbalo* (Op. 5). Printed by Gasparo Pietra Santa, Rome, 1700. British Museum, London.

The plate shows the title and frontispiece of the first edition of Corelli's celebrated set of 12 violin sonatas (including the Chaconne), which was reprinted innumerable times all over Europe. The frontispiece was designed by the painter Francesco Antonio Meloni (1676–1713) and engraved by Giovanni Girolamo Frezza (1659–1741), both of Rome. It features the coat-of-arms of the Electors of Brandenburg (note the dedication to the Electress on the title page).

ARCANGELO CORELLI

109 *Sonate a Violino e Violone o Cimbalo* (Op. 5). Estienne Roger, Amsterdam, *c.* 1706. Collection of G. S. Fraenkel.

This is a very early republication of the *Opera Quinta* (see preceding plate) by the important music publisher Roger in Amsterdam, who also printed several editions of Corelli's other works.

MICHEL LAMBERT

110 *Les Airs*. Charles de Sercy, Paris, 1660.
British Museum, London.

Father-in-law of Lully (1633?–1687), Lambert (*c.* 1610–1696) was a celebrated lute and theorbo virtuoso and a composer of airs in the service of Louis XIV. The Richer who engraved this work was possibly the Pierre Richer active in Paris between 1630 and 1670 as designer and engraver.

CANTANTIBUS ORGANIS CŒCILIA DOMINO DECANTABAT
Premier Liure dOrgue Composé par G. Jullien Organiste
de Léglise Cathédralle nostre dome de chartres, Contenant les huit tons de lEglise pour les festes Solemnels Auec Vn
Motet de Ste Cœcille atrois Voix et Simphonie, Se Vend a paris chez le Sr. Richar maistre Coustelier Rue des poulies
proche lhóstel de Crequy, Chéz le Sr. lEsclop facteur dOrgue Rue au Maire proche St. Nicolas des champs et a chartres chez
Lauteur Rue des Change, auec priuilege du Roy,
Graueé par Henry Lesclop facteur dOrgue á Paris.

GILLES JULLIEN

111 *Premier Livre d'Orgue.* Paris, *c.* 1690.
Bibliothèque Nationale, Paris.

This is a collection of 80 organ pieces in the eight ecclesiastical modes by the Chartres Cathedral organist Jullien (*c.* 1653–1703). The engraver's signature is "Henry Lesclop facteur d'Orgue."

JACQUES CHAMPION DE CHAMBONNIÈRES

112 *Les Pieces de Clavessin. Livre Premier.* Jollain, Paris, 1670. Bibliothèque Nationale, Paris.

Court harpsichordist to Louis XIII and Louis XIV and in his day the most celebrated French performer on that instrument, Chambonnières (b. after 1601, d. between 1670 and 1672) was the direct teacher or source of inspiration for most of the next generation of French harpsichordists: the three Couperin brothers Louis (*c.* 1626–1661), François (1630–before 1701) and Charles (1638–1678/9, father of François Couperin le Grand); Robert Cambert (*c.* 1628–1677); Nicolas Lebègue (1630–1702); and Jean-Henri d'Anglebert (see Plate 116). Chambonnières' compositions are marked by a youthful grace not apparent in the work of his immediate followers. The title page of this first book of harpsichord pieces by the master was engraved by Gérard Jollain, active in Paris between *c.* 1660 and 1683 (the year of his death), member of a noted family of engravers.

Les
Pieces de Claueßin
de Monsieur
de Chambonnieres
Se Vendent a Paris
Chez Jollain rue S.t Jacques
a la ville de Cologne
Liure Second
Jollain sculpsit.

JACQUES CHAMPION DE CHAMBONNIÈRES

113 *Les Pieces de Clavessin. Livre Second*. Jollain, Paris (n.d.).
Bibliothèque Nationale, Paris.

This is the second book of Chambonnières' harpsichord pieces.

MARIN MARAIS

114 *Pieces a une et a deux violes*. Paris, 1686.
British Museum, London.

Marais (1656–1728) was a virtuoso gambist in the royal orchestra in Paris and a composer of operas and music for viols. The title page of this first book of his viol pieces was designed by Pezey—possibly Antoine Pezey, mentioned as being a painter in Paris between 1695 and 1710—and engraved by the celebrated graphic artist Antoine Trouvain (1656–1708).

MARIN MARAIS

115 *Alçione*. Paris, 1705/6.
Bibliothèque Nationale, Paris.

This is one of the operas of Marais, who was a student of Lully in this genre. First produced in 1706, *Alcione* is known for its pioneering musical storm sequence.

Pieces de Clavecin
Composées par J. Henry d'Anglebert
Ordinaire de la Musique de la Chambre du Roy
avec la maniere de les Joüer.
Diverses Chaconnes, Ouvertures, et autres airs
de Monsieur de Lully mis sur cet Instrum[t].
Quelques Fugues pour l'Orgue.
Et
les Principes de l'Accompagnement.
Livre premier.
AVEC PRIVILEGE DU ROY.
A Paris Chez l'Autheur Rüe Ste Anne près S[t]. Roch
Au bout de la Ruë du hazard.

JEAN-HENRI D'ANGLEBERT

116 *Pieces de Clavecin*. Published by the composer, Paris, 1689.
Bibliothèque Nationale, Paris.

Probably a pupil of Chambonnières (see Plates 112 and 113), d'Anglebert (1628–1691) was a harpsichordist at the court of Louis XIV. The harpsichord suites in this collection were the only works of d'Anglebert published in his lifetime. They are arranged in three series by keys (*G* major, *G* minor and *D* minor), with 30 or 40 pieces in each; there are also five organ fugues. One feature of the book is its listing—the first really complete one—of the ornaments used in it, together with their resolutions; some of the notation was invented by the composer.

Livre de Musique pour le Lut.
Contenant Vne Metode nouvelle et facile pour aprendre à toucher
le Lut sur les notes de la musique, avec des regles pour exprimer par
les mémes notes toutes sortes de pieces de Lut dans leur propre mouv.t
Vne Demonstration generale des Intervalles qui se trouvent dans la
musique et sur le Lut, avec leur diverse composition et division.
Des Cartes par lesquelles les proportions armoniq.ues du Lut sont expliquées
Et Vne Table pour aprendre à toucher le Lut sur la basse continüe pour
accompag.nes la Voix avec les Regles generales et les principes de la musique.
Dedié
A Monseigneur Le Tellier Archevéque de Reims &c.
Par le S.r Perrine.
Avec Privilege du Roy.
J. le Pautre sculp.

JEAN (?) PERRINE

117 *Livre de Musique pour le Lut*. Published by the composer, Paris, 1680. Bibliothèque Nationale, Paris.

This was the first French lute book to use modern notation in place of tablatures. Perrine (?–after 1698) was a teacher of and composer for the lute in Paris. The title page was engraved by the master Jean Lepautre (1618–1682), who is considered one of the most brilliant and original engravers of book illustrations.

EDME FOLIOT

118 *Motets.* Published by the composer, Paris, 1710. Bibliothèque Nationale, Paris.

This is a collection of motets by Foliot (d. between 1735 and 1752), a composer and director of choir schools at Troyes and Paris. The work is dedicated to the composer Michel-Richard de La Lande (1657–1726), chief musical figure at court (see also Plate 125). The title was designed by Jean Bérain the Elder (1637–1711) or the Younger (1678–1726), both well-known graphic artists in Paris. The engraver was Gérard Jean-Baptiste Scotin (1671–1716), member of a Parisian family of engravers and a frequent collaborator with the Bérains.

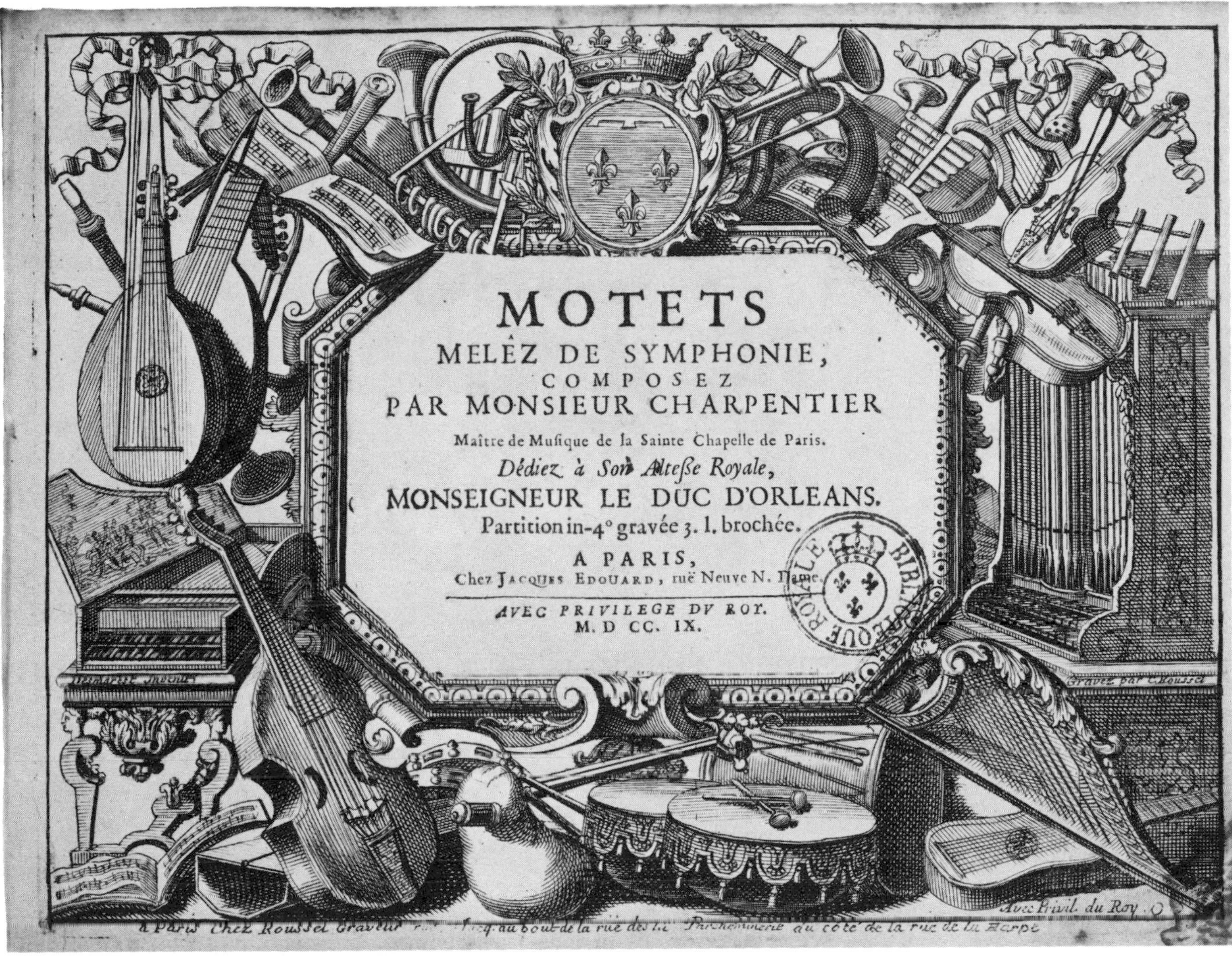

MOTETS
MELÊZ DE SYMPHONIE,
COMPOSEZ
PAR MONSIEUR CHARPENTIER
Maître de Musique de la Sainte Chapelle de Paris.
Dédiez à Son Altesse Royale,
MONSEIGNEUR LE DUC D'ORLEANS.
Partition in-4° gravée 3. l. brochée.
A PARIS,
Chez JACQUES EDOUARD, ruë Neuve N. Dame.
AVEC PRIVILEGE DV ROY.
M. D CC. IX.

MARC ANTOINE CHARPENTIER

119 *Motets melêz de symphonie.* Jacques Édouard, Paris, 1709. Bibliothèque Nationale, Paris.

Charpentier (1636?–1704), a major French composer of operas and sacred works, was music director to the Duke of Orleans and later at the Sainte-Chapelle. A student of Carissimi (*c.* 1604–1674), he wrote the incidental music for several of Molière's productions. This posthumous collection of motets, selected by the composer's nephew Édouard Charpentier from the *Meslanges* (28 folio manuscript volumes of compositions), was one of the handful of Charpentier's works printed in the seventeenth and eighteenth centuries. The title design is by a Desmarest; the engraver was a C. Roussel. The address of "Roussel Graveur" is given in full below; in another publication using the same compartment this address is actually placed within the title design itself.

JOSEPH-HECTOR FIOCCO

120 *Pieces de clavecin.* Brussels, 1730.
Bibliothèque Nationale, Paris.

Fiocco (1703–1741), one of a family of musicians, was active in the royal chapel at Brussels and later as music director of the cathedral of Antwerp. This work contains two harpsichord suites in the manner of Couperin (1668–1733), with some tendencies toward sonata form. The title was engraved by the Brussels master Jan Lauwryn (Jean Laurent) Krafft (1694–after 1765).

JEAN-JOSEPH CASSANÉA DE MONDONVILLE

121 *Pieces de Clavecin Avec Voix ou Violon.* Published by the composer, Paris, 1748. Bibliothèque Nationale, Paris.

A renowned violin virtuoso, attached to the court from 1739, conductor of the "Concert spirituel" from 1755 to 1762, Mondonville (1711–1772) was also a composer of instrumental music, oratorios and operas. His works were attacked by the Encyclopedists. The title was designed by the great portraitist Hyacinthe Rigaud (1659–1743) and engraved by Aubert—most likely Michel Aubert (1700–1757). Other credits that appear on this title are "F. Baillieul Scripsit" (this must refer to the calligraphy) and "Hue Sculpsit" (was Hue the music engraver?—see Plates 129 and 130).

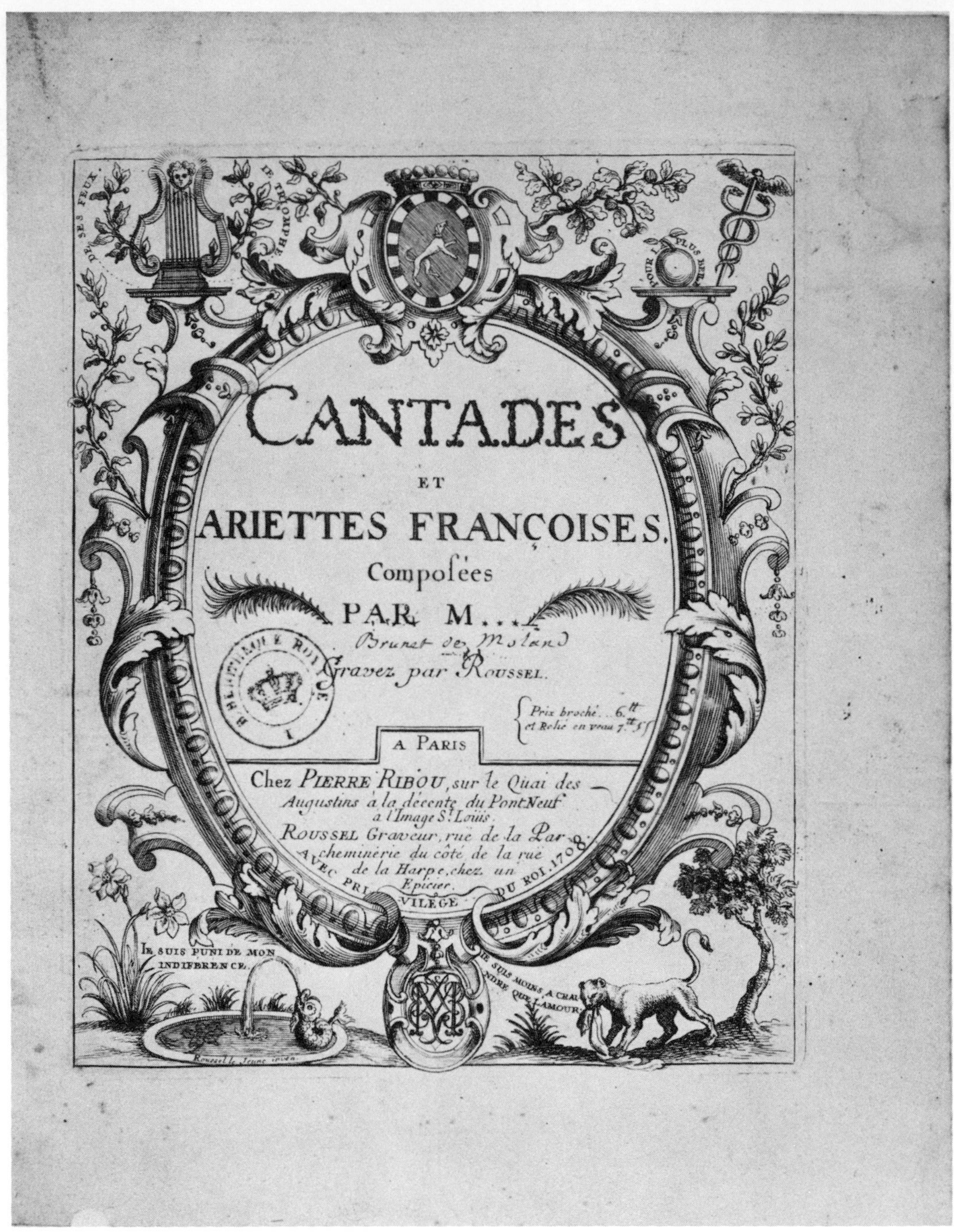

CANTADES
ET
ARIETTES FRANÇOISES.
Composées
PAR M...
Brunet de Moland
Gravez par ROUSSEL.
Prix broché .. 6.tt
et Relié en veau 7.tt 5s
A PARIS
Chez PIERRE RIBOU, sur le Quai des Augustins à la décente du PontNeuf à l'Image S.t Louis.
ROUSSEL Graveur, ruë de la Parcheminérie du côté de la ruë de la Harpe, chez un Epicier.
AVEC PRIVILEGE DU ROI. 1708.

BRUNET DE MOLAND (?)

122 *Cantades et Ariettes françoises*. Pierre Ribou, Paris, 1708.
Bibliothèque Nationale, Paris.

Nothing is known about Brunet de Moland, to whom this anonymous publication is attributed. In addition to six "ariettes," the book contains three "pièces": *Apollon et Daphné*, *Pyrame et Tisbé* and *Le destin de Narcisse*. The whimsical title, designed by Roussel "le Jeune" (son of the Roussel Graveur whose address appears here as also on Plate 119?), contains references to the classical subjects of these cantatas: at the upper left, Daphne, now a laurel bough encircling Apollo's lyre, says, "I triumph over his flames"; at the lower right, the lion mangles Thisbe's cloak (his saying is "I am less to be feared than love"); at the lower left, Narcissus, "punished for my indifference" and already a flower, still sees his reflection in the water. Mercury's caduceus and the apple of discord fill the upper right.

B. 325.

LES PLAISIRS DE LA PAIX
BALET.
mis en Musique Par Mr. BOURGEOIS
Cy-devant Maître de Musique
des Catédrales de Toul et Strasbourg
Le Prix est de 8.tt 10 s. broché
Et de 10.tt relié en veau.
A PARIS
Chez P. Ribou à la Décente du Pontneuf
proche les grands Augustins à l'Image S.t Louis,
Avec Privilege du Roi 1715.

THOMAS [LOUIS, JOSEPH] BOURGEOIS

123 *Les plaisirs de la paix*. Pierre Ribou, Paris, 1715.
British Museum, London.

This work, an opera-ballet, had its première in April, 1715 at the Paris Opéra. The singer and composer Bourgeois (1676–1750) wrote several such works, as well as cantatas.

JEAN-FRANÇOIS DANDRIEU

124 *Livre de Sonates en Trio.* Published by the composer, Paris, 1705. British Museum, London.

The composer and organist Dandrieu (1682–1738) was very careful about the pictorial ornamentation of his publications, and many fine artists were associated with them. His first published work was this collection of trio sonatas. On the designer Desmarest and the engraver Roussel credited on this title page, compare Plate 119.

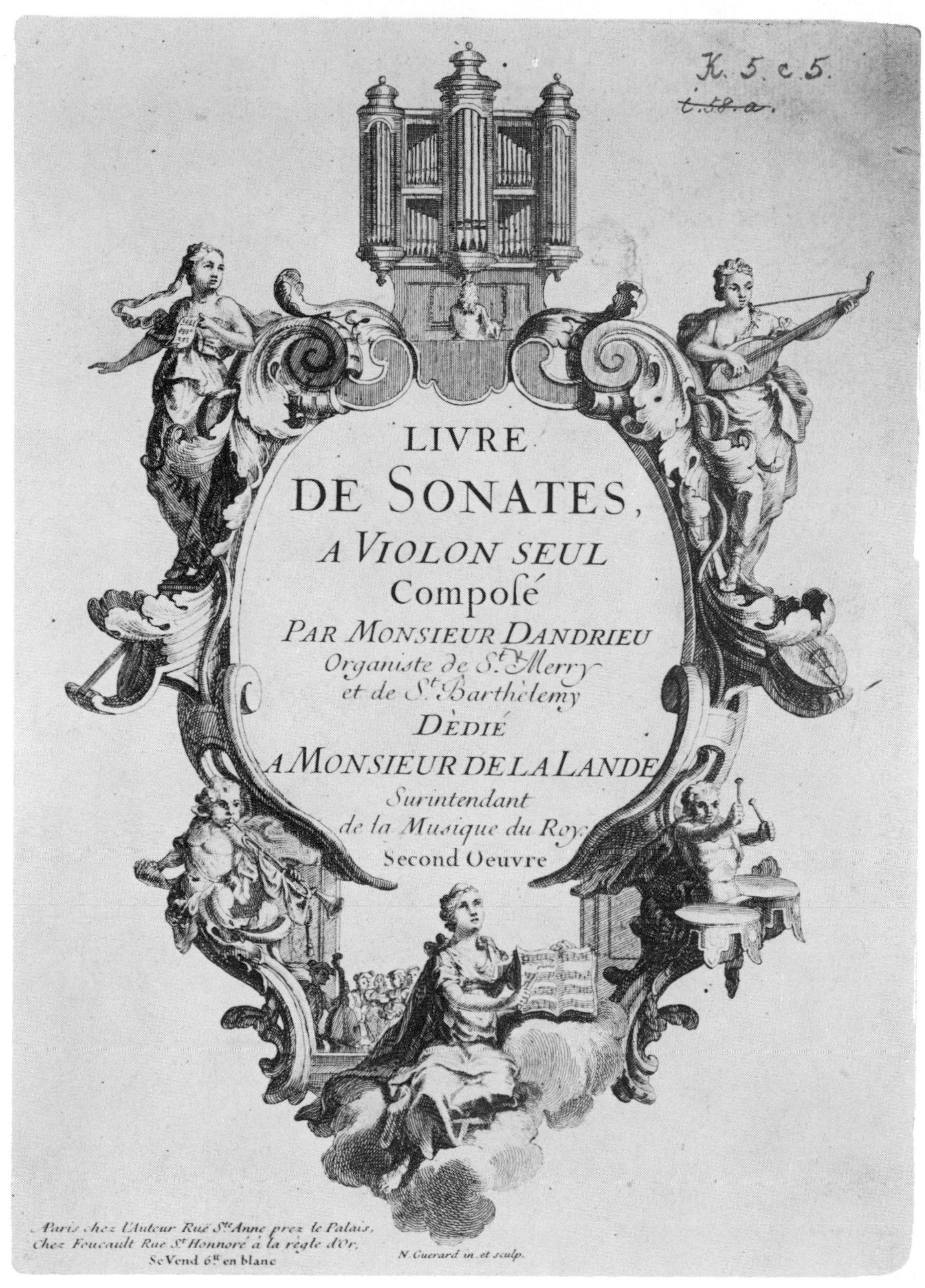

K. 5. c. 5.
LIVRE
DE SONATES,
A VIOLON SEUL
Composé
PAR MONSIEUR DANDRIEU
Organiste de S.t Merry
et de S.t Barthélemy
DÈDIÉ
A MONSIEUR DE LA LANDE
Surintendant
de la Musique du Roy
Second Oeuvre
Paris chez l'Auteur Ruë S.te Anne prez le Palais,
Chez Foucault Rue S.t Honnoré à la règle d'Or.
Se Vend 6.lt en blanc
N. Guerard in. et sculp.

JEAN-FRANÇOIS DANDRIEU

125 *Livre de Sonates, a Violon seul.* Published by the composer, Paris, *c.* 1720. British Museum, London.

This set of unaccompanied violin sonatas, dedicated to La Lande (see Plate 118), has a title designed and engraved by Nicolas Guérard of Paris (d. 1719).

Troisième Livre
de Pièces de Clavecin
Composées par Mr. Dandrieu
Organiste de la Chapele du Roi
N. Lancret pinx.
1734.
S.H. Thomassin sculp.
A Paris chés l'Auteur rue Ste Anne prés le Palais; chés la Veuve du Sr. Boivin
rue St. Honoré à la Regle d'Or et chés le Sr. Le Clerc rue du Roule à la Croix d'Or.
Prix, 12tt
en blanc.

JEAN-FRANÇOIS DANDRIEU

126 *Troisième Livre de Pièces de Clavecin*. Published by the composer, Paris, 1734. British Museum, London.

The title of this collection of 36 harpsichord pieces arranged in eight suites was designed by the famous painter of *fêtes galantes* Nicolas Lancret (1690–1745) and engraved by Simon Henri Thomassin (1687–1741), one of a well-known family of engravers.

NICOLAS CHÉDEVILLE THE YOUNGER [LE CADET]

127 *Amusemens de Bellone.* Published by the composer in association with Boivin & Le Clerc, Paris, 1735.
Bibliothèque Nationale, Paris.

One of the musical family of the Chédevilles, relatives of the famous family of woodwind virtuosos, the Hotteterres, Nicolas (1705–1782) was himself a noted oboist and performer on the musette (bagpipe), an instrument very popular at the time.

This collection of compositions for musette, viol, flute and oboe has a pretty Rococo title designed and engraved by Jacques Philippe Lebas of Paris (1707–1783), who is best known for his engravings after paintings.

VI CONCERTO
A TRÉ VIOLINI, ALTO, E BASSO
PER ORGANO, E VIOLONCELLO.
Composés
PAR M. LECLAIR L'AINÉ
Gravés par son Epouse.
Dédiés
A SON A. R. LE PRINCE
DOM PHILIPPE
Infant D'Espagne.
prix en blanc 24.ll
On trouvera deux parties de Basse.
Parte Seconda
OEUVRE X.me
A PARIS
Chez l'Auteur, rue St. Benoit au dessus de la porte de l'Abaïe,
La Ve. Boivin, rue St. honoré a la Régle d'or,
et chez Le Sr. Le clerc, Marchand
rue du roule a la Croix d'or.
Avec Privilege du Roy.

JEAN-MARIE LECLAIR THE ELDER

128 *VI Concerto.* Published by the composer in association with Boivin & Le Clerc, Paris, 1743/4. Bibliothèque Nationale, Paris.

Leclair (1697–1764), who started his musical career as a dancer, composed important music for the violin (in France and Holland), which is still studied today. His concertos are the first in France that are of international importance and value. The style of the title design is very similar to that of the preceding plate, also done for Boivin and Le Clerc, and this, too, may be a Lebas page.

L'Estro Armonico

CONCERTI

DA D'ANTONIO VIVALDI

Musico di violino è Maestro de concerti

del Pio ospidale della Pieta di Venezia

OPERA TERZA

Gravé par L.Hüe

Prix 21 ₶

A PARIS

Chez { Mr. Le Clerc le cadet rüe St. Honoré vis-a-vis l'Oratoire chez le Bonnetier au second.
Le Sr. Le Clerc Md. rüe du Roule à la Croix d'or.
Mme. Boivin Mde. rüe St. Honoré à la Regle d'or. }

Avec Privilege du Roy.

Bourgoin Scripsit

ANTONIO VIVALDI

129 *L'Estro Armonico.* Le Clerc & Boivin, Paris, *c.* 1750.
British Museum, London.

This is an early French edition of one of the best-known works, the twelve string concerti, Op. 3, by Vivaldi (1678–1741). The calligraphy is by Bourgoin. The "gravé par L. Hüe" probably refers to the music engraving; is this the "Hue" of Plates 121 and 130? The original publication of *L'Estro* by Estienne Roger in Amsterdam, *c.* 1712, established the composer's contemporary fame.

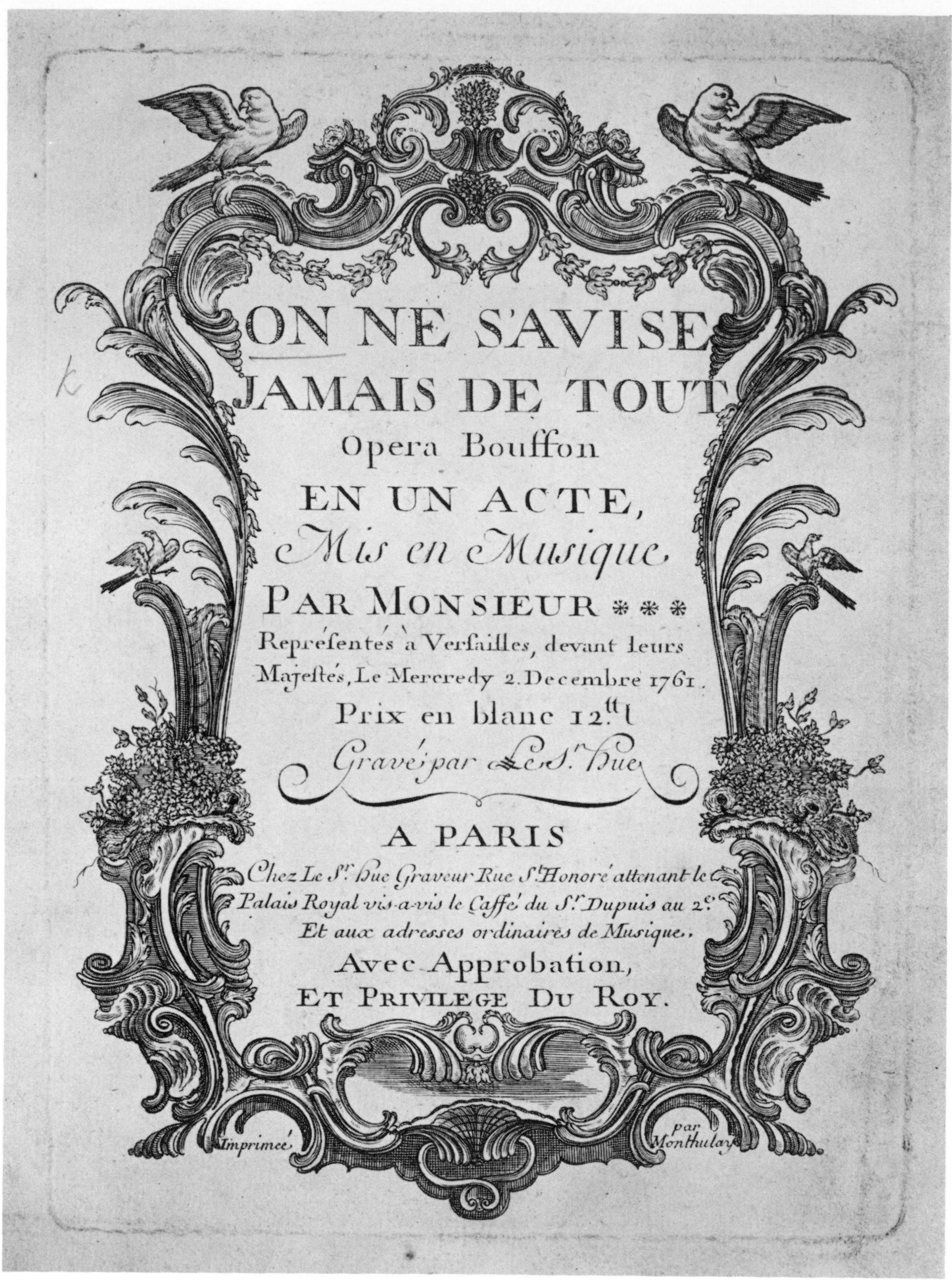

PIERRE-ALEXANDRE MONSIGNY

130 *On ne s'avise jamais de tout.* Published by Hue (printed by Monthulay), Paris, 1762. British Museum, London.

Monsigny (1729–1816) was a prolific and popular operatic composer, one of the creators of the French *opéra comique*. This opera marked the beginning of his fruitful collaboration with the librettist Jean-Michel Sedaine. The Versailles performance mentioned in the title to this edition was not the première, which took place in September, 1761 at the Théâtre de la Foire St. Laurent in Paris. The publisher and (music?) engraver of the present print was Hue (see preceding plate).

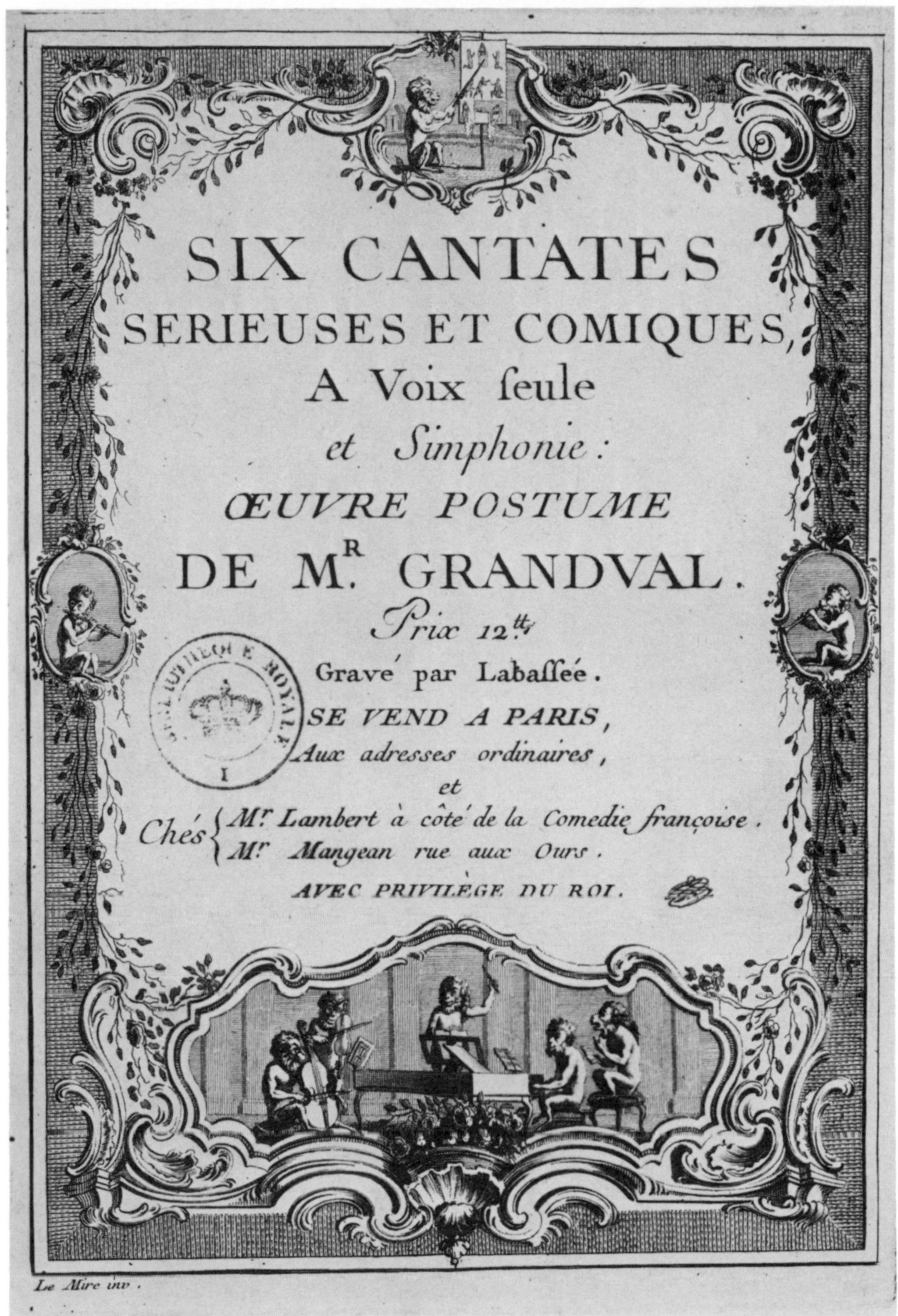

SIX CANTATES
SERIEUSES ET COMIQUES,
A Voix ſeule
et Simphonie:
ŒUVRE POSTUME
DE MR GRANDVAL.
Prix 12.^{tt}
Gravé par Labaſſée.
SE VEND A PARIS,
Aux adresses ordinaires,
et
Chés { *M.*^{r} *Lambert à côté de la Comedie françoise.*
{ *M.*^{r} *Mangean rue aux Ours.*
AVEC PRIVILEGE DU ROI.

Le Mire inv.

NICOLAS RACOT DE GRANDVAL

131 *Six cantates serieuses et comiques.* Lambert & Mangean, Paris, after 1755. Bibliothèque Nationale, Paris.

The organist and harpsichordist Grandval (1676–1753) wrote prose comedies and parodies, as well as musical divertissements for the Comédie-Française and other popular burlesque vocal music. The title design is by Noël Lemire (1724–1801), one of the most celebrated French engravers—especially of book illustrations—of his time. The engraving (probably of the music) was by Labassée.

PANCRACE ROYER

132 *La Fortune*. Paris, 1747 (?).
Reproduced from von zur Westen, *Musiktitel aus vier Jahrhunderten.*

Harpsichordist, composer of operas and *opéras comiques*, opera conductor and concert entrepreneur, Royer (*c.* 1705–1755) was also music teacher to the Dauphin from 1734 on. This is a musical setting of the *Ode à la Fortune* by the poet Jean-Baptiste Rousseau (1670–1741), first performed at the "Concert spirituel" on Christmas Day, 1746. The Roy who designed and engraved the title page may very well be Claude Roy (*c.* 1712–1792), active as a portrait engraver in Paris. On the Labassée who engraved the music, compare the preceding plate.

CHRISTOPH WILLIBALD GLUCK

133 *L'Arbre enchanté.* Des Lauriers, Paris, 1775. British Museum, London.

This one-act opera by the great German master Gluck (1714–1787) was first performed in Vienna in 1759, but was not published at that time. This first publication of *L'Arbre enchanté, ou le tuteur dupé* (text by P. L. Moline) is based on the new version first given at Versailles in 1775. The title decoration, by Hubert François Gravelot (1699–1733; see also Plate 157), one of the most celebrated French book illustrators, was originally prepared for the dedication page of the musical joke *Le Privilège* by La Borde. The calligraphy is by L. Aubert. Other copies of this page show Lemarchand as publisher.

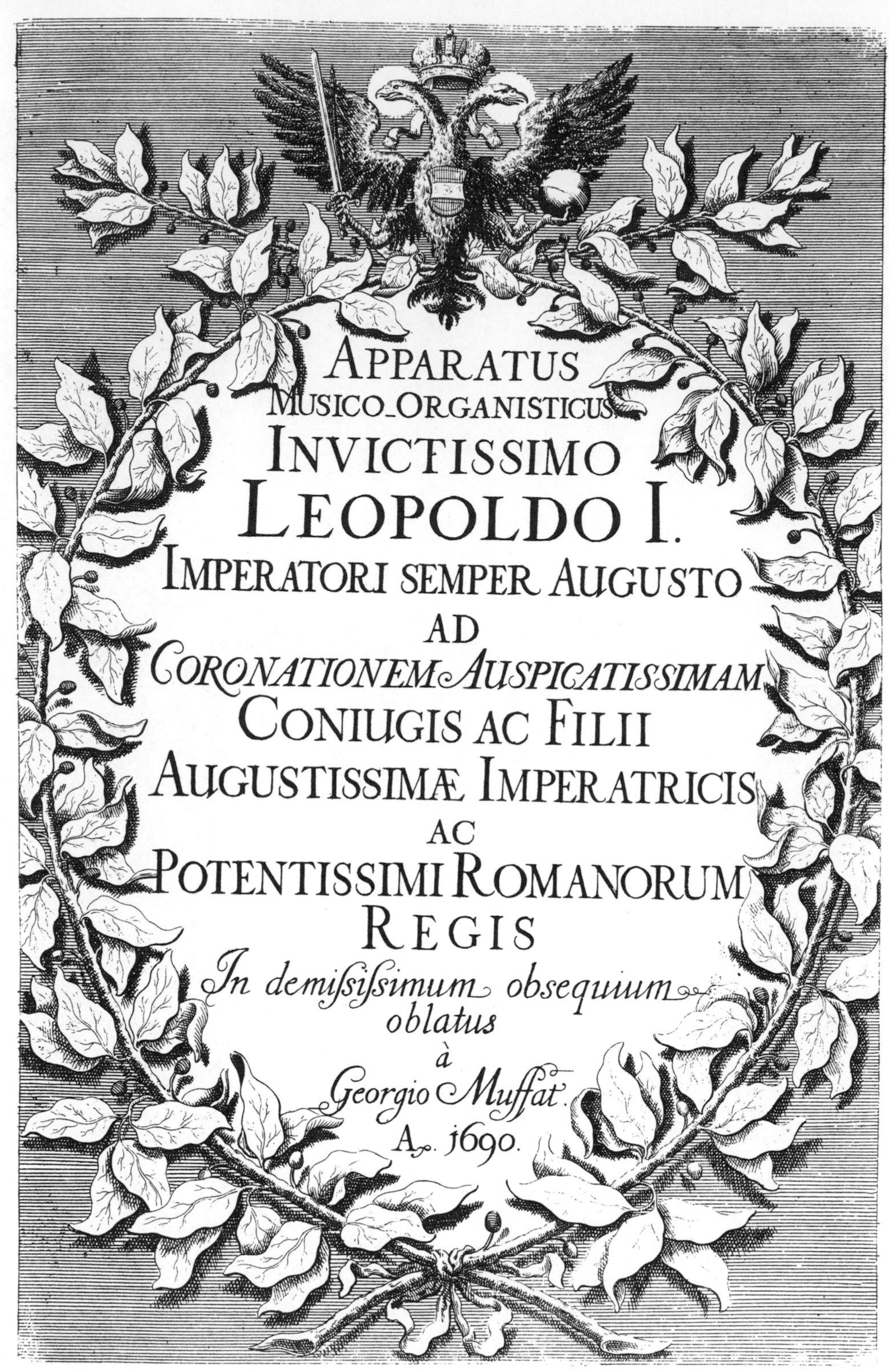

APPARATUS
MUSICO-ORGANISTICUS
INVICTISSIMO
LEOPOLDO I.
IMPERATORI SEMPER AUGUSTO
AD
CORONATIONEM AUSPICATISSIMAM
CONIUGIS AC FILII
AUGUSTISSIMÆ IMPERATRICIS
AC
POTENTISSIMI ROMANORUM
REGIS
In demississimum obsequium
oblatus
à
Georgio Muffat.
Ao. 1690.

GEORG MUFFAT

134 *Apparatus Musico-Organisticus*. Vienna, 1690.
British Museum, London.

The German composer Georg Muffat (1653–1704) studied in Paris as a young man, was active as organist in Strassburg, Salzburg and Passau, and also traveled to Rome. His music represents a synthesis of the various traditions he investigated. The most famous of his musical sons was Gottlieb Muffat (see Plate 141). The *Apparatus* contains twelve toccatas and other pieces for organ. It is dedicated to Leopold I, and the eagle of the Holy Roman Empire is prominent on the title. The first edition, published by the composer and J. B. Mayr, appeared in Salzburg in 1690. The later editions in Passau and Vienna all retained the 1690 date on their titles.

JOHANN JAKOB WALTHER

135 *Hortulus Chelicus Waltherianus*. Mainz, 1695.
Civico Museo Bibliografico Musicale, Bologna.

Walther (*c.* 1650–1717) was a violin virtuoso active in Dresden and later employed by the Elector of Mainz as secretary for Italian affairs. His violin pieces, like those in this collection, demand the same virtuoso technique as those of Biber (1644–1704)—in fact they verge on the acrobatic—but they are less traditional and more programmatic. Moreover, in the preface to the *Hortulus* Walther condemns the use of scordatura. The first edition of this work appeared in 1688.

HEXACHORDVM APOLLINIS
SEX ARIAS EXHIBENS
Organo pnevmatico, vel clavato cymbalo, modulandas,
quarum singulis suæ sunt subjectæ
VARIATIONES,
Philomusorum in gratiam adornatum.
Studio ac industria:
JOANNIS PACHELBEL NVRENBERGENSIS,
in Aede Patria Sebaldina Organœdi.

JOHANN PACHELBEL

136 *Hexachordum Apollinis.* W. M. Endter, Nuremberg, 1699.
British Museum, London.

The celebrated organist Pachelbel (1653–1706) was active in many German cities, for the last ten years of his life at St. Sebald's in Nuremberg. This collection of six sets of variations for organ or harpsichord was his only work printed during that final period. The title was engraved by Cornelius Nicolaus Schurtz (second half of seventeenth century), a graphic artist in Nuremberg. On the publisher Endter, see Plate 96.

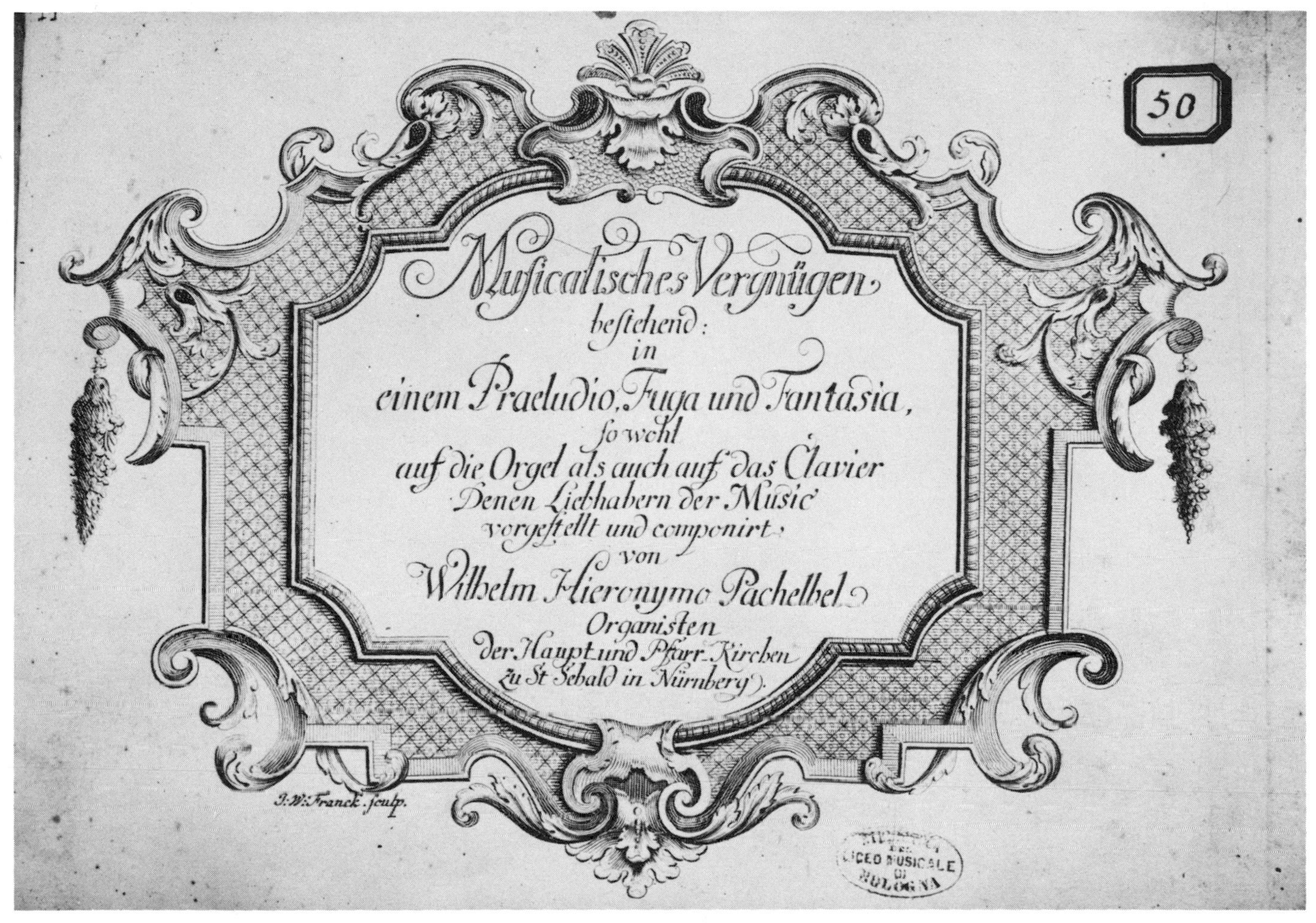
50

Muſicaliſches Vergnügen
beſtehend:
in
einem Praeludio, Fuga und Fantasia,
ſo wohl
auf die Orgel als auch auf das Clavier
Denen Liebhabern der Music
vorgeſtellt und componirt
von
Wilhelm Hieronymo Pachelbel
Organiſten
der Haupt und Pfarr-Kirchen
zu St Sebald in Nürnberg.

J. W. Franck. sculp.

WILHELM HIERONYMUS PACHELBEL

137 *Musicalisches Vergnügen*. Nuremberg, 1725 (?). Civico Museo Bibliografico Musicale, Bologna.

Elder son of Johann Pachelbel (see preceding plate), Wilhelm Hieronymus Pachelbel (1686–1764) was organist at several Nuremberg churches, primarily St. Sebald's. This work—a prelude, fugue and fantasy—is heavily influenced by Domenico Scarlatti (see Plate 150) and in some ways approaches the classical sonata. J. W. Franck is given as engraver of the title.

Johann Kuhnauens Neue
CLAVIR-UBUNG.
LEIPZIG

Johann Kuhnauens
Neüer Clavier Übung
Andrer Theil.
das ist:
Sieben Partien aus dem Re, Mi, Fa,
oder Tertia minore eines jedweden Toni, bene
benst einer Sonata aus dem B.
Denen Liebhabern dieses Instruments
Zu gar besondern Vergnügen
auffgesetzet.
Leipzig.
In Verlegung des Autoris.

JOHANN KUHNAU

138 *Neue Clavier-Ubung*. Published by the composer, Leipzig, 1695 (?).
British Museum, London (first part).
Deutsche Staatsbibliothek, Berlin (second part).

A universal scholar, successful lawyer, writer, organist, conductor, composer, Kuhnau (1660–1722) was the immediate predecessor of J. S. Bach as Cantor of St. Thomas' in Leipzig. His clavier works were a model for Handel and others. The first part (*above*) of the *Neue Clavier-Übung*, which first appeared in 1689 and was reprinted several times, contains seven suites ("Partien"). The title background probably represents Kuhnau's native town Geising. The second part (*below*; no date on title of first edition, but preface dated 1692; reprinted several times) offers seven more suites and a "Sonata aus dem B." This is the first appearance in Germany of the term "sonata" in a printed work for the clavier—but this sonata is merely a conglomeration of separate pieces.

JOHANN KUHNAU

139 *Frische Clavier Früchte*. Johann Christoph Zimmermann, Dresden & Leipzig, 1703.
British Museum, London.

The seven "Suonaten" contained in this work, like the "Sonata aus dem B" of Plate 138, are not yet classical sonatas. The collection was first published by J. C. Mieth, along with Zimmermann, in Leipzig in 1696. The title illustrated here is from one of the various editions that followed within the next years.

Müsicalisch-Italienischer Arien Crantz.
Aüs denen berühmten Authoribus Aldrovandini/Bassani/
Besechi/ ünd Scarlati. In Cant: Transponiert/
ünd Züsamen getragen/
Von Joh: Ludwig Steiner. Und dürchaus in Holtz geschnitten, v.
David Redinger/ Züfinden bey beiden in Zürich, 1724.
J. Melch: Füss: del.

JOHANN LUDWIG STEINER

140 *Musicalisch-Italienischer Arien Crantz.* Published by the composer and David Redinger, Zurich, 1724. British Museum, London.

Steiner (1688–1761) was a town trumpeter, musical pedagogue and minor composer in Zurich. This compilation apparently first introduced Italian solo vocal music to Switzerland. It contains seven solo pieces with general bass (to new German texts) by the composers Giuseppe Antonio Vincenzo Aldrovandini (*c.* 1673–1708), Giovanni Battista Bassani (*c.* 1657–1716), Besecchi and a Scarlatti, presumably Alessandro (1660–1725). The woodcutting throughout is by the co-publisher Redinger, the title design probably by Melchior Füssli (1677–1736) of Zurich.

Componimenti Musicali per il Cembalo
Di Theofilo Muffat
Organiſta di Corte e Camera
Di Sua Sacra, Cesarea, Cattolica, e Real Maestà
CARLO VI Imperadore
Di Sua Maestà L'Imperadrice AMALIA Vedova
E Maestro di Cembalo D'Ambidue
Le Sereniſsime Arci - Ducheſse Regnanti,
E Parimente
Di Sua Altezza Reale Duca di Lorena
E Gran Duca di Toscana.
Scolpit in rame et fatti Stampare
Da Giovanni Christiano Leopold Intagliatore in Augusta.
Con Gratia e Privilegio di sua Sacra Cesarea
Cattolica e Real
Maesta.

GOTTLIEB MUFFAT

141 *Componimenti Musicali per il Cembalo*. Johann Christian Leopold, Augsburg, 1736 (?). Library of Congress, Washington.

Son of Georg Muffat (Plate 134), the eminent Gottlieb Muffat (1690–1770), organist in Vienna, correspondent of Handel, composed almost exclusively for the keyboard. This collection of six "Partien" and one "Ciaccona" for clavier was one of the two published during his lifetime. The important Augsburg artist Jacob Andreas Fridrich the Elder (1684–1751) engraved this title.

Clavir Übung
bestehend in
Præludien, Allemanden, Couranten, Sarabanden, Giguen,
Menuetten, und andern Galanterien;
Denen Liebhabern zur Gemüths Ergoetzung verfertiget
von
Johann Sebastian Bach
Hochfürstl: Sächsisch-Weisenfelsischen würcklichen Capellmeistern
und
Directore Chori Musici Lipsiensis.
OPUS I.
In Verlegung des Autoris.
1731.

Zweyter Theil
der
Clavier Ubung
bestehend in
einem Concerto nach Italiænischen Gusto,
und
einer Overture nach Französischer Art,
vor ein
Clavicÿmbel mit zweÿen
Manualen.
Denen Liebhabern zur Gemüths-Ergötzung verferdiget
von
Johann Sebastian Bach.
Hochfürstl: Sæchsl: Weißenfelsl: Capellmeistern
und
Directore Chori Musici Lipsiensis.
in Verlegung
Christoph Weigel Junioris.
Zu Nürnberg

N: 16.

Clavier Ubung
beſtehend
in einer
ARIA
mit verſchiedenen Verænderungen
vors Clavicimbal
mit 2 Manualen.
Denen Liebhabern zur Gemüths-
Ergetzung verfertiget von
Johann Sebaſtian Bach
Königl. Pohl. u. Churfl. Saechſ. Hoff-
Compoſiteur, Capellmeiſter, u. Directore
Chori Muſici in Leipzig.
Nürnberg in Verlegung
Balthaſar Schmids.

JOHANN SEBASTIAN BACH

142 *Clavir Ubung* (first part). Published by the composer, Leipzig, 1731.
University of Illinois, Urbana.
Zweyter Theil der Clavier Ubung. Christoph Weigel the Younger, Nuremberg, 1735.
British Museum, London.

Only a small fraction of the music of J. S. Bach (1685–1750) was printed in his lifetime, almost all of it clavier music. The first (1731) and third (1739) parts of the *Clavier Übung* were published, and perhaps even partially engraved, by the composer. The first part (*above*) contains the partitas in *B*-flat major, *C* minor, *A* minor, *D* major, *G* major and *E* minor, all of which had been published separately between 1726 and 1731. The second part (*below*) consists of the *Italian Concerto* and the partita ("Overture") in *B* minor.

JOHANN SEBASTIAN BACH

143 *Clavier Ubung* (fourth part). Balthasar Schmid, Nuremberg, 1742.
British Museum, London.

This fourth part of the *Clavier Übung* consists of the *Goldberg Variations*. For a very different sort of Bach title see Plates 200 and 201.

SPERONTES (pseudonym of JOHANN SIGISMUND SCHOLZE)

144 *Singende Muse an der Pleisse.* Published "auf Kosten der lustigen Gesellschaft," Leipzig, 1736. Bayerische Staatsbibliothek, Munich.

Sperontes (1705–1750), in the legal profession in Leipzig, supplied all the texts in this extremely popular song collection dealing with love, friendship, nature and rural pleasures. The melodies were derived from the works of such composers as Bach, Handel and Telemann. This much-imitated work went into many continuations and a revision; from 1740 on it was published by B. C. Breitkopf (see next plate). It gave great impetus to the development of the lied and the singspiel. This original title, with its view of Leipzig (which is on the Pleisse), was designed by a Richter—possibly the Saxonian architect Johann Adolf Richter (1682–1768)—and engraved by the noted Leipzig artist Christian Friedrich Boëtius (1706–1782). Identified as *b* in the city view is the Thomaskirche, made famous by such luminaries of music as Schein (Plates 94 and 95), Kuhnau (Plate 138) and Bach (Plates 142 and 143).

GEORG CHRISTIAN SCHEMELLI

145 *Musicalisches Gesang-Buch*. Bernhard Christoph Breitkopf, Leipzig, 1736. Bayerische Staatsbibliothek, Munich.

This collection of 952 devotional songs, with 69 melodies, compiled by Schemelli (*c.* 1680–1762), has acquired fame through the cooperation of J. S. Bach, who provided the figured bass and contributed musically. Only one of the melodies is now considered as surely by Bach, with two other possibilities; 47 were once ascribed to him. Like the title of the preceding plate, this was engraved by Boëtius. This book was among the earliest music publications of the noted printer B. C. Breitkopf (1695–1777; see also Plate 164).

A Compleat Method,
for
Attaining to Play a Through Bass upon either Organ, Harpsichord or Theorbo Lute
by the late Famous
M^r. GODFRY KELLER
with
Variety of Proper Lessons & Fuges, Explaining the several Rules through-out the whole Work; & a Scale for Tuning ye Harpsichord or Spinet, all taken from his own Copies which he design'd to Print. Note in this Celebrated Work for ye ease of Practitioners all ye Chords are correctly explain'd both with Figures & Notes.
London,
Printed for Richard Meares Musicall Instrument Maker at the Golden Viol & Hautboy in S^t. Pauls Church Yard.

GOTTFRIED [GODFRY] KELLER

146 *A Compleat Method.* Richard Meares, London, 1717.
British Museum, London.

Keller (d. 1704), born in Germany, was a highly respected music teacher in England. This instruction book for the execution of a figured bass on keyboard instruments, lutes and theorbos was the first work of its kind to appear since Matthew Locke's *Melothesia* in 1673, and it remained popular well into the eighteenth century. It was originally published in 1705 by Walsh & Hare, London, under the title *Rules for playing a Thorough Bass.* Its first appearance as *A Compleat Method* was in 1707 (published by Walsh, Hare & Randal). There were further London editions in 1707 and 1717. The title page of the latter is the one illustrated.

JOHN ERNEST [JOHANN ERNST] GALLIARD

147 *The Hymn of Adam and Eve*. London, 1728.
British Museum, London.

Galliard (*c.* 1680–1749) was an English composer of German birth. For a time oboist to George of Denmark, consort of Queen Anne, he later wrote for the London theater. Burney wrote caustically: "With respect to his compositions in general, I must say, that I never saw more correctness or less originality in any author that I have examined, of the present century, Dr. Pepusch always excepted."

One of Galliard's real claims to fame is his excellent translation (*Observations on the Florid Song*, J. Wilcox, London, 1742) of Pietro Francesco Tosi's *Opinioni de' Cantori . . . o sieno Osservazioni sopra il Canto Figurato* (Bologna, 1723). The title page illustrated was designed and engraved by John Pine (1690–1756).

STABAT
MATER.
Compos'd by Sig.r
PERGOLESI.
I:Collins, sculp
London Printed for & Sould by I: Walsh Musicall Instrument maker in Ordinary to His Majesty

GIOVANNI BATTISTA PERGOLESI

148 *Stabat Mater*. John Walsh, London, 1749. Collection of G. S. Fraenkel.

Together with the comic opera *La Serva Padrona*, the *Stabat Mater* is probably the most celebrated work of the legendary Neapolitan composer Pergolesi (1710–1736), European favorite and idol of the French Encyclopedists. Tradition has it that this setting of the *Stabat* for soprano, alto, strings and bass was Pergolesi's last work. The first known edition seems to be the one by Bayard, Le Clerc & Castegneri in Paris, and apparently there were other editions in Paris and Lyons before this earliest English one. The title, engraved by J. Collins (active in London between 1670 and 1690), was first used before 1700 and subsequently adorned the title pages of many Walsh publications.

JOHANN MATTHESON

149 *Pieces de Clavecin.* I. D. Fletcher, London, 1714.
Library of Congress, Washington.

A major figure of eighteenth-century Hamburg, Mattheson (1681–1764) was a singer, an important composer of operatic, sacred and keyboard works and a voluminous writer on music. His books are a superb source for the lives of contemporary composers, the current practice of thorough bass, and so on. The title of this clavier collection was engraved by Michiel van der Gucht (1660–1725), a Flemish artist who produced many book illustrations in London. Fletcher issued this collection in the same year with a German title page as well (same design): *Harmonisches Denckmahl aus zwölf erwählten Clavier-Suiten.*

ESSERCIZI PER GRAVICEMBALO
di
Don Domenico Scarlatti
Cavaliero di S. GIACOMO e Maestro
dè
SERENISSIMI PRENCIPE e PRENCIPESSA
delle Asturie &c.

DOMENICO SCARLATTI

150 *Essercizi per gravicembalo.* London, 1738.
British Museum, London.

These are the first thirty of the sparkling harpsichord sonatas by the great Italian composer Domenico Scarlatti (1685–1757). In 1738 Scarlatti made his home in Madrid, where an ambassador of John V made him a knight of the Portuguese Order of Santiago (thus the "Cavaliero di S. Giacomo" of the title). In return, the composer dedicated this book to the Portuguese king. The title was designed by the painter Jacopo Amigoni (1675–1752, active in London 1729–1736). The engraver was B. Fortier.

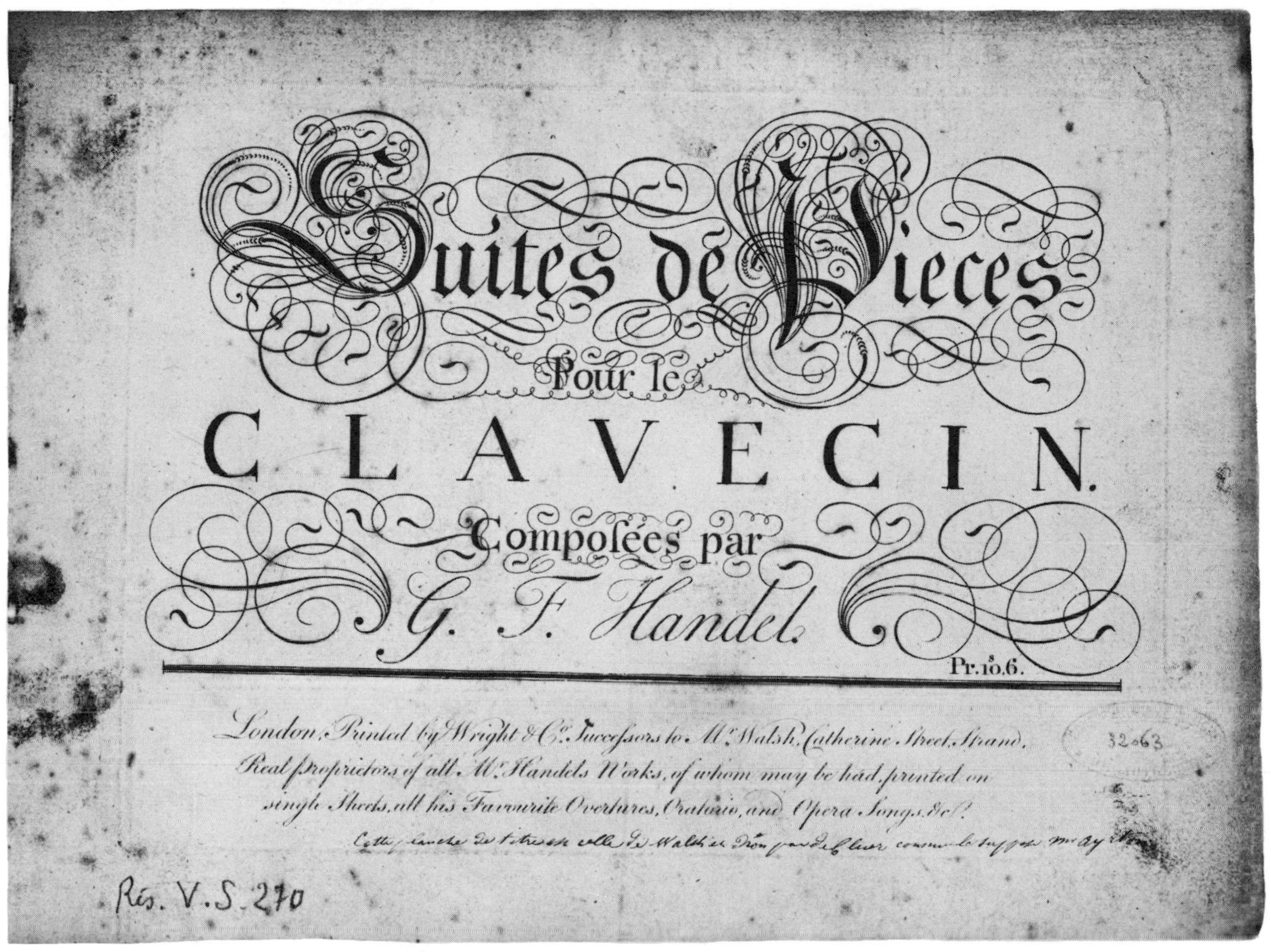

Suites de Pieces

Pour le

CLAVECIN.

Composées par

G. F. Handel.

Pr. 10.6.

London, Printed by Wright & Co. Successors to Mr. Walsh, Catherine Street, Strand, Real Proprietors of all Mr. Handels Works, of whom may be had, printed on single Sheets, all his Favourite Overtures, Oratorio, and Opera Songs &c.

GEORGE FRIDERIC HANDEL

151 *Suites de Pieces Pour le Clavecin*. Printed by Wright & Co., London, *c*. 1784. Bibliothèque Nationale, Paris.

This is a reissue of the principal harpsichord compositions of George Frideric Handel (Georg Friedrich Händel, 1685–1759) from the plates printed in 1720 by the publishers Christopher Smith (Johann Christoph Schmidt) and Richard Meares, and in 1733 by John Walsh.

GEORGE FRIDERIC HANDEL

152 *Julius Caesar* (*Giulio Cesare*). John Cluer, London, 1724.
British Museum, London.

This is the vocal score of the opera (libretto by Nicola Haym, 1679–1729). While much of Handel's music was first published by John Walsh (d. 1736; see Plates 151, 154 and 155), *Julius Caesar* and *Alexander* were published by John Cluer in a smaller format. The music is beautifully engraved. In this year, 1724, and in editions of Handel, Cluer introduced the use of engraving on pewter rather than copper plates. Both Grand-Carteret and von zur Westen (see Introduction, p. 1) attribute this page to an engraver named James. Were they confused by the projecting "James's" at the end of the address at the lower right?

G.168.d.
ALEXANDER,
AN
OPERA,
Compos'd by Mr. Handel.
Engrav'd, Printed and Sold by J. Cluer in Bow-Church-Yard, London.

GEORGE FRIDERIC HANDEL

153 *Alexander* (*Alessandro*). John Cluer, London, 1726.
British Museum, London.

This opera (libretto by Paolo Antonio Rolli), like *Julius Caesar* (Plate 152), was published by Cluer.

GEORGE FRIDERIC HANDEL

154 *Rinaldo.* John Walsh, London, 1711.
British Museum, London.

Rinaldo (libretto by Giacomo Rossi) was one of the first operas Handel produced in London. The publication was reprinted many times in rapid succession. Walsh used the same compartment for later Handel operas.

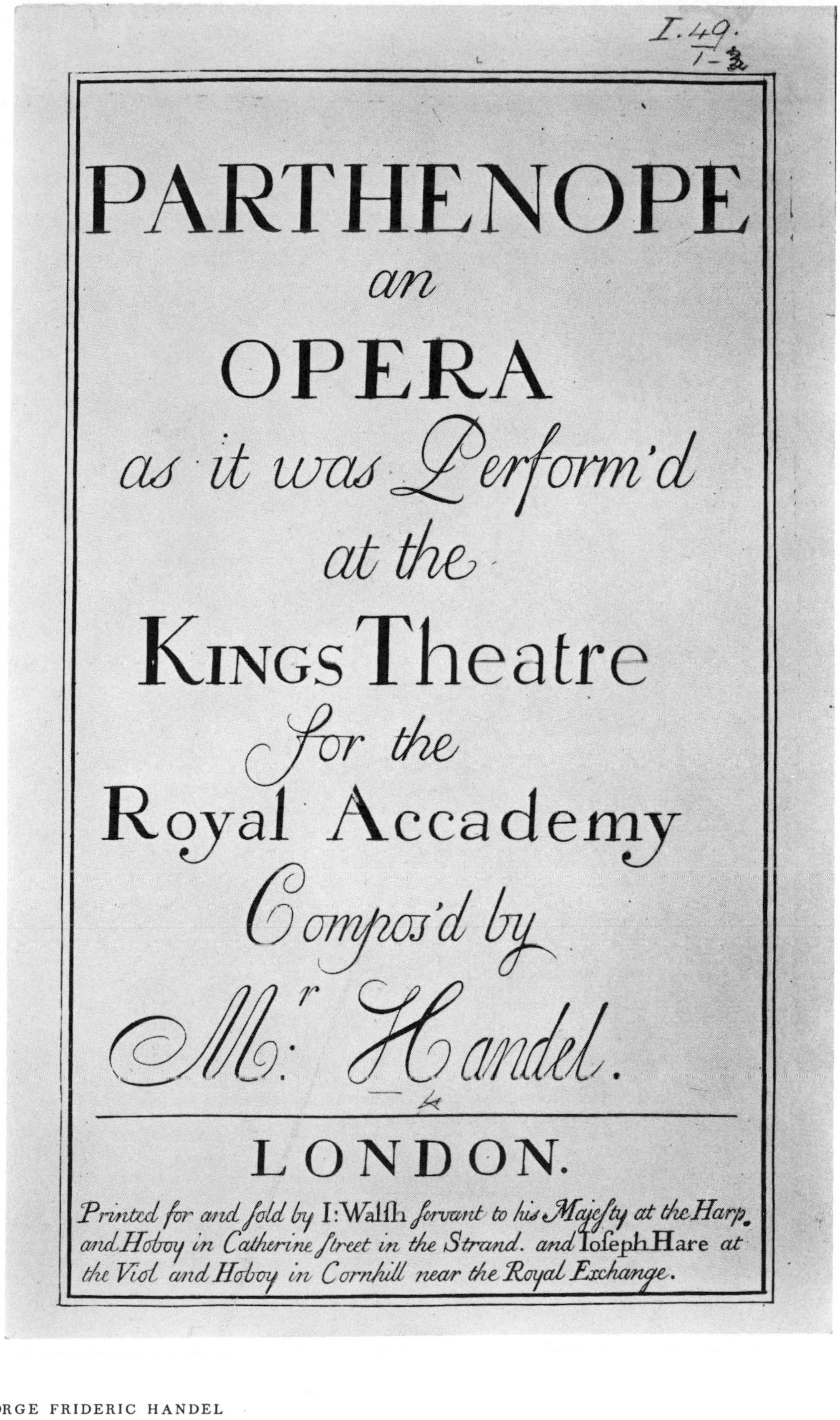

PARTHENOPE

an

OPERA

as it was Perform'd

at the

KINGS Theatre

for the

Royal Accademy

Compos'd by

Mr: Handel.

LONDON.

Printed for and sold by I: Walsh *servant to his Majesty at the Harp and Hoboy in Catherine street in the Strand. and* Ioseph Hare *at the Viol and Hoboy in Cornhill near the Royal Exchange.*

GEORGE FRIDERIC HANDEL

155 *Parthenope* (*Partenope*). John Walsh & Joseph Hare, London, 1730.
British Museum, London.

This opera (libretto by Silvio Stampiglia) was not an immediate success. The monumental script of this title is typical of many Walsh publications.

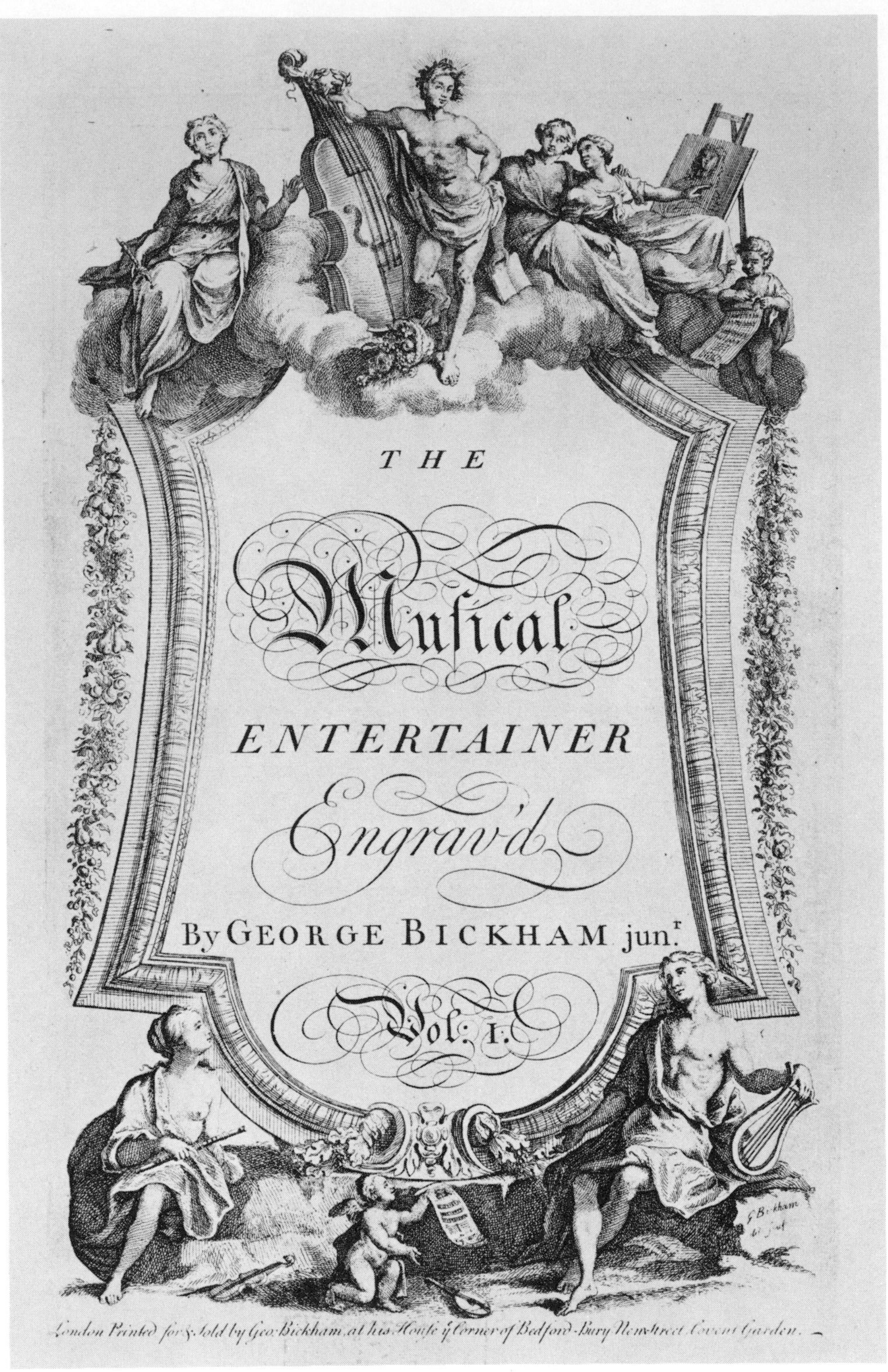

GEORGE BICKHAM, JR.

156 *The Musical Entertainer. Vol. I.* George Bickham, London, 1737.
Reproduced from partial facsimile reprint, Chiswick Press, London, 1942.

This work, a collection of songs by Purcell, Handel and many other composers, is considered one of the most beautiful ornamental music books ever printed. It consists of 200 leaves, printed on one side only, each containing one song adorned with its own vignette. The first two parts (1737–8) were published by George Bickham, Sr. (*c.* 1684–1769), the engraver-publisher of *The Universal Penman.* Another part appeared in London *c.* 1740 as *Bickham's Musical Entertainer*, published by Charles Corbett. The engraver of *The Musical Entertainer* (who also designed this title page) was George Bickham, Jr. (d. 1758), probably the son of the publisher.

GEORGE BICKHAM, JR.

157 *The Musical Entertainer*. George Bickham, London, 1738.
Reproduced from partial facsimile reprint, Chiswick Press, London, 1942.

The chief stylistic influence on the *Musical Entertainer* vignettes was that of Gravelot (see Plate 133), who was living in England at the time and himself designed some of the vignettes, like the one (from the second part) illustrated here. The composer of "The Invitation to Mira" was Thomas Gladwin, organist at St. George's in Hanover Square and at the Vauxhall Gardens in the mid-eighteenth century.

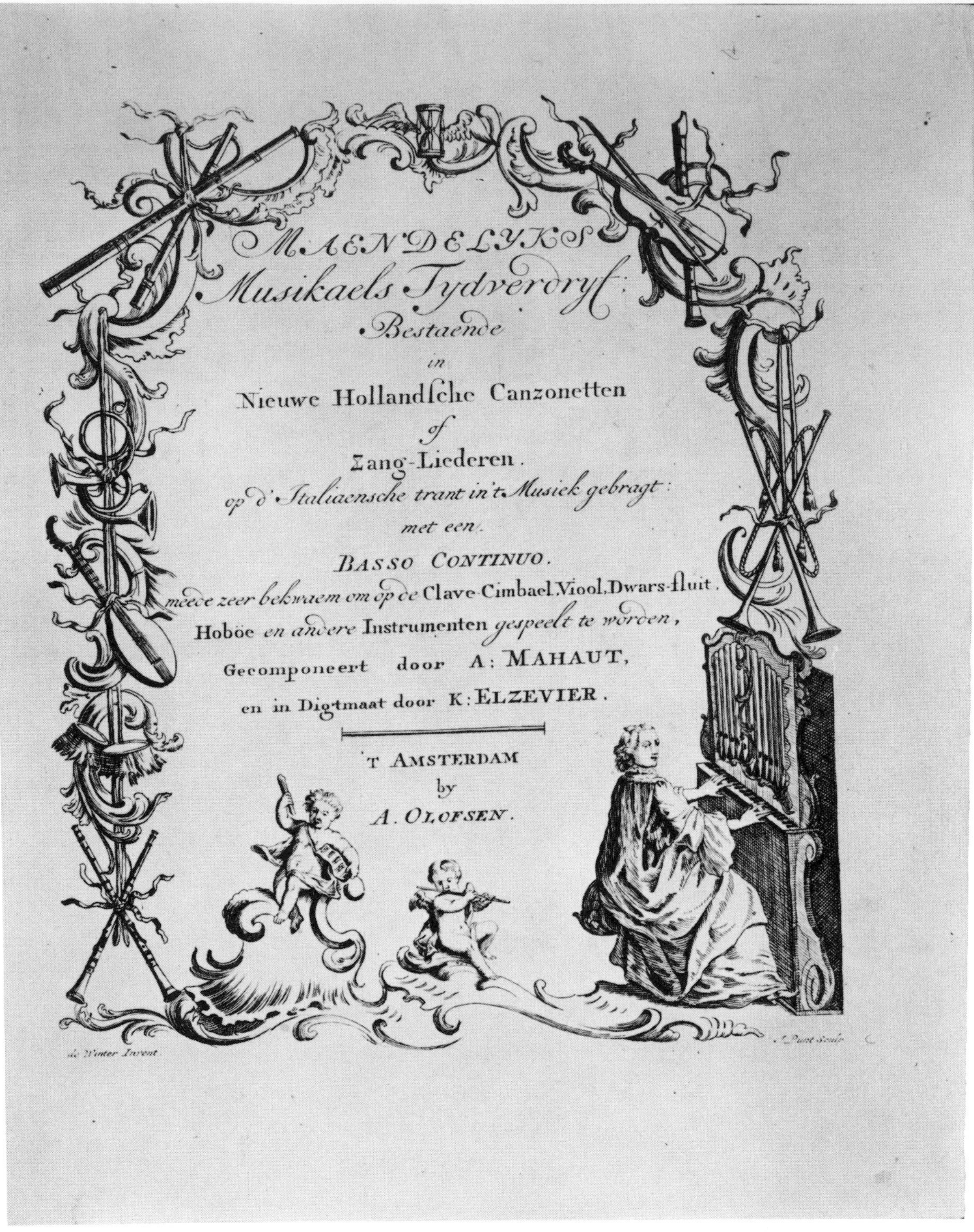

ANTOINE MAHAUT

158 *Maendelyks Musikaels Tydverdryf.* A. Olofsen, Amsterdam, 1751/2. British Museum, London.

Mahaut was a composer of instrumental and vocal music in Antwerp, and the author of an excellent flute method. This is a collection of canzonettas and songs in Dutch. The de Winter who designed this title was most likely Hendrik de Winter of Amsterdam (1717–1782), although there are other possibilities. The engraver (who was also a painter and a successful actor) was Jan Punt (1711–1779).

JEAN-JACQUES ROUSSEAU

159 *Les consolations des miseres de ma vie.* De Roullède de la Chevardière, Paris, 1781. Bibliothèque Nationale, Paris.

Rousseau (1712–1778) not only gave music a place within the framework of his philosophy, but composed as well. This is a posthumous collection of airs, romances and duos. The title was designed and engraved by a C. Benazech. (An artist named Richomme engraved the music within the book, an André part of the text underlays.) Medallions tied to the laurel sprigs bear the names of works by Rousseau. The small inset over the imprint represents the Isle of Poplars at Ermenonville, where Rousseau was buried.

ANDREA BASILI

160 *Musica universale*. Venice, 1776.
British Museum, London.

This instruction book for harpsichordists, organists and students of counterpoint was written by Basili (*c.* 1703–1777), music director of the Loretto shrine from 1740 until his death.

ORFEO
AZIONE TEATRALE
RAPPRESENTATA
NEL NOBILIS.mo TEATRO DI S. BENEDETTO DI VENEZIA
NEL CARNOVALE DELL ANNO MDCCLXXVI
Composta in Musica dal
SIG.r FERDINANDO BERTONI
MAESTRO DEL PIO CONSERVATORIO DE MENDICANTI
ACCADEMICO FILARMONICO.
IN VENEZIA
A SPESE DI INNOCENTE ALESSANDRI E PIETRO SCATTAGLIA
Incisori e venditori di Musica stampata sopra il Ponte di Rialto.

FERDINANDO GIUSEPPE BERTONI

161 *Orfeo*. Innocente Alessandri & Pietro Scattaglia, Venice, 1776. Library of Congress, Washington.

From 1785 on the Venetian composer Bertoni (1725–1813) was music director at San Marco. This is the vocal score of one of his 40-odd operas, *Orfeo*, composed to the same Calzabigi libretto that Gluck had set in 1762. Bertoni's version was first produced during the Venetian carnival season of 1776 with the same castrato, Gaetano Guadagni, who had created the role of Orpheus in Gluck's opera. The publishers Alessandri and Scattaglia were also engravers, and may be responsible for this title page.

VINCENZO MANFREDINI

162 *Sonate da Clavecimbalo.* Accademia Imperiale delle Scienze, St. Petersburg, 1765. Civico Museo Bibliografico Musicale, Bologna.

One of an Italian family of musicians and composers, Manfredini (1737–1799) was active in Russia from 1758 to 1769 and returned there in 1798. Music at the Russian court was almost exclusively in the hands of Italians in the eighteenth century. Manfredini, whose theoretical works are considered more important than his compositions, was music director to Catherine the Great and clavier teacher to her son, the future Paul I.

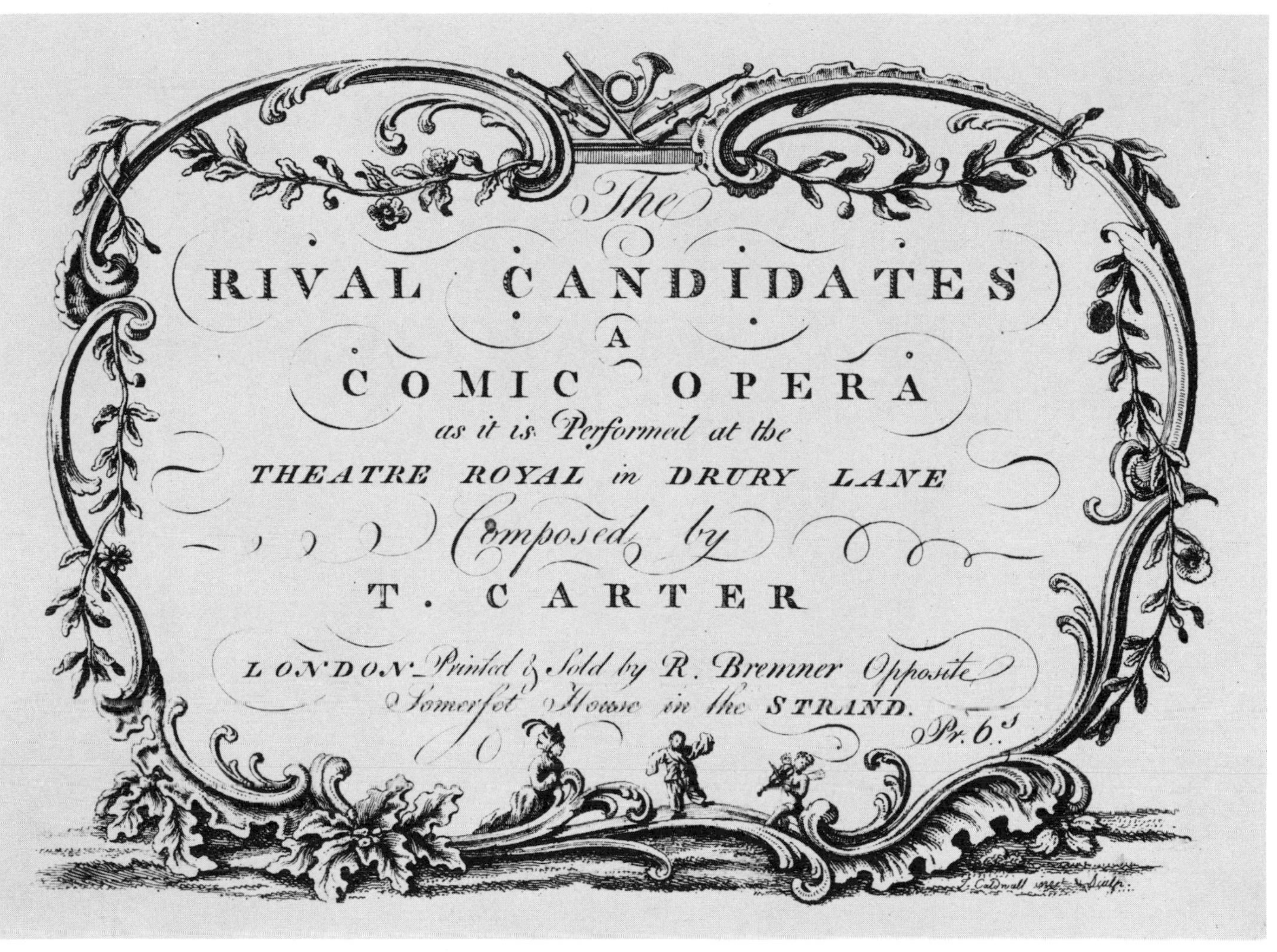

THOMAS CARTER

163 *The Rival Candidates*. Robert Bremner, London, 1775.
Collection of G. S. Fraenkel.

The Irish composer Carter (active between 1769 and 1800 in London) wrote songs, theatrical interludes and comic operas. For a time he was musical director of a theater in Calcutta. The title page was designed and engraved by James Caldwall of London (1739–after 1789).

TALESTRI
REGINA DELLE AMAZZONI
DRAMMA PER MUSICA
DI
E. T. P. A.

IN LIPSIA
DALLA STAMPARIA di BERNARD CRISTOFORO BREITKOPF e FIGLIO
1765

E. T. P. A. [MARIA ANTONIA WALPURGIS]

164 *Talestri, Regina delle Amazzoni.* Bernhard Christoph Breitkopf & Son, Leipzig, 1765. British Museum, London.

Eldest daughter of Karl Albert, Elector of Bavaria, and by this time widow of Friedrich Christian, Elector of Saxony, the poetess, painter and singer Maria Antonia Walpurgis (1724–1780) composed music under the pseudonym E[rmelinda] T[alia] P[astorella] A[rcada] ("Arcadian shepherdess"). This score of one of her operas appeared during 1765, the first year that B. C. Breitkopf (see Plate 145) added "and Son" to his title pages. The son was the great Johann Gottlob Immanuel Breitkopf (1719–1794), under whose management the firm really became a music house. Another E. T. P. A. opera, *Il trionfo della fedeltà*, was the first important publication (1755–6) printed with the younger Breitkopf's own new musical type that permitted more complicated setting than had ever been possible.

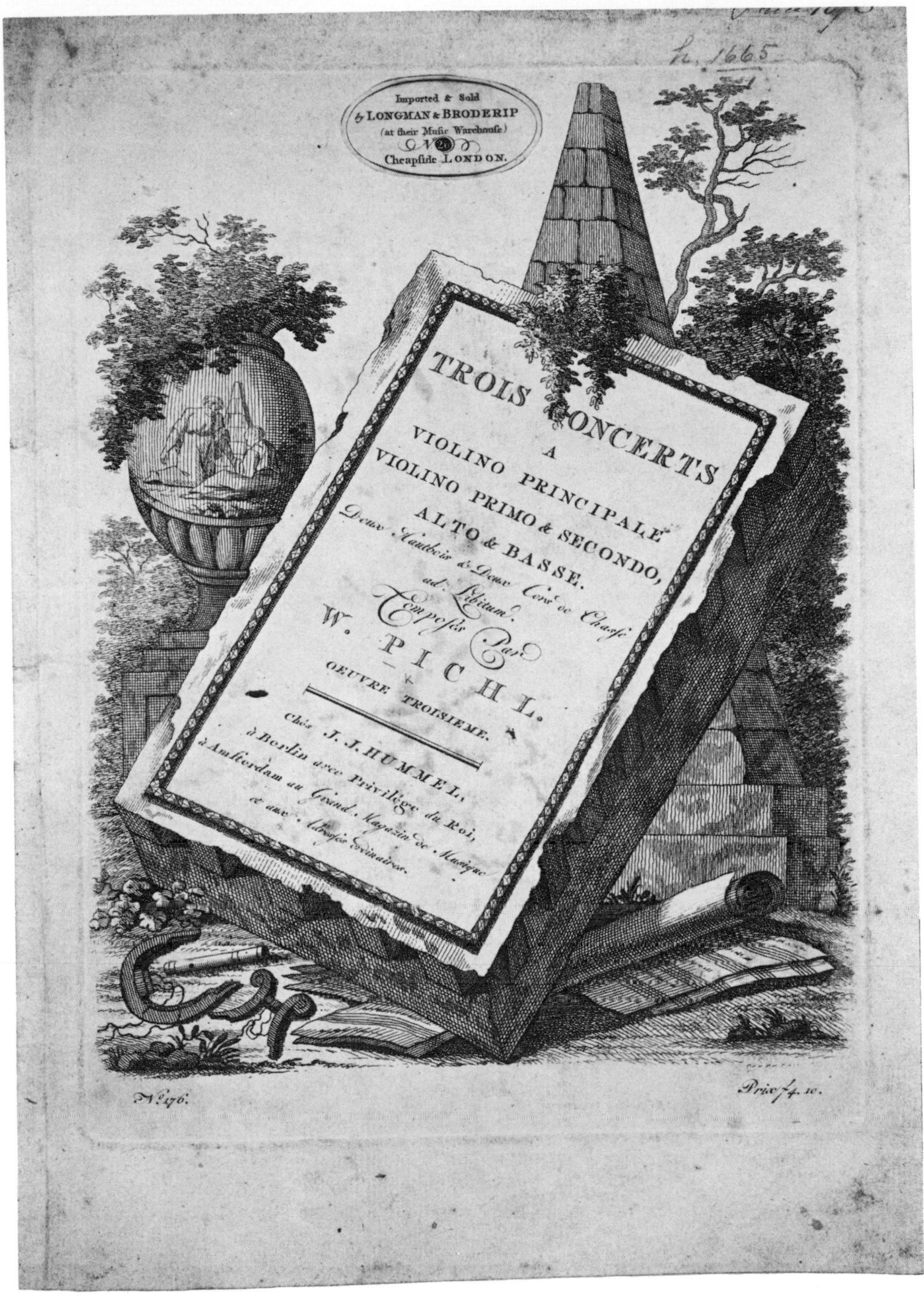

WENZEL PICHL

165 *Trois concerts*. Johann Julius Hummel, Berlin, 1775.
British Museum, London.

Pichl (1741–1805), a Czech violinist, poet and dramatist active in many cities including Vienna and Milan, was a prolific composer, especially of instrumental music. The title page of these violin concerti is in the romantic style of Piranesi. J. J. Hummel (1728–1798) was one of the most important music publishers and dealers of his time, specializing in chamber music, and publishing many early editions of Haydn. His Amsterdam house (see Plates 172 and 173) began operations in 1756. In 1770 he opened a branch in Berlin and moved there in 1774.

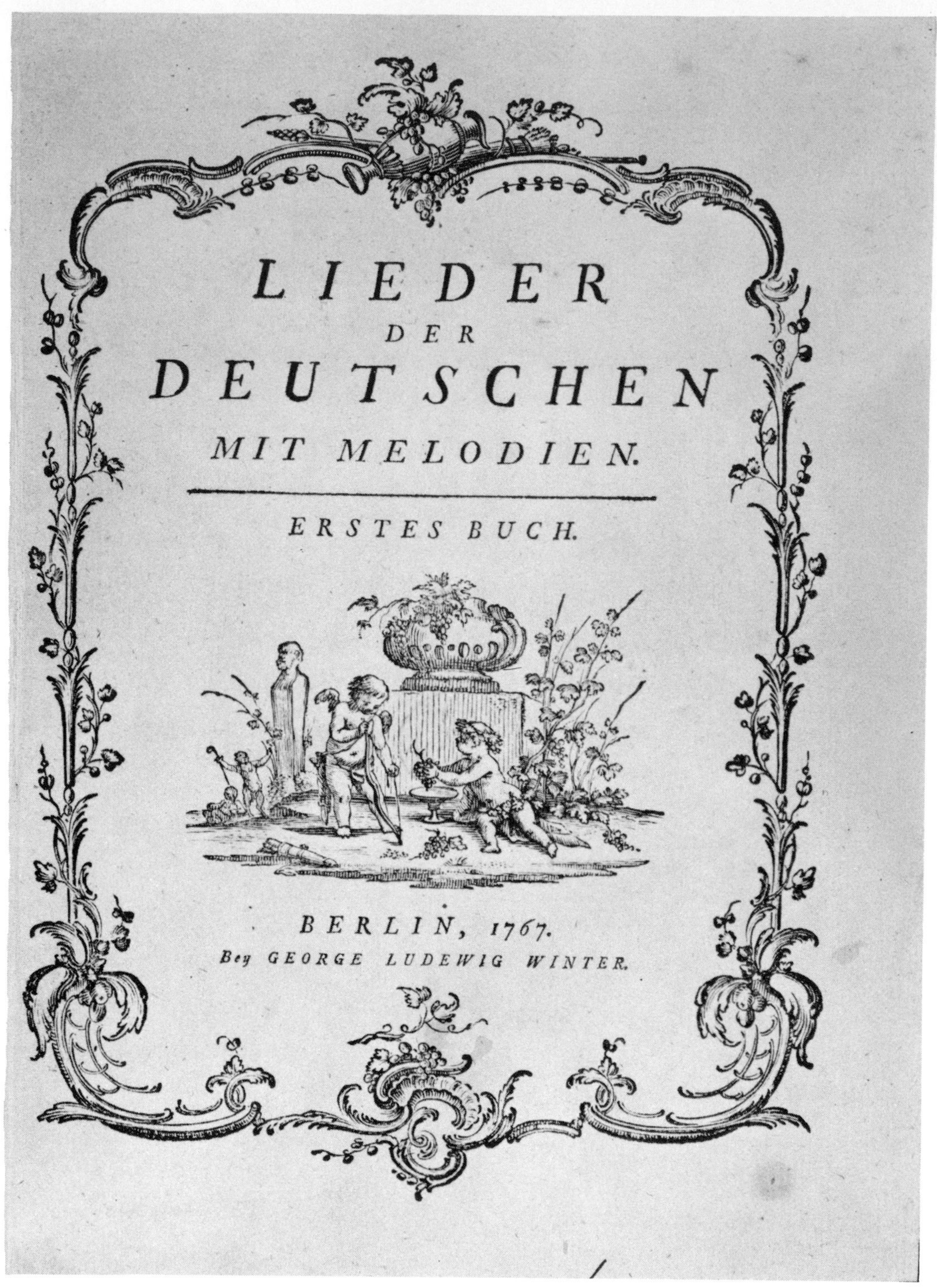
LIEDER
DER
DEUTSCHEN
MIT MELODIEN.
ERSTES BUCH.
BERLIN, 1767.
Bey GEORGE LUDEWIG WINTER.

166 *Lieder der Deutschen.* George Ludewig Winter, Berlin, 1767.
British Museum, London.

This is the title page of the first book of four (1767–8) of the *Lieder der Deutschen*, one of the chief publications of the "first school of Berlin," a major musical movement of the eighteenth century which established the importance of the German lied. Christian Gottfried Krause (1719–1770), a contributor to this book, had written the treatise *Von der musicalischen Poesie* in 1752 and had compiled the ground-breaking collection *Oden mit Melodien* in 1753. Other contributions to the *Lieder der Deutschen* and the many similar collections it inspired were Johann Friedrich Agricola (1720–1774), Carl Philipp Emanuel Bach (1714–1788), Franz Benda (1709–1786), Johann Gottlieb Graun (1702/3–1771) and his brother Carl Heinrich (1703/4–1759), Christoph Nichelmann (1717–1762), Johann Joachim Quantz (1697–1773)—all the foregoing were members of the chapel of Frederick the Great—Johann Christian Bach (see Plates 170 and 171), Johann Adam Hiller (see next plate), Friedrich Wilhelm Marpurg (1718–1795), (Christian Ernst?) Rosenbaum, Georg Philipp Telemann (1681–1767) and Ernst Wilhelm Wolf (1735–1792).

Cantaten und Arien

verschiedener Dichter,

in Musik gesetzt

von

Johann Adam Hiller.

Leipzig,

im Schwickertschen Verlage.

JOHANN ADAM HILLER

167 *Cantaten und Arien verschiedener Dichter*. Schwickert, Leipzig, 1781.
British Museum, London.

Hiller (1728–1804), composer of many songs and arias, is famed chiefly for his *Singspiele*. Active musically in Leipzig, he was the founder and first conductor of the celebrated Gewandhaus concerts.

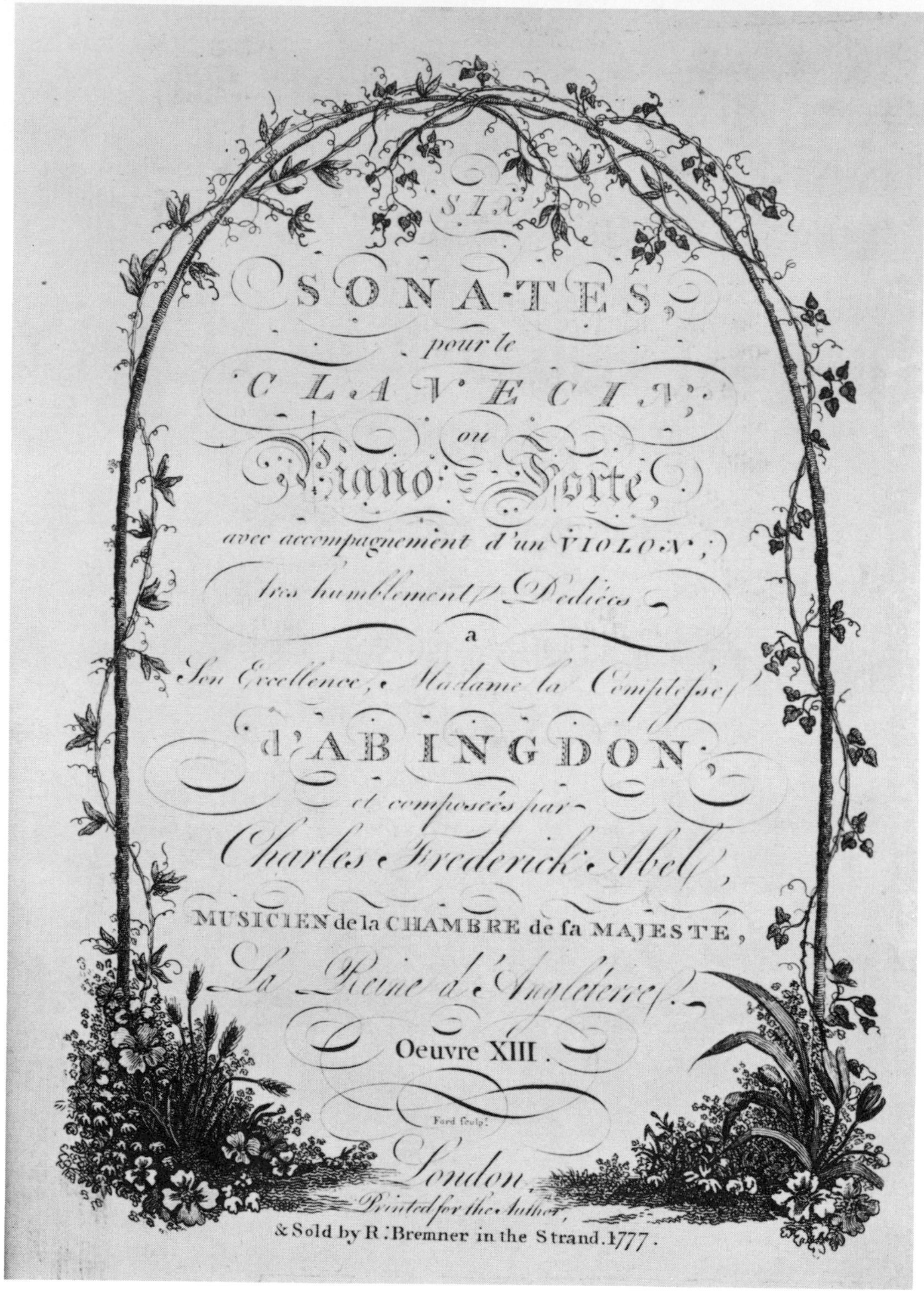

SIX
SONATES,
pour le
CLAVECIN;
ou
Piano-Forte,
avec accompagnement d'un VIOLON;
tres humblement Dediées
a
Son Excellence, Madame la Comtesse
d'ABINGDON,
et composées par
Charles Frederick Abel,
MUSICIEN de la CHAMBRE de sa MAJESTÉ,
La Reine d'Angleterre.
Oeuvre XIII.
Ford sculp!
London
Printed for the Author,
& Sold by R! Bremner in the Strand.1777.

KARL FRIEDRICH ABEL

168 *Six Sonates pour le Clavecin, ou Piano-Forte, avec accompagnement d'un Violon.* Published by the composer, London, 1777.
British Museum, London.

Born in Germany, Abel (1723–1787) lived in London from 1759 on, leading a busy life as gambist—he was the last virtuoso on that instrument to gain European renown—as manager and conductor of concerts in association first with J. C. Bach (see Plates 170 and 171), later with John Peter Salomon (1745–1815); and as a successful composer of instrumental music. The Ford who engraved the title of this set of violin sonatas was possibly John Ford, active in London between 1764 and 1797.

KARL FRIEDRICH ABEL

169 *Six Quartetto.* Printed by Robert Bremner, London, 1760's.
British Museum, London.

This title page is by the celebrated team Cipriani-Bartolozzi. The designer Giovanni Battista Cipriani (1727–1785) settled in England in 1755; the engraver Francesco Bartolozzi (1727–1815) arrived in 1764. They became *the* graphic artists à la mode in London, as well as sought-after teachers (see also Plate 170).

SIX SONATES
POUR LE
CLAVECIN OU LE PIANO FORTE,
DEDIÉES A
SON ALTESSE SERENISSIME
MONSEIGNEUR LE DUC ERNEST,
DUC DE MECKLENBOURG &c. &c.
CHEVALIER DE L'ORDRE DE L'AIGLE BLANC,
ET MAJOR GENERAL DES ARMÉES
DE S·M·BRITANNIQUE ;
COMPOSÉES PAR
JEAN CRETIEN BACH, MAITRE DE MUSIQUE
DE S·M·LA REINE D'ANGLETERRE.
OEUVRE V.

JOHANN CHRISTIAN BACH

170 *Six sonates pour le clavecin ou le piano forte*. London, *c.* 1770.
British Museum, London.

Youngest son of J. S. Bach, Johann Christian (1735–1782), who had studied and worked in Milan, settled in England in 1762 and became a well-liked composer and concert manager (with Abel; see Plate 168). His keyboard compositions, like this set of sonatas, were particularly elegant and brilliant. This title design by Cipriani and Bartolozzi (see preceding plate) was also used for the comic opera *Rosina* (1783) by William Shield (1748–1829), published by William Napier.

JOHANN CHRISTIAN BACH

171 *Six Sonatas for the Harpsichord or Piano Forte; with an Accompagnament for a Violin.* Welcker, London, 1775 (?). British Museum, London.

This graceful title page was engraved by an artist named Mango.

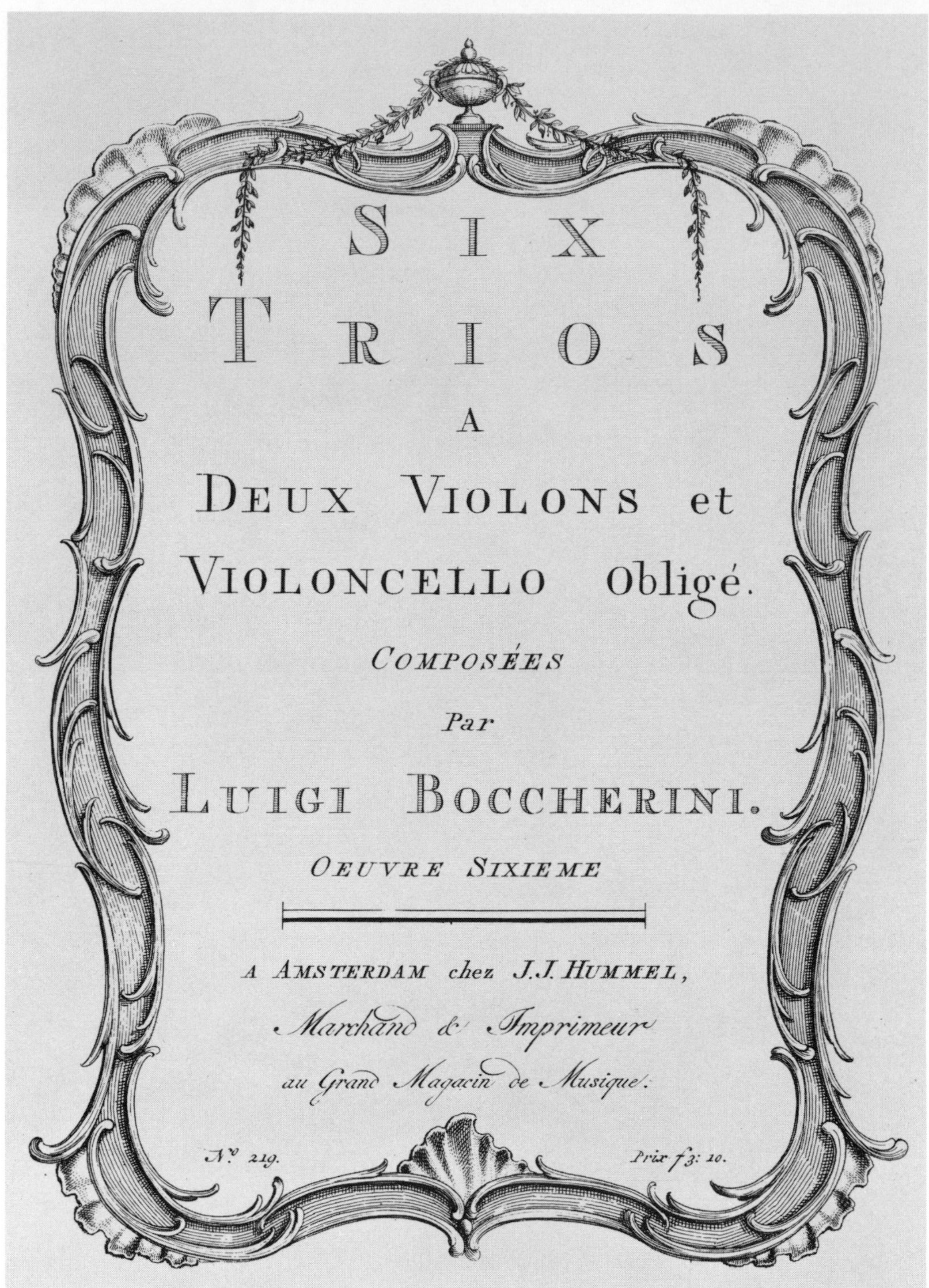

LUIGI BOCCHERINI

172 *Six Trios*. Johann Julius Hummel, Amsterdam, *c.* 1785. Collection of G. S. Fraenkel.

The cello virtuoso and prolific chamber music composer Boccherini (1743–1805) was active in Spain beginning in 1768/9. The musicologist Yves Gérard, whose thematic catalogue of Boccherini's works is to be published by Oxford University Press, has kindly furnished the following information: In the composer's autograph catalogue of his works, these trios are noted as Op. 4 and dated 1766 (the order of the six trios is different in the Hummel edition). They were first published, as Op. 4, by Vénier in Paris in March of 1768, the same month in which Boccherini made his first public appearance in that city at a "Concert spirituel." Three London editions and a Paris reprint appeared before the Amsterdam edition illustrated here. On the publisher Hummel, see Plate 165, as well as Plate 173.

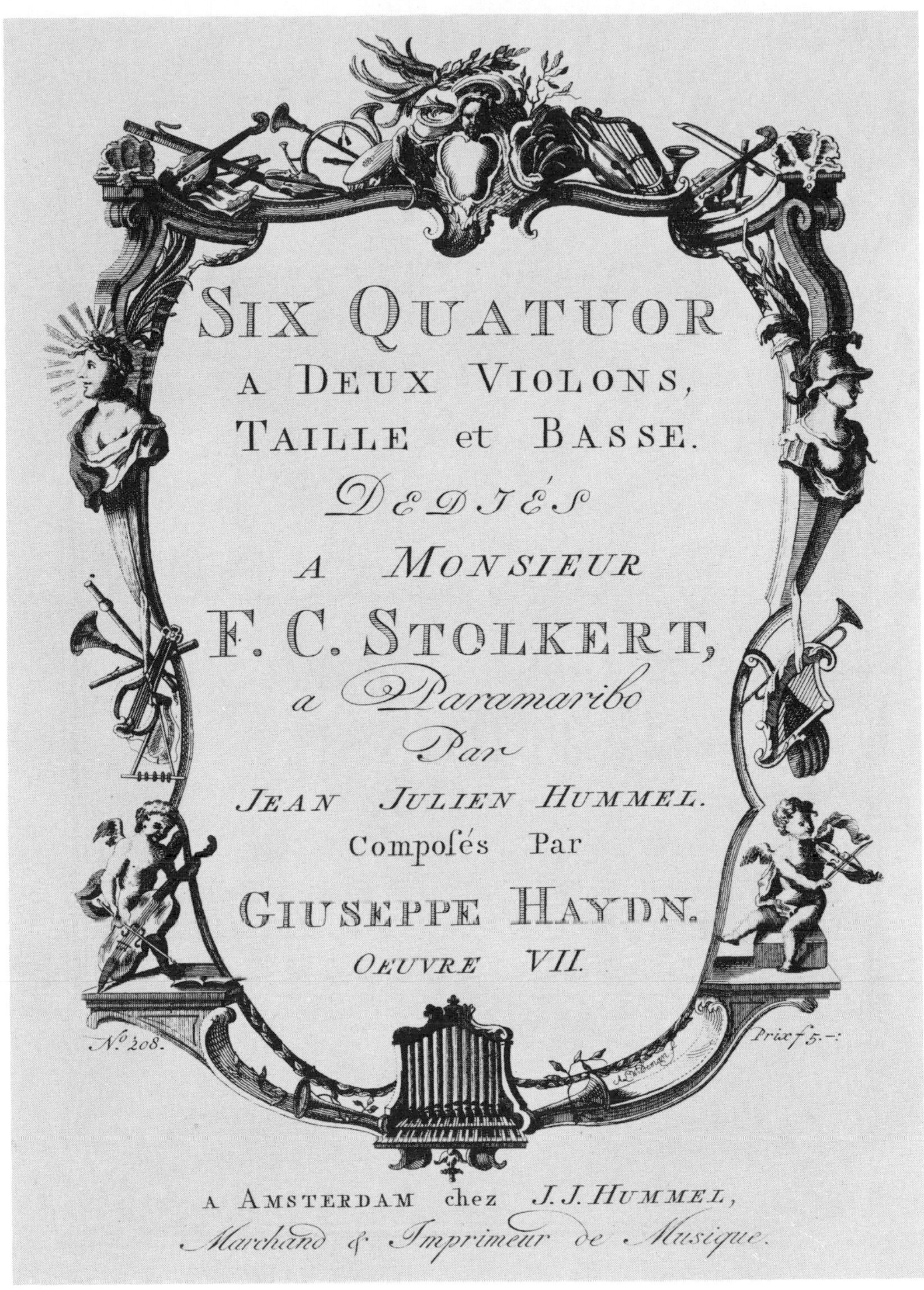
SIX QUATUOR
A DEUX VIOLONS,
TAILLE et BASSE.
DEDIÉS
A MONSIEUR
F. C. STOLKERT,
a Paramaribo
Par
JEAN JULIEN HUMMEL.
Composés Par
GIUSEPPE HAYDN.
OEUVRE VII.
No. 208.
Prix f 5.-:
A AMSTERDAM chez J. J. HUMMEL,
Marchand & Imprimeur de Musique.

JOSEPH HAYDN

173 *Six Quatuor*. Johann Julius Hummel, Amsterdam, 1769. Collection of G. S. Fraenkel.

This is the first edition of a set of early string quartets (Hoboken III 19, 24, 20–23*) by Haydn (1732–1809) which was reprinted by over a dozen publishers in Austria, Germany, Holland, France and England within the next few years. This title page is signed A. L. Wildeman. On the publisher Hummel, see Plate 165, as well as Plate 172.

* The Haydn compositions in Plates 172–180 will be identified here by the catalogue numbers assigned to them by Anthony van Hoboken in his *Joseph Haydn: Thematisch-bibliographisches Werkverzeichnis*, Band I [instrumental works], B. Schott's Söhne, Mainz, 1957. The information given here on editions and dates of works is also based on this standard reference by Hoboken. The reader is warmly urged to consult the *Werkverzeichnis* for further details which could not be furnished here.

SEI
QUARTETTI
CONCERTANTE
á Flauto, Violino, Alto et Baſſo.
COMPOSTE
DEL SIG.RE HAYDEN
Maestro di Capella del Principe
ESTERHASI.
OPERA 16.A
Prezo 9.tt di Francia
Mis au Jour par M.R HUBERTY
Cy devant de l'Académie Royale de Musique.
Gravés par Melle Laurencin.
A PARIS
Chez l'Editeur, rue des deux Ecus, au Pigeon blanc,
Ou l'on trouve un grand Magazin de Musique moderne.
A·P·D·R.
Ecrit par Ribiere

JOSEPH HAYDN

174 *Sei quartetti concertante.* Huberty, Paris, 1773.
Collection of G. S. Fraenkel.

Some of these six quartets for flute, violin, viola and cello (Hoboken II 1, D11, 11, D9, G4, D10) were published for the first time in this edition. The title-page calligraphy is by an artist named Ribière.

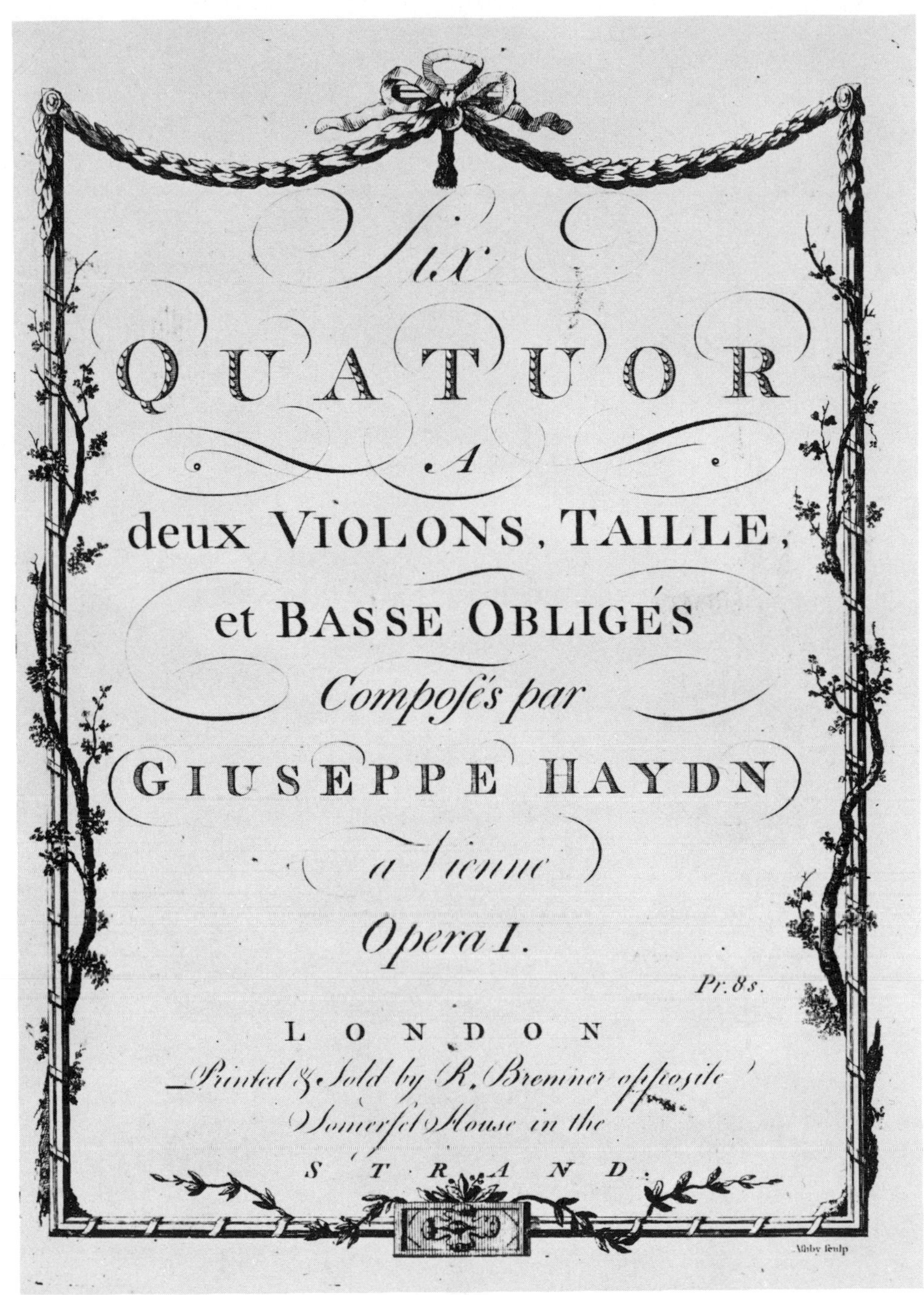
Six
QUATUOR
A
deux VIOLONS, TAILLE,
et BASSE OBLIGÉS
Composés par
(GIUSEPPE HAYDN)
a Vienne
Opera I.
Pr. 8s.
LONDON
Printed & Sold by R. Bremner opposite
Somerset House in the
STRAND.
Athby sculp

JOSEPH HAYDN

175 *Six Quatuor*. Robert Bremner, London, after 1765.
Collection of G. S. Fraenkel.

This is the first English edition of Haydn's earliest set of quartets (Hoboken II 6, III 6, 1–4), which had first been printed a few years before (1762?) by la Chevardière in Paris. The edition illustrated here, with a title engraved by an artist named Athby, must be later than Hummel's of 1765.

JOSEPH HAYDN

176 *Three Quartettos.* William Forster, London, after 1785. Collection of G. S. Fraenkel.

These are the first three of the six "Russian" Quartets (Hoboken III 37–39), dedicated to the Grand Duke Paul (later Paul I), who visited Vienna in 1781. The design of this English title page is the mirror image of that of the first edition issued by Artaria (see caption to Plate 179) in 1782. This (reversed) design had already been used by J. Kerpen in London before the Forster edition.

THREE
Quartetts,
for
TWO VIOLINS,
Tenor & Violoncello,
Composed by
JOSEPH HAYDN Mus. Doc.
Op. 76. Ent.d at Sta. Hall. Pr. 8s
Bowman sc.
London Printed by Longman Clementi & Compy.
No. 26 Cheapside

JOSEPH HAYDN

177 *Three Quartetts*. Longman, Clementi & Co., London, 1799. Collection of G. S. Fraenkel.

This is the first edition of the six late "Erdödy" Quartets Op. 76 (Hoboken III 75–80), the second of which is known as the "Quinten," the third as the "Emperor" and the fourth as the "Sunrise." This London issue was in two books of three quartets each, the first book appearing in 1799 five weeks earlier than the Vienna Artaria edition. The calligraphy of this title is by an artist named Bowman.

JOSEPH HAYDN

178 *Trois simphonies*. Christoph Torricella, Vienna, 1784.
Library of Congress, Washington.

This is the first edition of the symphonies numbered I 76–78 by Hoboken. The coat-of-arms at the top is that of the Prince of Esterházy, Haydn's patron for many years.

JOSEPH HAYDN

179 *Sei Sonate*. Artaria, Vienna, 1780.
Library of Congress, Washington.

This edition of keyboard sonatas (Hoboken XVI 35–39 and 20) was the seventh music publication of the celebrated Viennese house of Artaria (1769–1932) and their first original Haydn publication. The cousins Carlo (1747–1808) and Francesco (1744–1808) Artaria, whose fathers, two brothers, had come to Vienna from Blevio on Lake Como, ran a business of printing and selling art reproductions there. When they started to publish music in 1778, they adorned their title pages with consistent good taste (see also Plates 180, 186, 187, 188, 189, 190 and 197).

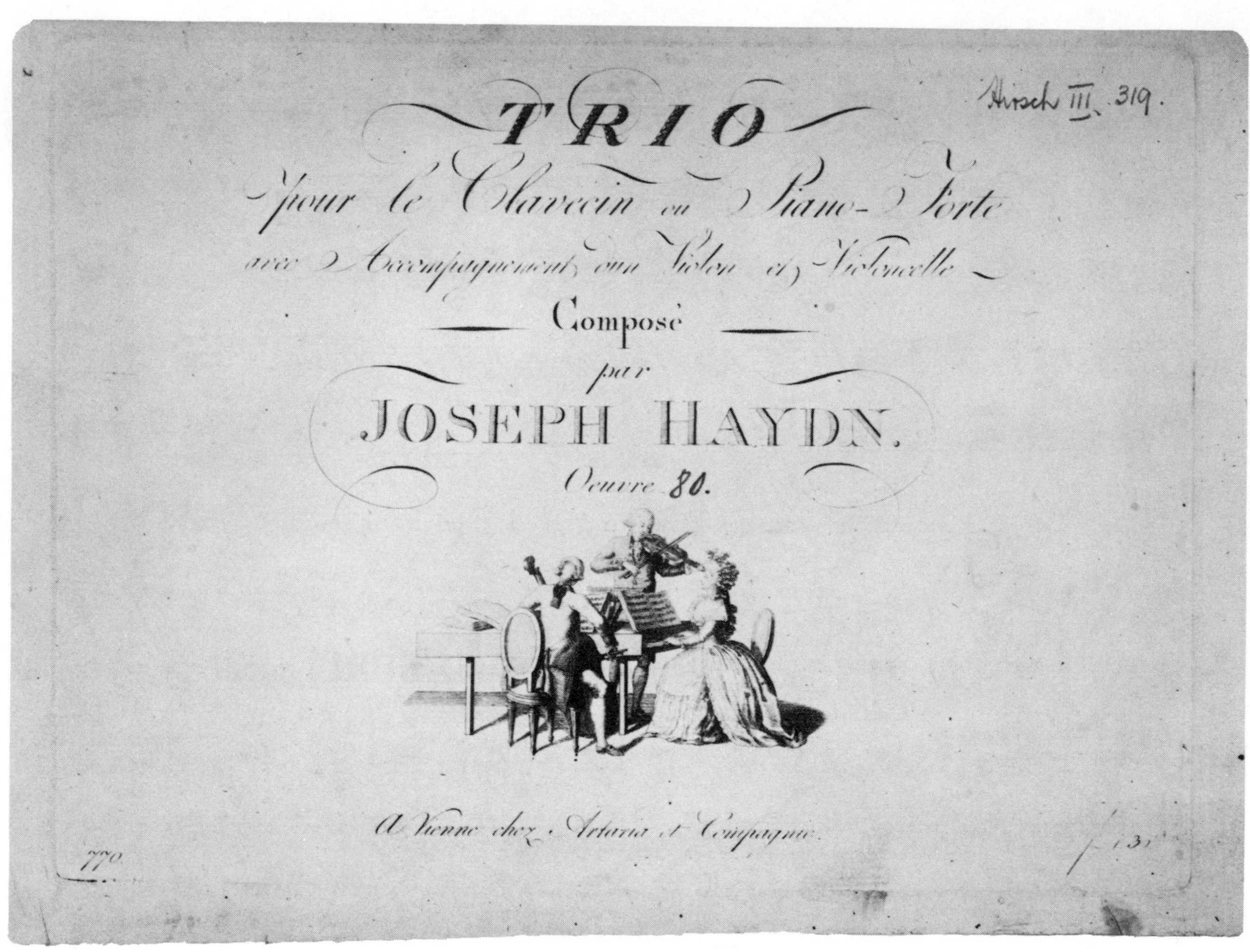

JOSEPH HAYDN

180 *Trio.* Artaria, Vienna, 1798.
British Museum, London.

This trio (Hoboken XV 10), composed in 1785, was probably first published in Vienna in 1785/6 by Hoffmeister, whose plates Artaria used to print the music of this edition. The title design is particularly fitting and felicitous.

DIE JAHRESZEITEN
nach Thomson,
in Musik gesezt von
JOSEPH HAYDN.
PARTITUR.
Originalausgabe.
Bey Breitkopf & Hærtel in Leipzig.

JOSEPH HAYDN

181 *Die Jahreszeiten. Partitur*. Breitkopf & Härtel, Leipzig, 1802. Bayerische Staatsbibliothek, Munich.

This is the first edition of the full score of *The Seasons*. Christoph Gottlob Breitkopf (1750–1800), younger son of Johann Gottlieb Immanuel (see Plate 164), had inherited the business in 1794, but gave it up to Gottfried Christoph Härtel (1763–1827) the next year. This was the origin of the world-famous imprint Breitkopf & Härtel. The "G. V. Kininger" who designed the title is the same as V. G. Kininger (see Plate 184). The engraver was Amadeus Wenzel Böhm (1769–1823).

JOSEPH HAYDN

182 *The Seasons* (*Die Jahreszeiten*). *Klavierauszug*. Breitkopf & Härtel, Leipzig, 1801. Collection of G. S. Fraenkel.

This is the wrapper, in brick red with decorative border, of the original piano score of *The Seasons*, which Breitkopf & Härtel issued in the same style and format as the *Oeuvres Complettes* (Plates 184 and 185): oblong, with wrapper and inner title page (see next plate) with classicistic vignette.

JOSEPH HAYDN

183 *The Seasons* (*Die Jahreszeiten*). *Klavierauszug*. Breitkopf & Härtel, Leipzig, 1801. Collection of G. S. Fraenkel.

This is the title page of the edition discussed in the preceding caption. The design, by Johann David Schubert (1761–1822) of Dresden, was engraved by Friedrich Wilhelm Nettling (active 1793–1824).

Oeuvres Complettes

de

JOSEPH HAYDN

Cahier I.

Au Magasin de Musique de Breitkopf & Härtel

à Leipsic.

JOSEPH HAYDN

184 *Oeuvres Complettes. Cahier I.* Breitkopf & Härtel, Leipzig, 1800.
Collection of G. S. Fraenkel.

Breitkopf & Härtel issued this first "collected" edition of Haydn's works between 1800 and 1806 with the cooperation of the composer himself. Only twelve volumes were actually published, all containing music for piano, solo or in various combinations. This first volume contains eight sonatas. Like the *Seasons* piano score (Plates 182 and 183) and the Mozart *Oeuvres Complettes* (Plate 196), this Haydn series was printed by a new process considered suitable for inexpensive mass production. The title of *Cahier I* features the well-known portrait of Haydn drawn from life by Vincenz Georg Kininger (1767–1851) and engraved by Carl Hermann Pfeiffer (1769–1829).

JOSEPH HAYDN

185 (*Oeuvres Complettes. Cahier 9.*) *Gesaenge.* Breitkopf & Härtel, Leipzig, after 1803.
Collection of G. S. Fraenkel.

This is the ninth volume of the series described in the foregoing caption. It contains 33 airs and chansons to German texts.

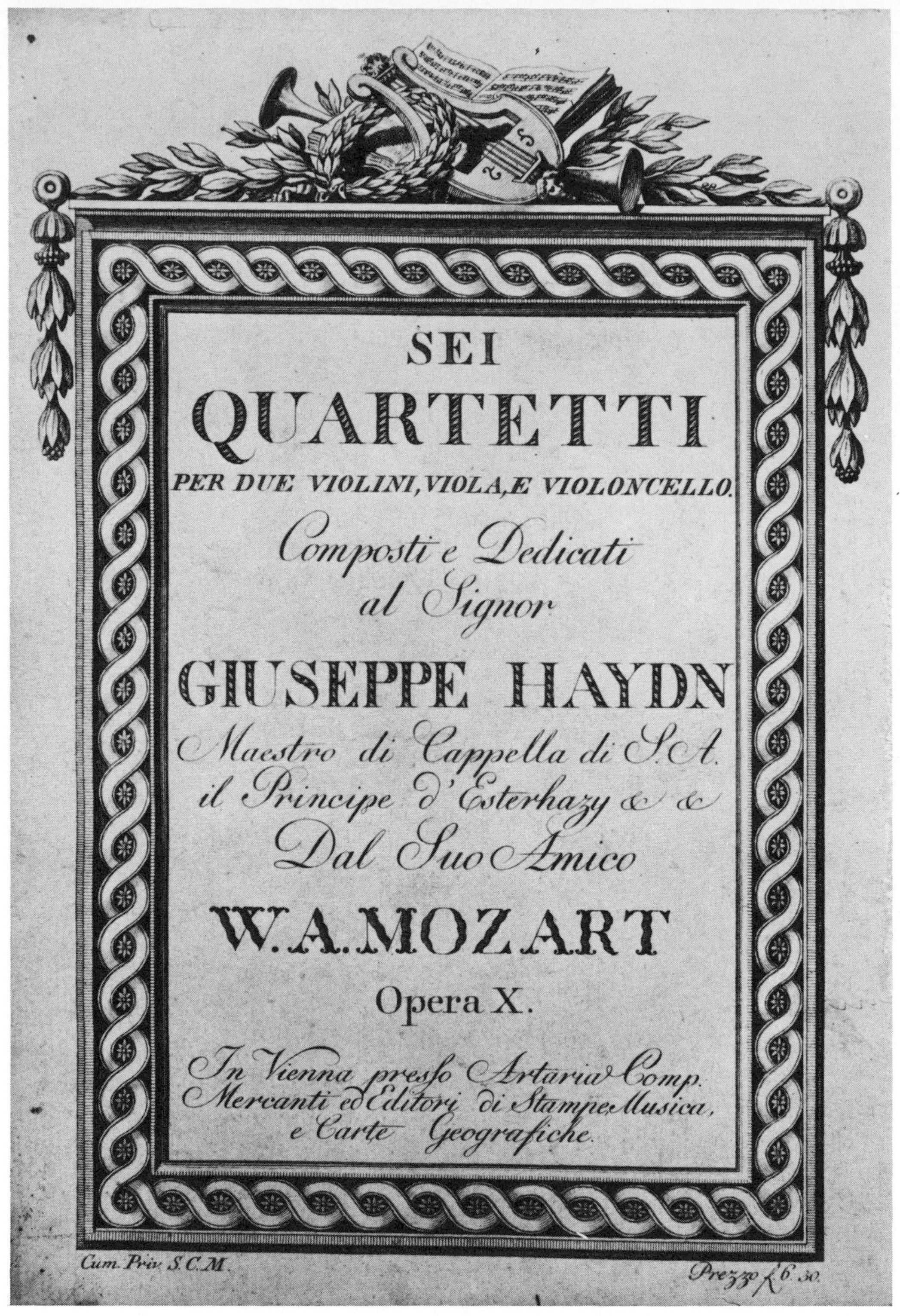

WOLFGANG AMADEUS MOZART

186 *Sei quartetti.* Artaria, Vienna, 1785.
British Museum, London.

This is the first edition of six of the most famous string quartets by Mozart (1756–1791), K. 387, 421, 428, 458, 464 and 465, dedicated to Joseph Haydn. The page following this title contains a touching address by the composer, in Italian, to his older colleague and friend. On the house of Artaria, Mozart's chief publishers during his lifetime, see Plate 179.

WOLFGANG AMADEUS MOZART

187 *Six Sonates Pour le Clavecin, ou Pianoforte avec l'accompagnoment d'un Violon*. Artaria, Vienna, 1781. Collection of G. S. Fraenkel.

One of the earliest music publications of Artaria, issued during the same year that Mozart moved permanently to Vienna, this is the first edition of the violin sonatas K. 376, 296 and 377–380. Josephine von Aurnhammer, to whom the sonatas were dedicated, was a pupil of the composer.

Hirsch IV. 65

GRAND CONCERT
pour
LE CLAVECIN ou FORTE-PIANO
avec l'accompagnement des deux Violons, Alto,
et Baſse, deux Hautbois, et deux Cors.
composé par
W. A. MOZART
Oeuvre IV. Livre
Publié a Vienne chez Artaria Comp.
Prix f 2. 30.

WOLFGANG AMADEUS MOZART

188 *Grand concert pour le clavecin ou forte-piano.* Artaria, Vienna, 1785. British Museum, London.

This is the first edition of the piano concerto K. 413.

WOLFGANG AMADEUS MOZART

189 *Fantaisie et Sonate Pour le Forte-Piano.* Artaria, Vienna, 1785.
British Museum, London.

This is the first edition of the fantasy K. 475 and the sonata K. 457. The dedicatee, Therese von Trattner, was a pupil of Mozart.

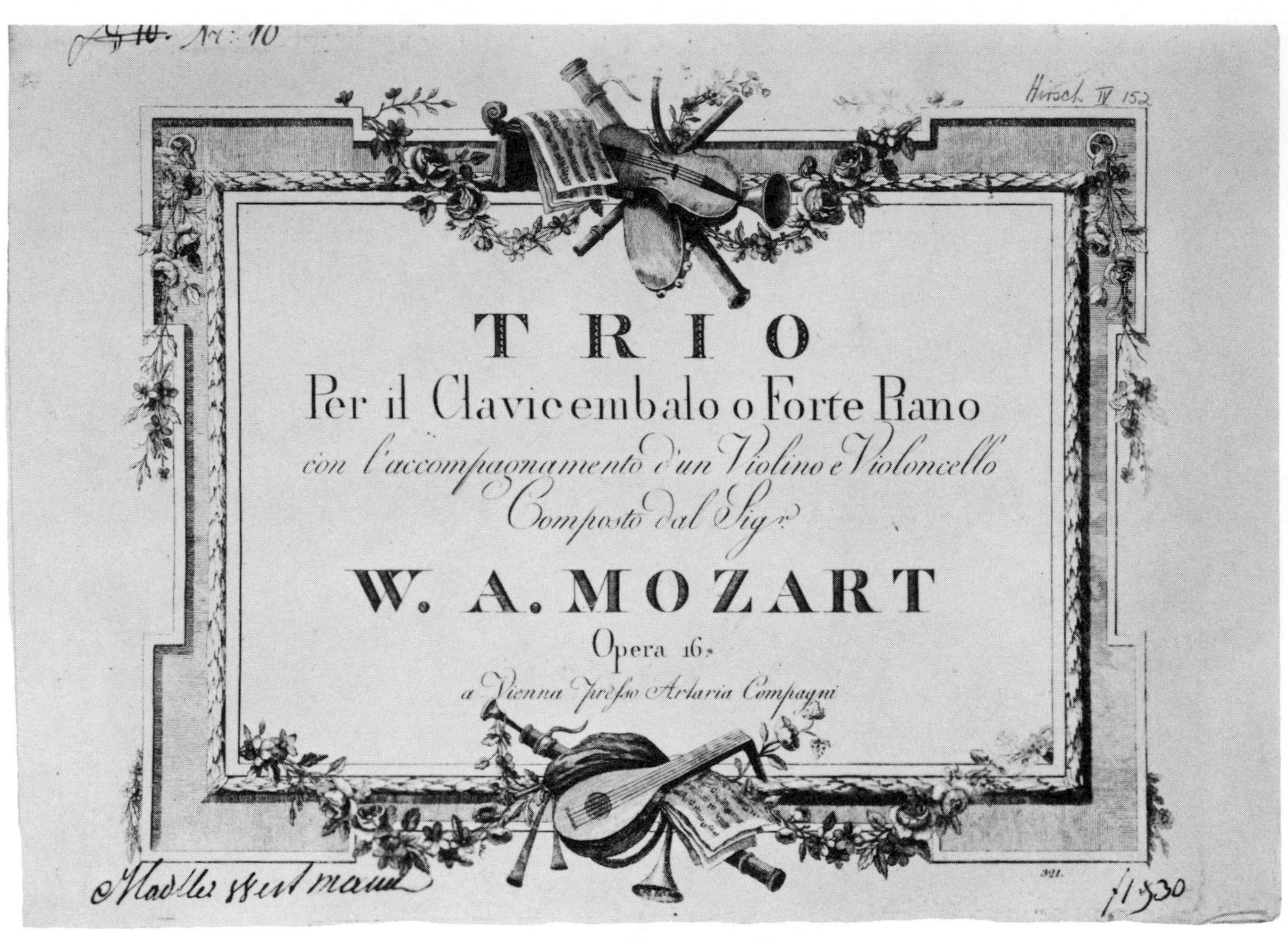

WOLFGANG AMADEUS MOZART

190 *Trio.* Artaria, Vienna, 1790.
British Museum, London.

This trio K. 564, composed in 1788, was first published in 1789 in the *Collection of Original Harpsichord Music,* Vol. 2, No. 5, by Stephen Storace in London.

Die Entführung aus dem Serrail

Ein komisches Sing=Spiel in drey Aufzügen.

Die Musick ist von dem vortreflichen Herrn Mozart,

und

Der Klavier=Auszug von Herrn Abbé Starck

gestochen und herausgegeben

von B. Schott, kurfürstlichen Hof=Musick Stecher in Main:

Der Preis ist drey Conventions Thaler.

11.

WOLFGANG AMADEUS MOZART

191 *Die Entführung aus dem Serrail*. Bernhard Schott, Mainz, 1785 (?).
Collection of G. S. Fraenkel.

This was the first full piano score of the *Seraglio* (K. 384), which had its première in July of 1782. This pirated edition was one of the early productions of the important music house of Schott in Mainz, founded in 1770 by Bernhard Schott (1748–1809).

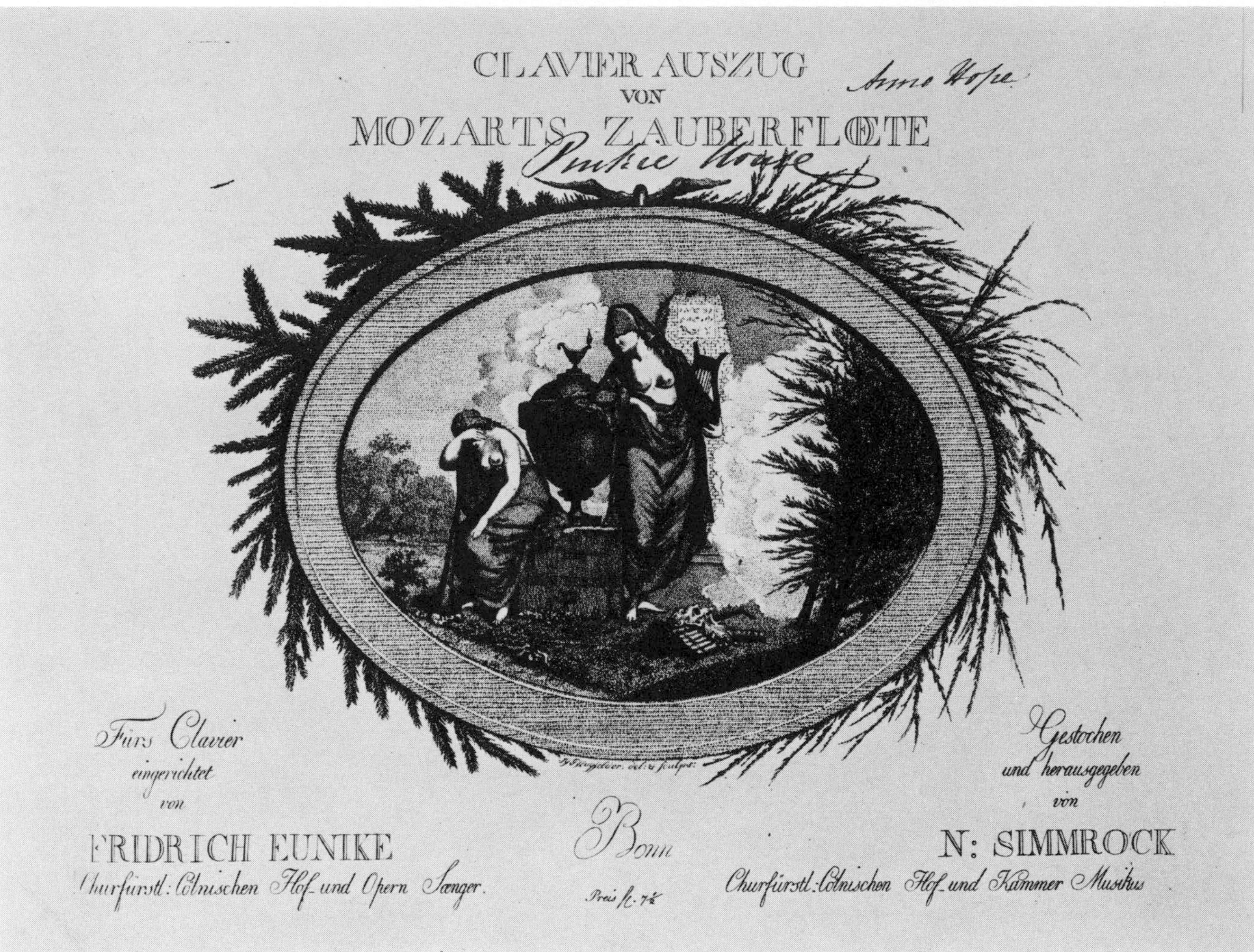

WOLFGANG AMADEUS MOZART

192 *Die Zauberflöte*. Nicolaus Simrock, Bonn, 1793.
Collection of G. S. Fraenkel.

One of the earliest piano scores of *The Magic Flute* (K. 620), this was also one of the first productions of the house of Simrock, founded in 1793 by Nicolaus Simrock (1751–1832). The title was designed and engraved by Johann Gottfried Pflugfelder (active in Bremen from 1805 to 1818).

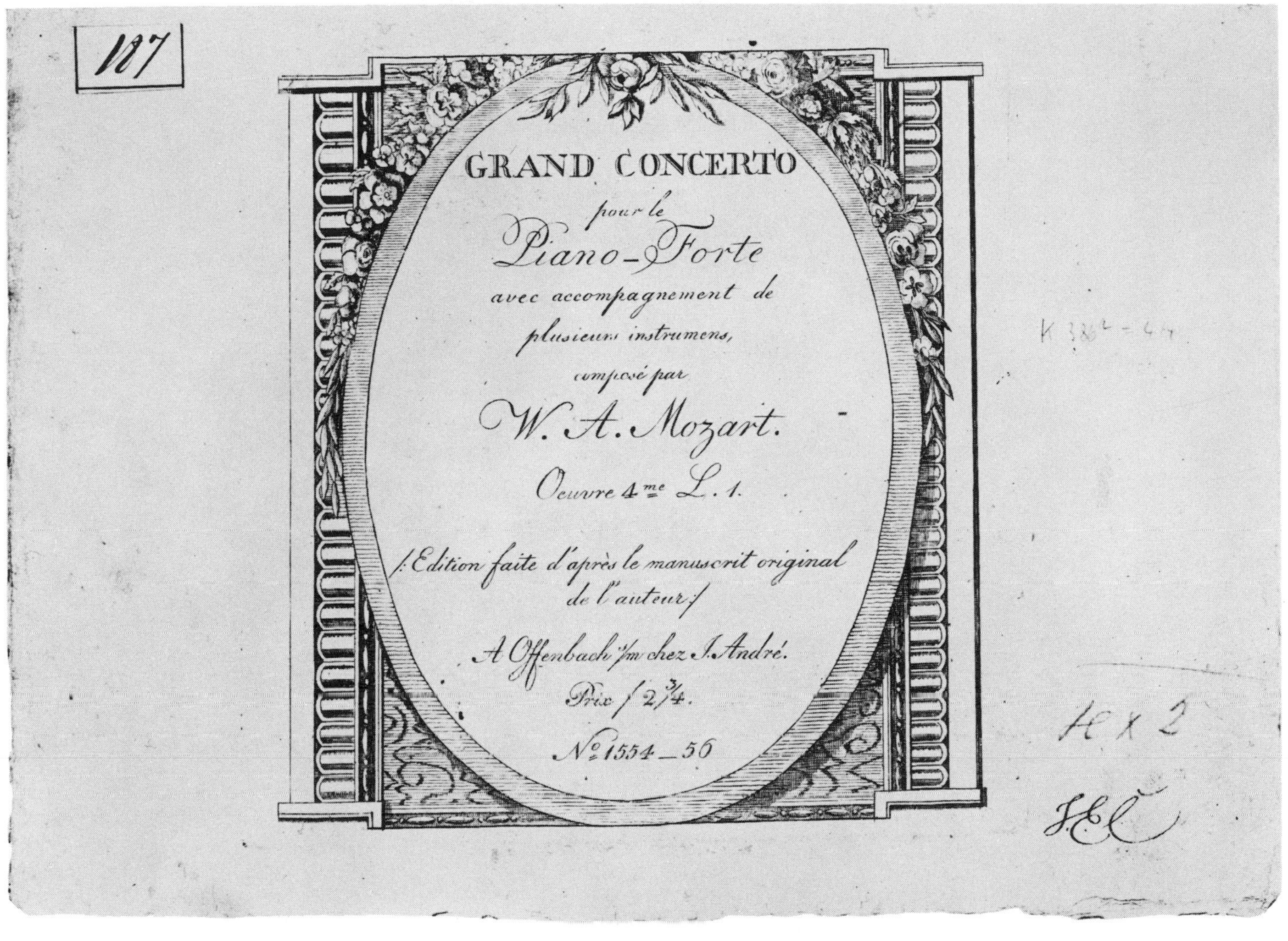

127
GRAND CONCERTO
pour le
Piano-Forte
avec accompagnement de
plusieurs instrumens,
composé par
W. A. Mozart.
Oeuvre 4me L. 1.
(Edition faite d'après le manuscrit original
de l'auteur.)
A Offenbach s/m chez J. André.
Prix f 2¾.
No. 1554_56

WOLFGANG AMADEUS MOZART

193 *Grand Concerto pour le Piano-Forte*. Johann Anton André, Offenbach, 1802. Collection of G. S. Fraenkel.

The first edition of this piano concerto K. 414 (probably composed in 1782) was issued by Artaria in 1785. The house of André, publishers of this edition, was founded in 1784 by Johann André (1741–1799). He was succeeded by his third son Johann Anton (1775–1842), who became one of the great Mozart publishers, purchasing the composer's manuscript remains in 1800 and publishing thematic catalogues of his works.

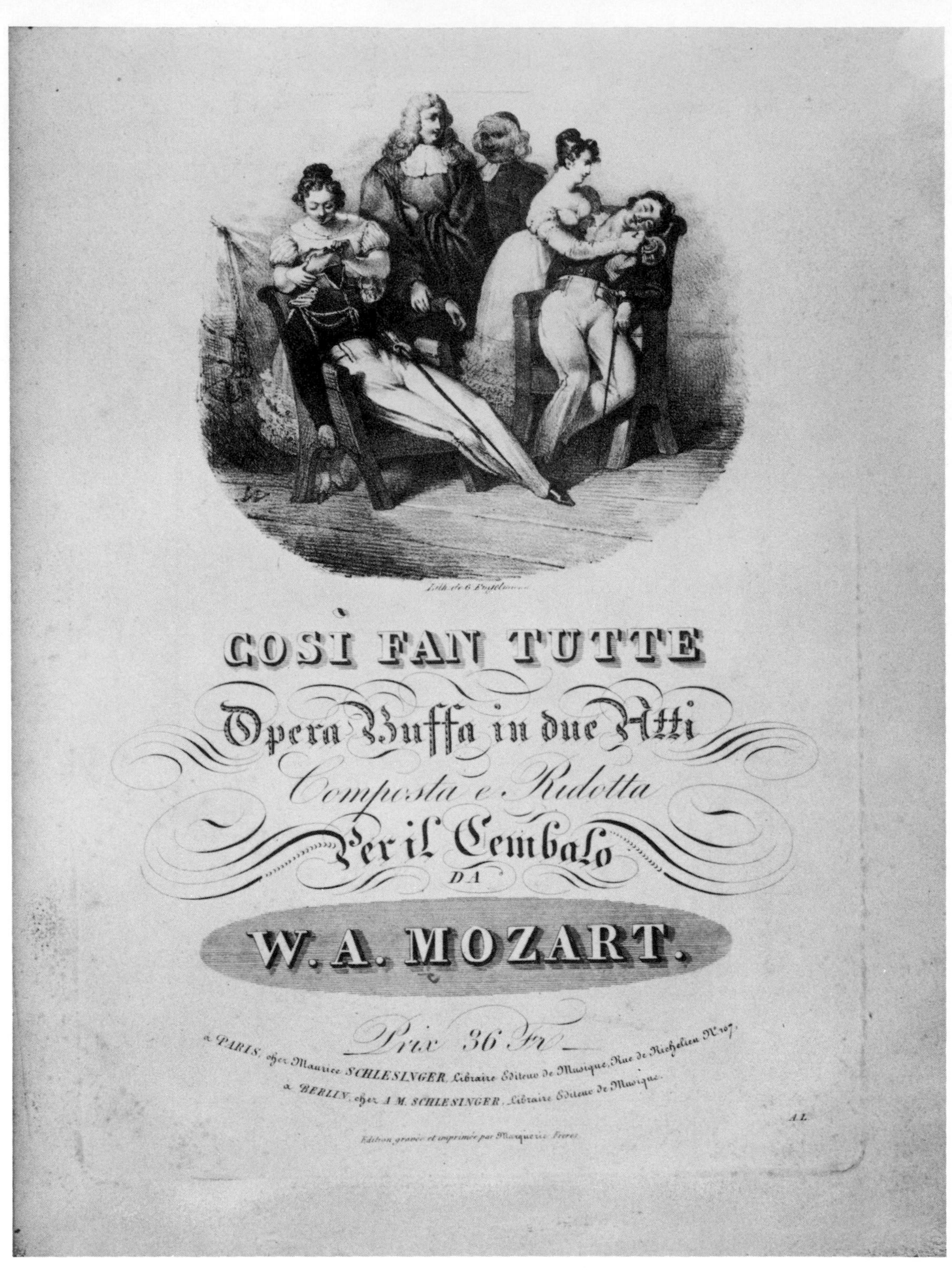
COSÌ FAN TUTTE
Opera Buffa in due Atti
Composta e Ridotta
Per il Cembalo
DA
W. A. MOZART.
Prix 36 Fr.
à PARIS, chez Maurice SCHLESINGER, Libraire Editeur de Musique, Rue de Richelieu No. 107.
à BERLIN, chez A. M. SCHLESINGER, Libraire Editeur de Musique.
A. L.
Edition gravée et imprimée par Marquerie Frères

WOLFGANG AMADEUS MOZART

194 *Così fan tutte* (piano score). Maurice Schlesinger, Paris, 1822. British Museum, London.

We make an exception to our own rule of excluding lithographic title pages in order to present this delightful and well-known Mozart page with its vignette apparently signed by a "W" and lithographed by G. Engelmann. The first full score of *Così* (K. 588) was not printed until 1810 (Breitkopf & Härtel, Leipzig), although the first piano score appeared before 1795 in three volumes published by the Breitkopfische Musikhandlung, Leipzig.

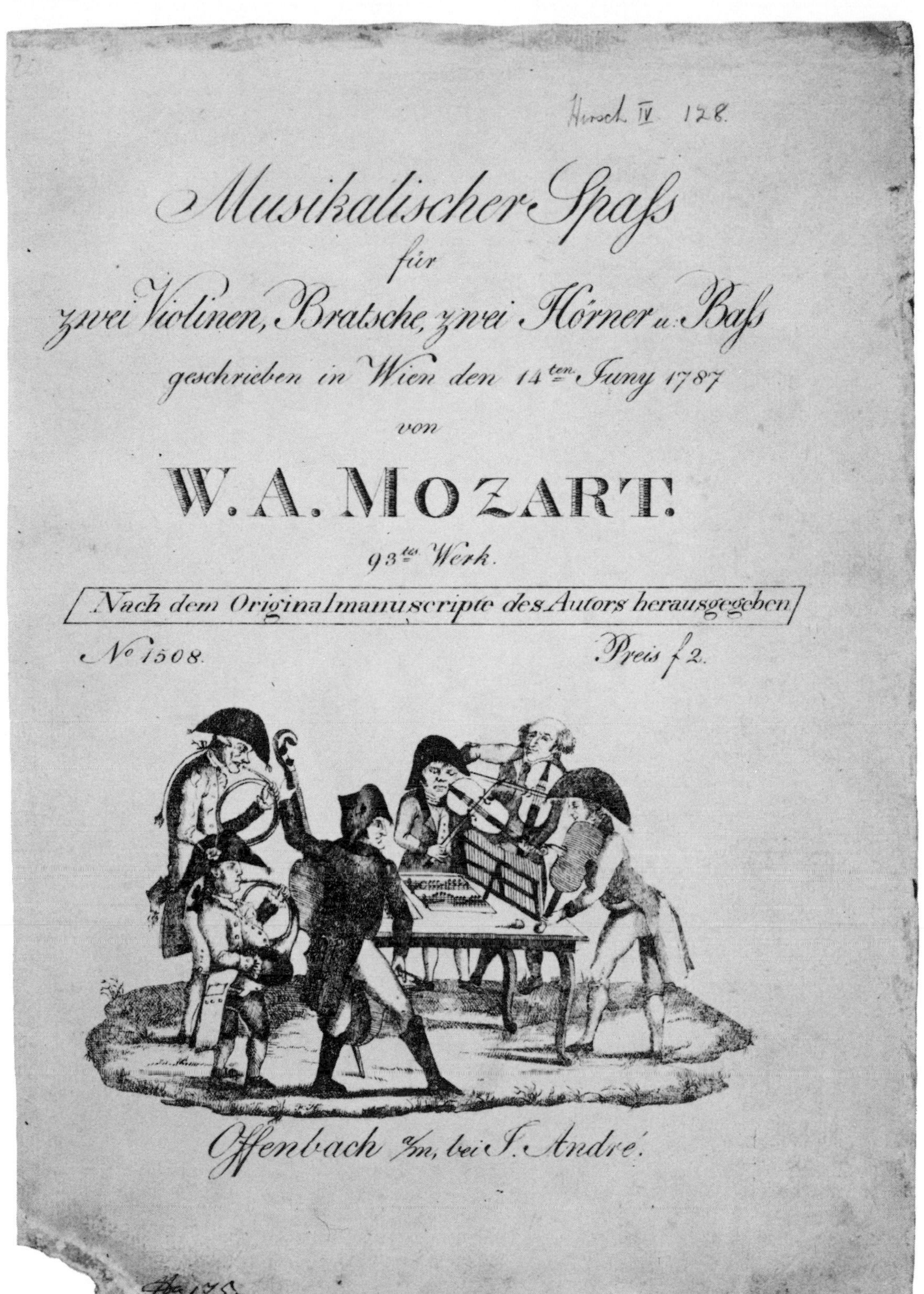
Hirsch IV 128.

Musikalischer Spass
für
zwei Violinen, Bratsche, zwei Hörner u. Bass
geschrieben in Wien den 14ten Juny 1787
von
W. A. MOZART.
93tes Werk.
Nach dem Originalmanuscripte des Autors herausgegeben
No 1508. Preis f 2.

Offenbach a/m, bei J. André.

WOLFGANG AMADEUS MOZART

195 *Musikalischer Spass*. Johann Anton André, Offenbach, 1802.
British Museum, London.

The famous *Musical Joke* (K. 522), also known as the "Dorfmusikanten-Sextett," was composed in 1787. On the publisher, see Plate 193.

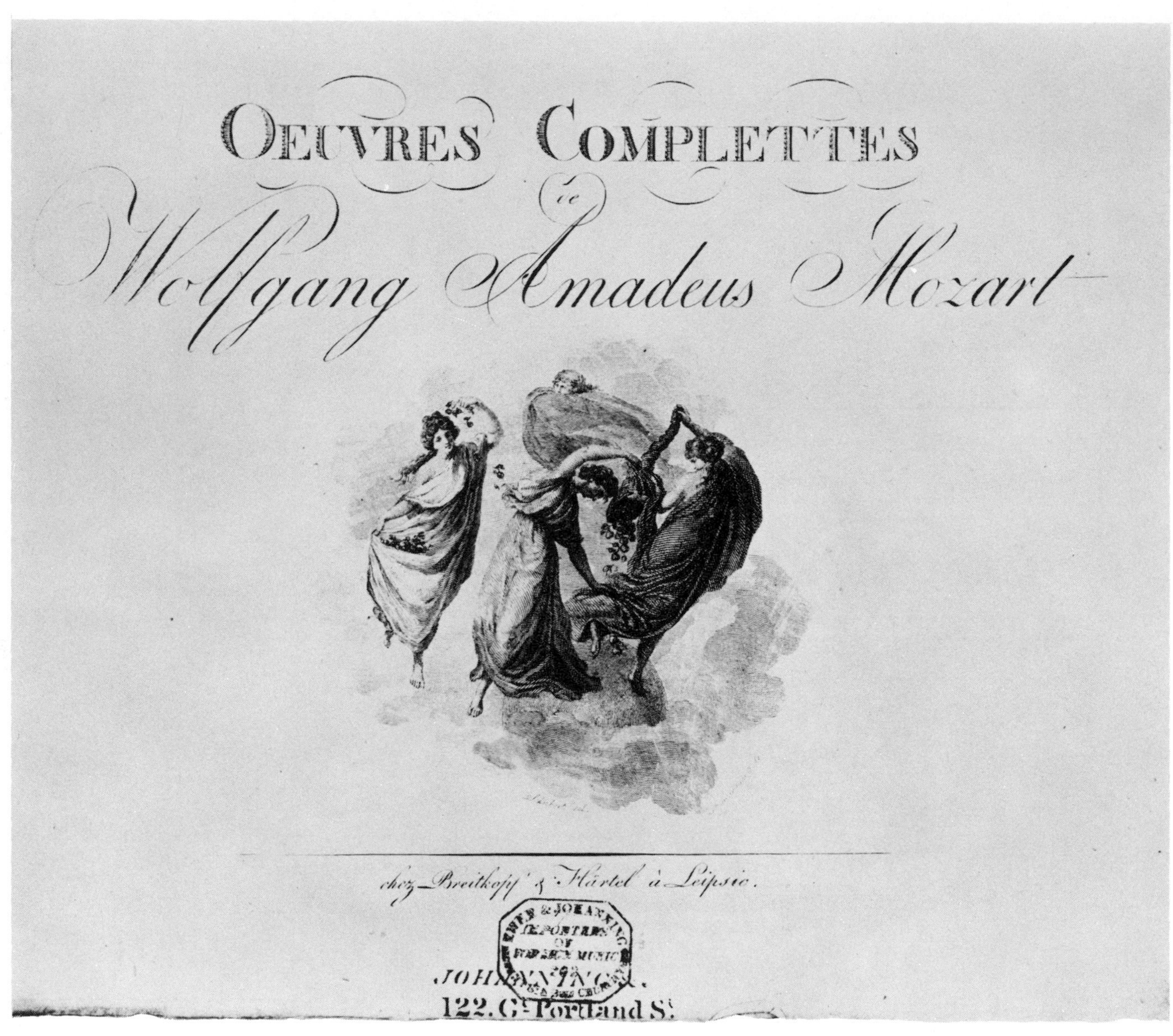

WOLFGANG AMADEUS MOZART

196 *Oeuvres Complettes*. Breitkopf & Härtel, Leipzig, 1806.
Collection of G. S. Fraenkel.

This is the title of the seventeenth and last volume of the most important early "collected" edition of Mozart's works, issued by Breitkopf & Härtel between 1798 and 1806. Like the corresponding Haydn collection (see Plates 184 and 185), this Mozart set contains music for piano, solo and in different combinations. The wrappers are green, and again the titles feature classicistic vignettes. That of Volume 17 was designed by J. D. Schubert (see Plate 183) and engraved by a "Jean Schmidt"—either Johann Gottfried Schmidt (1764–1803) or Johann Georg Schmidt (active in Leipzig *c.* 1802).

LUDWIG VAN BEETHOVEN

197 *Trois Trios*. Artaria, Vienna, 1795.
British Museum, London.

This first edition of Beethoven's Opus 1 was by no means the first of his works in print (about a dozen had appeared during the previous twelve years), but it was the first he considered important enough to have an opus number. At first it was printed by Artaria on a subscription basis, the composer himself bearing the publishing costs. The great care which composer and printer applied to this venture is evident from Beethoven's stipulation in their contract that the edition should be good-looking and have a decorative title ("rein und schön, auch mit einem zierlichen Titelblatte versehen"). This is all the more remarkable since hardly any of Beethoven's other first editions have title pages of distinction.

NICOLAS-MARIE DALAYRAC

198 *Le Poëte et le Musicien ou Je Cherche un Sujet*. Duhan, Paris, 1811 (?). Bibliothèque Nationale, Paris.

Dalayrac (1753–1809) was a prolific composer of *opéras comiques*. This opera, written (to a text by Emmanuel Dupaty) in the last year of the composer's life, was the last of some 60, and was published posthumously. The work appeared with several imprints; probably Pleyel was the first publisher. This passe-partout compartment was used by various publishers for various music titles in the first decade of the nineteenth century. The designer may have been Armand Charles Caraffe (1762–1822). A "Mlle. Gaucher" is credited with the engraving here, but on other copies Ruotte is named—Louis Charles Ruotte (1754–*c.* 1806).

JOHANN FRIEDRICH REICHARDT

199 *Schillers Lyrische Gedichte*. Breitkopf & Härtel, Leipzig, 1810.
Reproduced from von zur Westen, *Musiktitel aus vier Jahrhunderten*.

From 1775 on Reichardt (1752–1814) was court conductor in Berlin under Frederick the Great and his successor Friedrich Wilhelm II. A master of the lied and singspiel, Reichardt is particularly remembered for his settings of Schiller and Goethe, which influenced Schubert considerably. This title reflects the contemporary neoclassical style made popular in northern Germany by the outstanding architect and painter Karl Friedrich Schinkel (1781–1841).

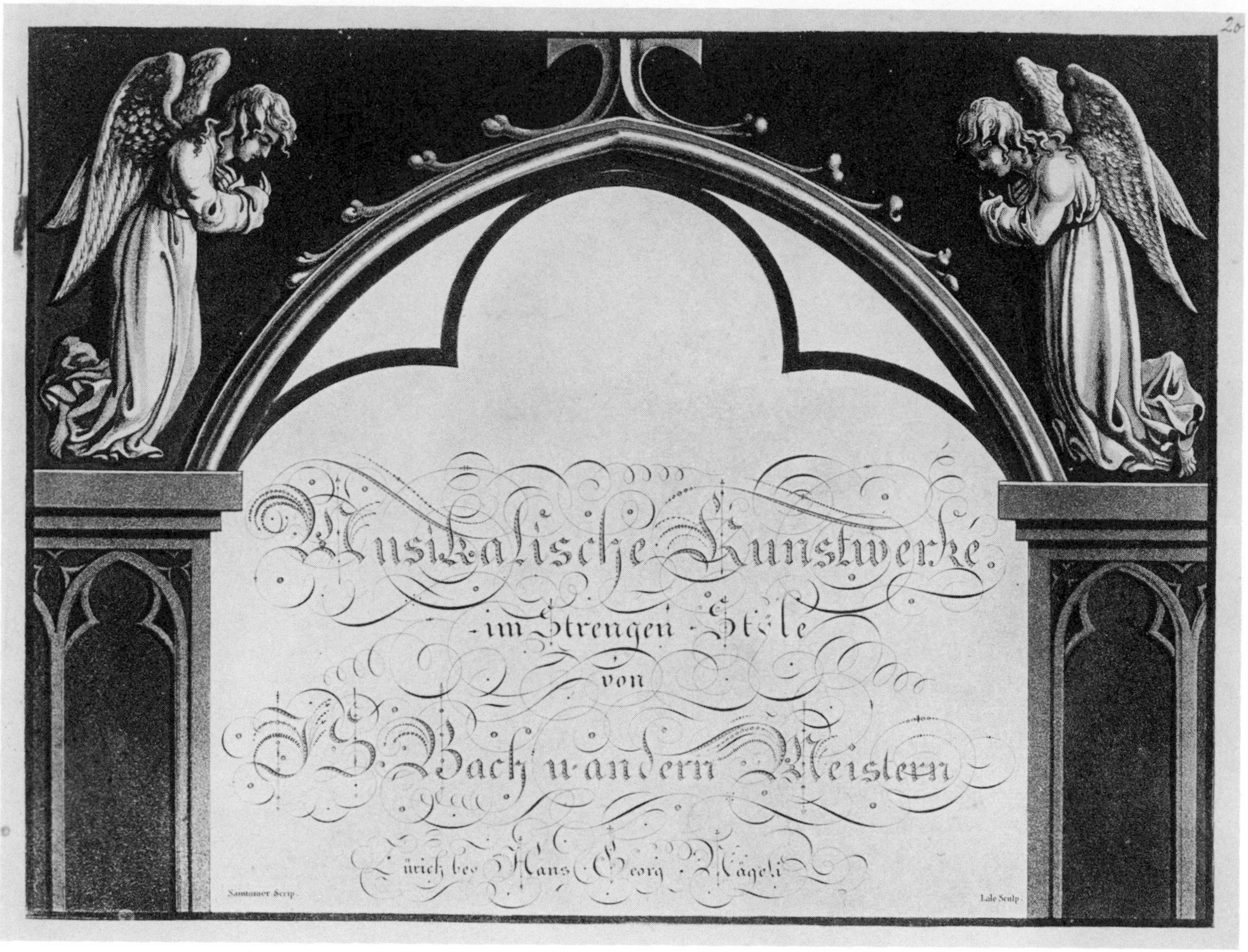

JOHANN SEBASTIAN BACH

200 *Clavier Sonaten Mit obligater Violine.* Hans Georg Nägeli, Zurich, 1804. Collection of G. S. Fraenkel.

This is the outer title of the first edition of Bach's violin sonatas. Bach (see also Plates 142 and 143) was almost forgotten during the later eighteenth century, but the beginning of the nineteenth—thanks largely to Forkel's 1802 monograph—saw a great Bach renaissance. The publisher and music dealer Nägeli (1773–1836) was also a composer, author and significant music educator. The calligraphy of this outer title is by Saintomer, the engraving by Lale.

JOHANN SEBASTIAN BACH

201 *Clavier Sonaten Mit obligater Violine.* Hans Georg Nägeli, Zurich, 1804. Collection of G. S. Fraenkel.

This is the main title of the work described in the preceding plate.

Sources of Illustrations

Museums, Libraries and Private Collections

Bayerische Staatsbibliothek, Munich:
Figs. 3 and 4, Plates 7, 12, 32, 38, 44, 47, 49, 93, 95, 144, 145, 181.

Bibliothèque Nationale, Paris:
Plates 16, 31, 34, 35, 39, 75, 84, 100, 111, 112, 113, 115, 116, 117, 118, 119, 120, 121, 122, 127, 128, 131, 151, 159, 198.

Boston Public Library:
Plate 68.

British Museum, London:
Fig. 2, Plates 4, 6, 14, 15, 17, 18, 19, 28, 29, 37, 40, 43, 46, 48, 51, 54, 55, 56, 57, 58, 59, 60, 61, 62, 63, 64, 65, 66, 67, 69, 71, 72, 74, 77, 82, 83, 85, 87, 88, 89, 90, 92, 94, 96, 97, 99, 102, 103, 104, 105, 107, 108, 110, 114, 123, 124, 125, 126, 129, 130, 133, 134, 136 138 (top), 139, 140, 142 (bottom), 143, 146, 147, 150, 152, 153, 154, 155, 158, 160, 164, 165, 166, 167, 168, 169, 170, 171, 180, 186, 188, 189, 190, 194, 195, 197.

Civico Museo Bibliografico Musicale, Bologna:
Fig. 1, Plates 1, 10, 11, 13, 20, 22, 24, 26, 27, 70, 76, 80, 106, 135, 137, 162.

Collection of G. S. Fraenkel (Urbana, Ill.):
Fig. 5, Plates 109, 148, 163, 172, 173, 174, 175, 176, 177, 182, 183, 184, 185, 187, 191, 192, 193, 196, 200, 201.

Deutsche Staatsbibliothek, Berlin:
Plate 138 (bottom).

Kungliga Musikaliska Akademiens Bibliotek, Stockholm:
Plate 53.

Library of Congress, Washington:
Plates 21, 23, 30, 73, 78, 79, 81, 141, 149, 161, 178, 179.

Österreichische Nationalbibliothek, Vienna:
Plates 5, 25, 33, 101.

Staats- und Stadtbibliothek, Augsburg:
Plates 2, 3, 86.

University of Illinois, Urbana:
Plate 142 (top).

Uppsala University Library:
Plates 36, 41, 42, 45, 50, 52, 91, 98.

Books

Bickham, George, Jr., *The Musical Entertainer*, London, 1737 and 1738 (partial facsimile reprint, Chiswick Press, 1942):
Plates 156, 157.

von zur Westen, Walter, *Musiktitel aus vier Jahrhunderten*, Festschrift anlässlich des 75-jährigen Bestehens der Firma C. G. Röder G.M.B.H., Leipzig, 1921:
Plates 9, 132, 199.

List of Dimensions

This listing shows all the title-page dimensions it has been possible to ascertain: in millimeters, height before width. When the abbreviations "(P)" and "(S)" are given, "(P)" indicates that the figures represent the picture (and/or type) area of the title page, whereas "(S)" indicates measurements of the entire sheet.

FIGURE

2	118 × 82 (P)
3	116 × 84 (P)
4	294 × 202 (S)
5	305 × 240 (S)

PLATE

1	(both) 164 × 235
2	219 × 148
3	217 × 145
4	385 × 235 (P)
5	410 × 300
8	144 × 94 (P)
9	280 × 185
10	143 × 200
11	144 × 200
12	(both) 147 × 190 (S)
13	150 × 216
14	135 × 184 (P)
15	146 × 206
17	214 × 145 (P)
18	375 × 235
19	400 × 260 (P)
20	425 × 275
21	240 × 170
22	224 × 160
23	189 × 137
24	207 × 156
25	150 × 205
26	545 × 390
27	220 × 163
28	223 × 159
29	180 × 145 (P)
32	130 × 176
33	425 × 285
36	128 × 179
38	500 × 350
40	170 × 116 (P)
41	272 × 185
42	134 × 180
43	143 × 186 (P)
44	464 × 300 (S)
45	137 × 174
46	132 × 170 (P)
47	226 × 158
48	315 × 200 (P)
49	282 × 180
50	190 × 135
52	122 × 160
53	155 × 195
54	132 × 178 (P)
55	119 × 186 (P)
56	102 × 132 (P)
57	322 × 207
58	213 × 155
59	178 × 122 (P)
60	257 × 159 (P)
61	205 × 150
62	213 × 150
63	290 × 190
65	252 × 164 (P)
66	334 × 210
67	133 × 73 (P)
68	337 × 208
69	200 × 138 (P)
70	222 × 165
71	260 × 173
76	220 × 158
77	267 × 185 (P)
78	398 × 262
79	398 × 262
80	330 × 215
81	240 × 170
82	254 × 200 (P)
86	181 × 142
88	190 × 150
89	190 × 149
91	183 × 141
93	250 × 164
94	160 × 120 (P)
95	160 × 130
96	223 × 142 (P)
97	230 × 152 (P)
98	186 × 154
99	202 × 144 (P)
101	195 × 305
102	102 × 185
104	151 × 192
105	226 × 168 (P)
106	220 × 160
107	248 × 170
108	(both) 192 × 287
109	255 × 345 (S)
110	145 × 170
114	148 × 236 (P)
116	242 × 280
124	368 × 253
125	272 × 186 (P)
126	285 × 202 (P)
128	385 × 270
129	323 × 250
130	317 × 232
135	195 × 285
136	157 × 197 (P)
137	247 × 326
138	(top) 119 × 194 (P)
139	122 × 193 (P)
142	(top) 250 × 290
143	228 × 162 (P)
144	245 × 157 (S)
145	171 × 99 (S)
146	337 × 228 (P)
147	165 × 240
148	240 × 170 (P)
149	370 × 205
150	322 × 395
151	230 × 320
152	218 × 135
153	284 × 212
154	345 × 226
155	353 × 214
156	430 × 260
157	430 × 260
158	276 × 227
160	202 × 271 (P)
162	244 × 335
163	231 × 327 (S)
164	280 × 360
165	250 × 194 (P)
166	191 × 145 (P)
167	172 × 219 (P)
168	247 × 172 (P)
170	178 × 219 (P)
172	320 × 240 (S)
173	330 × 240 (S)
174	320 × 243 (S)
175	320 × 230 (S)
176	318 × 240 (S)
177	318 × 240 (S)
180	242 × 353
181	350 × 247 (S)
182	265 × 340 (S)
183	265 × 340 (S)
184	255 × 325 (S)
185	255 × 325 (S)
186	340 × 242
187	240 × 340 (S)
188	225 × 319
189	200 × 238 (P)
191	123 × 180
192	200 × 270
193	220 × 119 (P)
195	336 × 242
196	255 × 325 (S)
197	188 × 248 (P)
199	200 × 270
200	250 × 325 (S)
201	250 × 325 (S)

Indexes

Only the captions to the plates and to the Introduction figures have been indexed. The latter are referred to as "Fig. 1," etc.; all numbers without the word "Fig." refer to the corresponding plates. Only those composers and artists are listed who are mentioned in connection with some specific publication.

Composers

PUBLISHERS AND PRINTERS

Graphic Artists

Dover Books on Art

VASARI ON TECHNIQUE, G. Vasari. Pupil of Michelangelo, outstanding biographer of Renaissance artists reveals technical methods of his day. Marble, bronze, fresco painting, mosaics, engraving, stained glass, rustic ware, etc. Only English translation, extensively annotated by G. Baldwin Brown. 18 plates. 342pp. $5\frac{3}{8}$ x 8. 20717-X Paperbound $2.75

FOOT-HIGH LETTERS: A GUIDE TO LETTERING, M. Price. 28 $15\frac{1}{2}$ x $22\frac{1}{2}''$ plates, give classic Roman alphabet, one foot high per letter, plus 9 other 2" high letter forms for each letter. 16 page syllabus. Ideal for lettering classes, home study. 28 plates in box. 20238-9 $6.00

A HANDBOOK OF WEAVES, G. H. Oelsner. Most complete book of weaves, fully explained, differentiated, illustrated. Plain weaves, irregular, double-stitched, filling satins; derivative, basket, rib weaves; steep, broken, herringbone, twills, lace, tricot, many others. Translated, revised by S. S. Dale; supplement on analysis of weaves. Bible for all handweavers. 1875 illustrations. 410pp. $6\frac{1}{8}$ x $9\frac{1}{4}$. 20209-7 Clothbound $7.50

JAPANESE HOMES AND THEIR SURROUNDINGS, E. S. Morse. Classic describes, analyses, illustrates all aspects of traditional Japanese home, from plan and structure to appointments, furniture, etc. Published in 1886, before Japanese architecture was contaminated by Western, this is strikingly modern in beautiful, functional approach to living. Indispensable to every architect, interior decorator, designer. 307 illustrations. Glossary. 410pp. $5\frac{5}{8}$ x $8\frac{3}{8}$. 20746-3 Paperbound $2.25

THE DRAWINGS OF HEINRICH KLEY. Uncut publication of long-sought-after sketchbooks of satiric, ironic iconoclast. Remarkable fantasy, weird symbolism, brilliant technique make Kley a shocking experience to layman, endless source of ideas, techniques for artist. 200 drawings, original size, captions translated. Introduction. 136pp. 6 x 9. 20024-8 Paperbound $2.00

COSTUMES OF THE ANCIENTS, Thomas Hope. Beautiful, clear, sharp line drawings of Greek and Roman figures in full costume, by noted artist and antiquary of early 19th century. Dress, armor, divinities, masks, etc. Invaluable sourcebook for costumers, designers, first-rate picture file for illustrators, commercial artists. Introductory text by Hope. 300 plates. 6 x 9. 20021-3 Paperbound $2.00

EPOCHS OF CHINESE AND JAPANESE ART, E. Fenollosa. Classic study of pre-20th century Oriental art, revealing, as does no other book, the important interrelationships between the art of China and Japan and their history and sociology. Illustrations include ancient bronzes, Buddhist paintings by Kobo Daishi, scroll paintings by Toba Sojo, prints by Nobusane, screens by Korin, woodcuts by Hokusai, Koryusai, Utamaro, Hiroshige and scores of other pieces by Chinese and Japanese masters. Biographical preface. Notes. Index. 242 illustrations. Total of lii + 439pp. plus 174 plates. $5\frac{5}{8}$ x $8\frac{1}{4}$.
20364-6, 20265-4 Two-volume set, Paperbound $5.00

LANDSCAPE GARDENING IN JAPAN, Josiah Conder. A detailed picture of Japanese gardening techniques and ideas, the artistic principles incorporated in the Japanese garden, and the religious and ethical concepts at the heart of those principles. Preface. 92 illustrations, plus all 40 full-page plates from the Supplement. Index. xv + 299pp. 8⅜ x 11¼.
21216-5 Paperbound $3.50

DESIGN AND FIGURE CARVING, E. J. Tangerman. "Anyone who can peel a potato can carve," states the author, and in this unusual book he shows you how, covering every stage in detail from very simple exercises working up to museum-quality pieces. Terrific aid for hobbyists, arts and crafts counselors, teachers, those who wish to make reproductions for the commercial market. Appendix: How to Enlarge a Design. Brief bibliography. Index. 1298 figures. x + 289pp. 5⅜ x 8½.
21209-2 Paperbound $2.00

THE STANDARD BOOK OF QUILT MAKING AND COLLECTING, M. Ickis. Even if you are a beginner, you will soon find yourself quilting like an expert, by following these clearly drawn patterns, photographs, and step-by-step instructions. Learn how to plan the quilt, to select the pattern to harmonize with the design and color of the room, to choose materials. Over 40 full-size patterns. Index. 483 illustrations. One color plate. xi + 276pp. 6¾ x 9½. 20582-7 Paperbound $2.50

LOST EXAMPLES OF COLONIAL ARCHITECTURE, J. M. Howells. This book offers a unique guided tour through America's architectural past, all of which is either no longer in existence or so changed that its original beauty has been destroyed. More than 275 clear photos of old churches, dwelling houses, public buildings, business structures, etc. 245 plates, containing 281 photos and 9 drawings, floorplans, etc. New Index. xvii + 248pp. 7⅞ x 10¾. 21143-6 Paperbound $3.00

A HISTORY OF COSTUME, Carl Köhler. The most reliable and authentic account of the development of dress from ancient times through the 19th century. Based on actual pieces of clothing that have survived, using paintings, statues and other reproductions only where originals no longer exist. Hundreds of illustrations, including detailed patterns for many articles. Highly useful for theatre and movie directors, fashion designers, illustrators, teachers. Edited and augmented by Emma von Sichart. Translated by Alexander K. Dallas. 594 illustrations. 464pp. 5⅛ x 7⅛.
21030-8 Paperbound $3.00